Combining Plants

Combining Plants

By the Editors of Time-Life Books
ALEXANDRIA, VIRGINIA

The Consultant

Robert S. Hebb is a horticultural consultant, garden designer, author, and frequent lecturer on gardening. He received a diploma of horticulture from the Royal Botanic Gardens in Kew, and then became assistant horticulturist for the Arnold Arboretum of Harvard University, where he wrote the pioneering book *Low Maintenance Perennials.* Hebb has been director of horticulture for the Mary Flagler Cary Arboretum of the New York Botanical Garden and executive director of the Lewis Ginter Botanical Garden in Richmond, Virginia. The recipient of the Massachusetts Horticultural Society Silver Medal for leadership in American horticulture, Hebb is the author of numerous works on low-maintenance gardening. He also oversees several estate gardens in the Richmond area.

Cover: *The lilac flowers of Campanula poscharskyana and the red bell-like blooms of Heuchera x brizoides create an eye-catching contrast in colors, accented by a lone strawberry blossom.* **Half title page:** *The blue-violet dwarf bearded iris and the mauve phlox combine high and low values of a single hue—violet.* **Title page:** *Dark blue 'Crystal Palace' lobelia (foreground) and blue ageratum surround a pink geranium in a vivid display of harmonious colors.*

Printed in U.S.A.
10 9 8 7 6 5 4 3 2 1

TIME-LIFE is a trademark of Time Warner Inc. and affiliated companies.

Library of Congress Cataloging in Publication Data
Combining plants / by the editors of Time-Life Books.
  p.   cm.—(The Time-Life complete gardener)
Includes bibliographical references (p.) and index.
ISBN 0-7835-4102-3 (hardcover)
ISBN 0-7370-0636-6 (softcover)
  1. Gardens—Design 2. Plants, Ornamental. 3. Landscape gardening
4. Gardens—United States—Design 5. Landscape gardening—
United States. 6. Plants, Ornamental—United States. I. Time-Life
Books. II. Series
SB473.C643 1995   94-49014
712—dc20   CIP

Books produced by Time-Life Trade Publishing are available at a special bulk discount for promotional and premium use. Custom adaptations can also be created to meet your specific marketing goals. Call 1-800-323-5255.

Time-Life Books is a division of TIME LIFE INC.

TIME LIFE INC.
Chairman and CEO: Jim Nelson
President and COO: Steven L. Janas

TIME-LIFE BOOKS
President: Larry Jellen

TIME-LIFE TRADE PUBLISHING
Vice President and Publisher: Neil Levin
Vice President, Content Development: Jennifer Pearce
Senior Sales Director: Richard J. Vreeland
Director of New Product Development: Carolyn Clark
Director of Marketing: Inger Forland
Director of Trade Sales: Dana Hobson
Director of Custom Publishing: John Lalor
Director of Design: Kate McConnell
Senior Editor: Linda Bellamy
Technical Specialist: Monika Lynde
Project Manager: Jennifer L. Ward
Cover Design: Jody Billert

Combining Plants
EDITOR-IN-CHIEF: John L. Papanek
Managing Editor: Roberta Conlan

Director of Design: Michael Hentges
Director of Editorial Operations: Ellen Robling
Director of Photography and Research: John Conrad Weiser
Senior Editors: Russell B. Adams Jr., Dale M. Brown, Janet Cave, Lee Hassig, Robert Somerville, Henry Woodhead
Special Projects Editor: Rita Thievon Mullin
Director of Technology: Eileen Bradley
Library: Louise D. Forstall

Vice President, Director of Marketing: Nancy K. Jones
Vice President, Director of New Product Development: Neil Kagan
Vice President, Book Production: Marjann Caldwell
Production Manager (hardcover): Marlene Zack
Production Manager (softcover): Virginia Reardon
Quality Assurance: James King, Stacy L. Eddy

SERIES EDITOR: Janet Cave
Deputy Editors: Sarah Brash, Jane Jordan
Administrative Editor: Roxie France-Nuriddin
Art Director: Alan Pitts
Picture Editor: Jane Jordan
Text Editors: Paul Mathless (principal), Darcie Conner Johnston
Associate Editors/Research-Writing: Sharon Kurtz, Robert Speziale, Mary-Sherman Willis
Technical Art Assistant: Sue Pratt
Senior Copyeditor: Anne Farr
Picture Coordinator: David A. Herod
Editorial Assistant: Donna Fountain
Special Contributors: Jennifer Clark (research); Susan S. Blair, Olwen Woodier (research-writing); Bonnie Kreitler (writing); Marge duMond (editing); John Drummond (art); Lina B. Burton (index).

Correspondents: Christine Hinze (London), Christina Lieberman (New York). Valuable assistance was also provided by Liz Brown (New York), Judy Aspinall (London).

Chapter One

COMPOSING WITH COLOR   6

Chapter Two

DECORATING WITH FOLIAGE   29

Gallery

GARDEN ARTISTRY   45

Chapter Three

COLOR FOR THE COLD SEASONS   59

Chapter Four

A SAMPLING OF GARDEN PLANS   76

Reference

Composing with Color

To give your garden the greatest visual impact, you have to decide not only where on your property a plant will thrive, but also where and with what companion plantings it will look its best. A garden whose colors, shapes, and textures are well matched will have an appeal far greater than the individual attributes of its plants. There is no mystery to designing such a garden; all you need is a little imagination and some grounding in the principles of combining plants.

Understanding color relationships will enable you to create inviting combinations like those in the California garden at right. Hot pink Agrostemma githago 'Milas' harmonizes with soft pink spikes of Jupiter's-beard and magenta-pink foxglove; a red poppy and blue delphiniums provide contrast, and silvery artemisia adds a cooling element. It will also enable you to link colors so they do not clash, create a serene ambience with pastels, capitalize on the qualities of white, green, silver, and gray flowers and foliage, and use dominant colors to dramatic effect.

A. *Centranthus ruber (Jupiter's-beard) (25)* **B.** *Centranthus ruber 'Albus' (white valerian) (6)* **C.** *Lychnis coronaria (rose campion) (12)* **D.** *Chrysanthemum parthenium (feverfew) (14)* **E.** *Agrostemma githago 'Milas' (common corn cockle) (many)* **F.** *Artemisia arborescens (fringed wormwood) (1)* **G.** *Delphinium (larkspur) (15)* **H.** *Papaver (poppy) (11)* **I.** *Hardenbergia violacea (vine lilac) (1)* **J.** *Betula pendula (European birch) (3)* **K.** *Digitalis (foxglove) (9)* **L.** *Lavatera arborea 'Tricolor' (tree mallow) (1)* **M.** *Tagetes lemmonii (Mexican bush marigold) (1)* **N.** *Pelargonium graveolens (rose geranium) (1)*

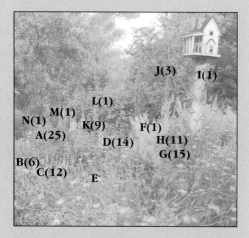

The key lists each plant type and the total quantity needed to replicate the garden shown. The diagram's letters and numbers refer to the type of plant and the number sited in an area.

Designing Your Garden with Color

Color is usually considered the predominant element in garden design. When used with skill, it can subtly direct attention to different focal points in the garden. For example, a single flower variety planted in a long swath forms a river of uniform color that draws the eye along its length and invites an exploration of the distance. Large drifts of bright color leap forward, foreshortening the garden; pale colors recede, creating the perception of depth. The interweaving of pale and bright colors that has traditionally characterized the planting schemes of perennial borders encourages the eye to linger over the artful pairings.

Different color match-ups affect the way people respond to a garden. What delights one viewer may seem jarring or monotonous to another. While any color scheme that pleases the gardener can be judged successful, there are some basic principles of color combination, and understanding them is one of the keys to converting your personal tastes into an effective garden design.

A TOOL FOR UNDER-STANDING COLOR
The color wheel shows how different hues interact. Adjacent colors relate harmoniously because they contain mixes of their neighbors. Colors situated across from each other are contrasting. Adding white to hues produces tints (inner circle); adding black produces shades (outer circle). Colors in the yellow and red ranges are considered warm colors; those in which green and blue predominate are called cool colors.

The Nature of Color

The primary characteristic of color is *hue*, which is the trait that distinguishes one color from another. By convention, red, yellow, and blue are the three primary hues. Mixing any two of these in equal amounts creates the three secondary hues: orange, composed of red and yellow; green, of yellow and blue; and violet, of red and blue.

The Color Wheel

A good way to understand how the various colors relate to each other is to look at a color wheel. The wheel may be divided any number of ways, but it is always based on the three primary hues. Every other color is produced by combining varied amounts of red, yellow, and blue. All the colors that lie between any two primary hues on the wheel and share these hues are said to be harmonious. For example, red-orange, orange, and yellow-orange all contain varying amounts of both red and yellow and are harmonious with both.

Any two of the primary and secondary colors directly opposite each other on the color wheel—blue and orange, violet and yellow, red and green—are called complementary colors. Unfortunately for novice colorists, "complementary" can be confused with "complimentary." Complementary hues create a strong, eye-catching contrast; they may also be complimentary, but are not necessarily so.

Located on either side of the primary and secondary colors are the intermediate colors—yellow-orange, yellow-green, blue-green, blue-violet, red-violet, and red-orange. When these are placed next to their opposites on the wheel, a less striking, more subdued contrast results.

Color Triads

In addition to harmony and contrast, the wheel includes a third set of relationships—the triad. A triad is a set of three colors spaced

at equidistant intervals around the color wheel. By virtue of encompassing all the sectors of the wheel, triads are compatible combinations that include elements of both harmony and contrast.

To find any triad, place a small circle of paper in the center of the wheel and mark its edge where it touches the center of the pure red, yellow, and blue sections. Rotate the circle to align one mark with any color; the other two marks will indicate its triadic mates.

Color Temperature

Another principle of organization on the color wheel is the division between warm and cool colors. Warm colors are inherently exciting and lively; cool colors are soothing and can be used to create a feeling of peacefulness.

To distinguish between the two on the color wheel, draw an imaginary line from the division between yellow-green (warm) and green (cool), straight across the wheel to the division between red (warm) and red-violet (cool). Contrasting combinations are made by marrying the warm and cool colors that face

A SOFTENING EFFECT OF SPLIT COMPLEMENTARIES
Yellow-green cypress spurge nestles comfortably next to red-violet and lavender varieties of phlox. The two phlox colors, coming from either side of pure violet on the color wheel, are split complementaries of the spurge color, which lies opposite them on the wheel. The grouping adds punch to this Iowa garden, but is not as vigorous or contrasting as combinations of complementary hues would be.

each other on the wheel. Cool violet, for example, contrasts with warm yellow.

When yellow is added to borderline-warm yellow-green, the latter becomes warmer; when green is added it becomes slightly cool. Borderline-cool red-violet becomes cooler when violet is added, but crosses over into the warm zone when red is added.

Color temperature also affects our perception of depth: Plantings of warm colors stand out and seem to advance toward the eye. Particularly strong warm colors—hot reds and oranges, and bright yellows—dominate the landscape and seem to reduce distance. Cool colors have a contrary effect; they appear to recede, giving way visually to other garden plantings and features.

You can exploit the optical effects of warm and cool colors to manipulate perceptions of space in your garden. A favorite technique of Gertrude Jekyll, the celebrated Victorian gardener who was also a talented painter, was to strengthen the impression of spaciousness by planting a gradation of colors ranging from cool to warm to cool. She recommended starting a long border with drifts of cool pastels, climaxing in the center with dominant

yellows, oranges, and reds, and then graduating back down through the pastels. In today's smaller gardens, a practical alternative is to start a short border with plantings of the warm colors and move into progressively cooler red-violets, blues, and related pastel tints.

Color Pairings in the Garden

Expert gardeners generally agree that good color combinations among plants are based on the principles of harmony and contrast. The farther apart plant colors are from each other on the color wheel, the greater is the contrast between them. The closer they are, the more harmonious their effect.

When flowers of one hue are grown next to different flowers of the complementary hue, they make intensely brilliant contrasting combinations. Planting large drifts of these flowers together can be overwhelming, however. You can soften the effect by replacing one or both of the pure hues with a color from either side of its complementary. Called split complementaries, these combinations will produce a more subdued contrast. Instead of planting masses of blue and orange flowers together, for example, combine blue with yellow-orange or orange with blue-violet.

Such combinations occur frequently in nature: *Solidago* (goldenrod) can be found in uncultivated areas growing alongside purple New England asters, which have bright yellow centers. The bell-shaped flowers of *Fritillaria michailovskyi* are red-violet tipped with bright yellow. Many species of iris have flowers of deep blue or deep violet, with a brush stroke of gold in their centers.

Even a triad of colors in your garden need not be limited to strong primaries or secondaries. You can choose plants that represent a triad of split complementary colors, such as red-orange, yellow-green, and blue-violet.

Other Dimensions of Color

Nature offers relatively few flowers in pure hues or even in mixes of pure hues. Far more often, plant colors are the result of variations in two other key color traits: value and intensity. *Value* is the amount of light reflected by a color. It is sometimes referred to as bright-ness or luminosity, and it can be understood as the place a given color occupies on a continuum from lightest to darkest. Of the primary and secondary hues, yellow, being the lightest, has the highest value; violet, the darkest, has the lowest value.

Intensity, also known as saturation, refers to a color's position on a scale ranging from strength, vividness, or clarity at one end to weakness, dullness, or dimness—and, regardless of the original color, ultimately to grayness—at the other.

A hue can be modified by the addition of white or black to become a *tone.* When white

Value and Intensity in Flowers

The varieties of achillea in the garden at right range from a deep shade of violet to pale tints of mauve and pink. This sequence of related tones shows how different values of the same hue can make a compatible combination. Even though the colors vary from dark to light, they match up well because they all are values of violet.

The difference between value and intensity is visible in the two bars of purple below. The upper bar displays changing values, from the low-value shade at left to the high-value tint at right. The lower bar shows gradations of intensity, from strong and saturated to weak and dim.

Values of Purple

Intensities of Purple

is mixed with a hue, the tone that results is called a tint; pink, for example, is a tint of red. The addition of black results in a *shade;* crimson is a shade of red. The addition of white or black changes the value of a hue. Pink and crimson both spring from red, but pink has a higher value than its parent color, while crimson has a lower value.

Applying Color Theory

While these terms have precise applications for an artist working at an easel, a gardener cannot be so exact. The painter can mix pigments to produce an infinite variety of colors, but the gardener must draw from a palette of living plant colors that are genetically predetermined. Moreover, in a garden those colors will be affected by growing conditions and neighboring plantings, but most of all by light.

Light varies from dawn to dusk and throughout the seasons. Colors will look quite different in the brilliant light of a summer afternoon, for example, than in the evening or on an overcast day. Grays, silvers, pastels, and whites seem to fade in bright summer sun and emerge in the diffused light of evening.

As you plan your garden, consider when you will be viewing your flowers. You might plant salmon pink impatiens or geranium to gleam in the early morning light; many orange, yellow, red, and deep blue blooms sparkle in the bleaching sun of midday; whites and pastels glow in the dim light of evening.

Colors to Suit the Season

Many flowers that bloom in the clear light of early spring, such as snowdrop and some varieties of crocus, Siberian squill, and early narcissus, are pale in color. Yet they lend a stark simplicity to a garden and stand out handsomely against the bright new growth of evergreens like spruce or boxwood and the dull shades of still-dormant ground covers.

As spring progresses, tulips, *Anemone blanda*, *Muscari botryoides* (grape hyacinth), *Hyacinthus orientalis*, *Fritillaria imperialis* (fritillary), and late daffodils can color the landscape with vivid reds, yellows, oranges, hot pinks, and deep blues. Their rich colors will complement the bright greens of new leaf growth on deciduous trees and shrubs.

Of the flowers that bloom during the sunni-

est time of the year—late spring through summer—vividly colored varieties will be the most effective. This does not mean, however, that paler colors have no place in a sunny plot—pastels, grays, silvers, and whites can separate and accentuate stronger hues. At the end of the growing season, the clear light of fall intensifies the muted colors found in such late-blooming flowers as chrysanthemum, New England aster, and several clematis cultivars.

Limitations of the Color Wheel

Although from a physiological point of view most of us see color the same way, each of us perceives what the eye takes in individually

SEEING YOUR GARDEN IN A DIFFERENT LIGHT
Demonstrating the variable effects of sunlight on flower colors, 'Blaze' roses (above) in Washington State appear a deeply saturated red when viewed in full sun but in shadow seem to tone down to a darker, less saturated shade.

and personally, especially when we are looking at plant combinations. While the color wheel can help you to arrive at pleasing match-ups, do not hesitate to violate its principles to accommodate your own color preferences. Colors that might clash if you wore them or chose them for your living-room decor often go together beautifully in the garden.

Of course, one rule does apply to garden planning. The plants you select to grow amid or near each other must have roughly the same cultivation requirements—the same needs for light, for soil fertility and pH balance, and for moisture. Once you have decided on color combinations, consult the Color Guide to Herbaceous Plants *(pages 100-103)* for specific flowers and foliage plants listed by color; then check the Encyclopedia *(pages 108-153)* for the cultivation needs of likely candidates.

Finally, to get the most out of your hard work of combining colors successfully, make your garden a tapestry of annual and perennial flowers and flowering shrubs *(Guide to Woody Plants, pages 104-105)*. By overlapping and interplanting different types of plants, you can keep your color arrangements in effect from late winter until the hard frosts of autumn.

COOPERATION AMONG DIVERGENT TONES

High and low values are seen in this Pennsylvania garden's combination of blue-violet dwarf bearded iris and mauve phlox (above). The strong shade and the pale tint work together because they share a single hue—violet—that is mediated by the addition of black or white.

WARM COLORS IN BRIGHT SUNLIGHT

Vivid green foliage is a backdrop for yellow-orange Papaver orientale 'Henfield Brilliant', which towers above red-orange helianthemum. Both vibrant flower colors retain their visual impact despite brilliant sunlight.

Managing Value and Intensity

Combining contrasting hues in large drifts can be colorful, but on a grand scale it can also be discordant. If you want to create a border of large plantings in both warm and cool hues, use colors that will unfold in a gradual sequence of changing value or intensity. Such a series could, for example, range from white to pale pink to deep pink, reaching its greatest intensity, or saturation, with magenta. It could then continue into the increasingly lower values of red-violet, violet, and deep blue.

You can also combine strong colors successfully by choosing a flower that expresses one of the colors in a lower value or with lower intensity. To temper a pairing of pure yellow and pure violet hues, for example, you might match the pure yellow with a lower-value deep violet—perhaps *Achillea* 'Coronation Gold' with *Salvia* x *superba* 'Lubeca'.

If you choose this kind of arrangement, though, it is best not to fight the inherent traits of the colors. Using yellow and violet as an example again, you should not combine a shade of the naturally high-value yellow with, say, a tint of the naturally low-value violet—the yellow would almost disappear from view.

Avoiding Garish Pairing

Attention to value and intensity will enable you to take risks with potentially garish combinations. Garishness is usually associated with the mismatching of bright hues, but you can confidently marry saturated colors such as scarlet and magenta because they are of the same intensity. A jarring note would creep in only if the magenta were replaced by a tint such as lavender, which would not stand up to the intense scarlet.

Orange and red can be paired successfully, but only in the lower values. Pairing pink, a high-value tint of red, with orange generally creates a discordant effect. On the other hand, you can combine a higher value of red with low values of violet, because the combination preserves the value relationship of pure red and pure violet. Red zinnia and pink garden phlox, for example, would coexist comfortably with violet *Verbena canadensis* 'Homestead Purple' and violet *Allium giganteum*.

Use such intense colors as brush strokes rather than in swaths or drifts—to accent, not overwhelm. You can be more certain of balance in the garden by surrounding a saturated color with larger plantings of lower-intensity flowers so that the dazzling hues make an eye-catching impact on a smaller scale.

Dampening Sunlight to Ease Intensity

Another way to control high intensity in flower colors is to choose varieties that do well in partial shade. Intense colors that might be overwhelming in full sun will behave in the shade, where they will become more restful to the eye without losing the appeal of their lush coloration. *Impatiens wallerana*, a wonderfully reliable annual, is an excellent choice for light shade. Another annual, *Nico-*

MATCHED INTENSITIES
Geranium 'Johnson's Blue' and Achillea x 'Moonshine' (above), both of which are highly saturated, make a successful pairing on Long Island, New York.

A COMBINATION BASED ON SHARED VALUES
High value and unusual form unite the two coneflower varieties in the garden at right, even though the yellow of the Rudbeckia laciniata is highly saturated while the Echinacea purpurea is much less intense.

A WEDDING OF LUMINARIES
*Metallic blue-violet sea holly and
an orange-yellow Alstroemeria Ligtu
Hybrids demonstrate how contrasting
colors that are equally intense make
a striking combination.*

tiana (flowering tobacco), also comes in a range of colors, including intense red, yellow, and violet. In hot climates, it lasts longer when planted in partial shade.

A brilliantly saturated red perennial for partial shade is *Potentilla atrosanguinea* 'Gibson's Scarlet'; *P. neumanniana* 'Nana', at just 3 inches tall, makes a beautiful bright golden yellow ground cover. For an orange version, there is 12-inch-high *P. fruticosa* 'Sunset'; its color changes from red-orange to vibrant yellow-orange as the summer wears on.

Trollius chinensis 'Golden Queen' (globeflower), with rose-shaped deep orange flowers, prefers light shade. And when a truly brilliant orange is desired, the vine *Bignonia* 'Tangerine Beauty' (cross-vine) offers the exceptional sight of many orange trumpet-shaped flowers and dark green foliage.

Bridging Clashing Colors

Clashing combinations can appear in the garden by the juxtaposition either of contrasting colors or of colors that, although they are closely related on the color wheel, are too strong and too saturated to work together comfortably. Such clashes can be tempered in many ways by the use of flowers and foliage.

Moderating with Bicolored Flowers

The simplest and most direct way to moderate color clashes is to interplant a bicolored flower composed of the hues of the two competing groups. This repetition of color integrates the plantings so that they are seen as a unit rather than as individual drifts. Repeating such echoes throughout the border or beds strongly unifies the garden design.

A surprising number of bicolored flowers are available. Many have centers of contrasting or related hues; others have petals that are splashed, streaked, or rimmed with a second and even a third color. The daisylike flowers of *Gaillardia* x *grandiflora* (blanketflower), for example, are red with yellow tips surrounding a dark brown eye. This combination makes them an ideal plant for bridging solid yellow and red flowers such as *Coreopsis lanceolata* and *Salvia splendens*.

To tone down a garden that is planted with an abundance of splashy primary colors such as yellow *Anthemis tinctoria* 'Beauty of Grallagh' (golden marguerite) and red *Pelargonium* x *hortorum* (common geranium), bridge them with *Potentilla* 'Red Robin' or *Paeonia* 'America'. Both of these selections produce red flowers with yellow centers.

Bicolored white flowers not only will bridge plants with combating hues but can also temper an oversaturated color scheme. Consider *Hemerocallis* 'Pandora's Box', a white daylily with a deep red-and-yellow center, or 'Golden Elegance', a white Oriental lily with yellow stripes and dark red flecks.

To bridge primary blues, plant yellow-centered Blackmore and Langdon Hybrids delphiniums or 'Russell Hybrids' lupines that have a color range of blue, red, yellow, and apricot, some of which are bicolored. Dependable low-growing annuals, such as pansy, *Nierembergia* (cupflower), and woodland forget-me-not, also offer pale and deep blues with yellow centers.

Sometimes the second color of a bicolored plant occurs in the stamen—as in certain daylilies, for example—or in the veins of its leaves, as in canna. Flowers such as *Penstemon digitalis* 'Huskers Red' (beardtongue) have stems of a contrasting color. In some plants the second color does not appear until seed heads or clusters of berries have ripened.

Linking Intense Colors

When strong colors predominate in the garden, you can link two potentially clashing hues with a middle color that has ingredients of both. This will help create a feeling of unity

JOINING STRONG, HOT COLORS
Orange daylilies and scarlet Crocosmia 'Lucifer' in this Bellevue, Washington, garden (above) are united by orange-yellow kniphofia and the yellow throats of the daylilies. Blue-violet salvia adds contrast.

GENTLY LINKED HUES
In a garden near San Francisco, yellow-tipped threadleaf cypress and silver echeveria bridge the clashing red roses, bronze Cymbidium pumilum orchids, and fuchsia Spanish shawl.

within groupings of sharply contrasting hues. Masses of such vivid flowers benefit when interplanted with masses of linking colors.

For example, when you plan a grouping of the strong primary colors, you can achieve greater harmony by separating each planting with a color occupying a middle position in the range from one strong hue to the other. Link yellow *Achillea* x 'Moonshine' and red *Monarda didyma* 'Gardenview Scarlet' (bee balm) with an orange *Calendula officinalis* (pot marigold), which contains both yellow and red. In turn, link the monarda and vivid *Agapanthus* 'Bressingham Blue' with violet *Salvia* x *superba* 'East Friesland', whose purple flowers contain both red and blue.

To add interest to small flowering trees that bear their blooms in long, pendulous clusters, such as *Wisteria sinensis* or *Laburnum* x *watereri* (golden-chain tree), underplant the trees with colors that hint at the hues of the overhanging flowers. A red-violet or lilac-blue wisteria, for example, could be underplanted with a progression of the more intense hues of blue-violet, violet, and red-violet found in ornamental onion, pansy, columbine, iris, and mountain pink. To enhance the deep yellow clusters of laburnum, choose underplantings of orange, scarlet, and crimson such as those found in gaillardia, *Potentilla* 'Gibson's Scarlet', daylily, pansy, and columbine.

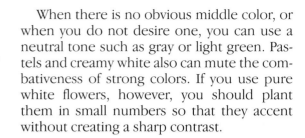

When there is no obvious middle color, or when you do not desire one, you can use a neutral tone such as gray or light green. Pastels and creamy white also can mute the combativeness of strong colors. If you use pure white flowers, however, you should plant them in small numbers so that they accent without creating a sharp contrast.

Linking with Foliage

Foliage can provide another subtle bridge between clashing bloom colors. After your perennials have spent their blossoms, the surviving greenery can work as a link between strongly contrasting flower colors. Explore the possibility of planting perennials that leave a legacy of beautiful variegated leaves. Look for those that combine cooling tones of green with lemon, cream, or white, such as sweet iris, hosta, or *Polygonatum* (Solomon's-seal).

You can also grow *Perovskia atriplicifolia* (Russian sage), *Gypsophila* (baby's-breath), or *Stachys byzantina* (lamb's ears) to bridge plantings of stronger colors. Their clouds of pale blue or mauve flowers are borne on silvery gray foliage, blooms and leaves sharing the same pale intensities. After the flowers are gone, the foliage will soldier on as faithful mediator.

Contrasting Foliage Textures

Foliage in the flower garden plays the important role of adding texture—meaning, in this usage, variations in leaf surfaces—as well as color. Sometimes foliage textures, like flower colors, can clash. When this happens, the contrasting textures can be bridged with flowering plants whose foliage texture takes the middle ground between the two.

For example, matte purple and shiny purple foliage might not work well together when sharing one area of your garden. Although both *Perilla frutescens* and *Iresine herbstii* 'Brilliantissima' (beefsteak plant) have purplish foliage, the perilla's leaves are furrowed and deeply veined, while those of the iresine are shiny. To bridge the contrasting textures, introduce *Sedum maximum* 'Atropurpureum', which has compact clusters of starry flowers and fleshy leaves in muted rose-purple tones. Such deep-value plantings of purple-red could also benefit from an accent of bright linked color—perhaps *Potentilla atrosanguinea* 'Gibson's Scarlet' or vibrant pink *Phlox paniculata* 'Starfire'.

When a cushion of the velvety soft, silvery gray-green leaves of *Stachys byzantina* 'Helene Von Stein' is growing near the crinkly, green-edged silver foliage of *Lamium maculatum* 'White Nancy' (dead nettle), the contrasting surface textures can be effectively bridged with a planting of *Achillea tomentosa*. Commonly known as woolly yarrow, *A. tomentosa* has fuzzy silver-gray foliage topped with small yellow flowers. To inject a dash of color into this planting arrangement, include a vibrant pink *Dianthus* x *allwoodii,* a plant that forms dense mats of spiky gray foliage, or a deep blue flower on gray-silver foliage, such as *Lavandula angustifolia* 'Dwarf Blue'.

Tempering Colors with Foliage

Sometimes the relationship between the color of a plant's foliage and the color of its flowers works beautifully to cool a vibrant color. For instance, the soft silvery gray foliage of *Lychnis coronaria* (rose campion) is a perfect foil for its own intense magenta flowers. Silvery gray or silvery green leaves also work well with strong pinks, crimsons, blues, and violets. The velvety silver-gray foliage of *Stachys byzantina* blends effectively with pinks, blues, and violets.

Other plants with silver-green leaves and blue-violet flowers include common sage, catmint, and lavender, all of which provide a soothing background for flowers that have bright hues. When brilliant reds are teamed as accent plantings with subdued blue-greens and blue-grays, the reds appear fierier and the blue-cast leaves more tranquil.

Yellow-green foliage is a better choice when separating a sequence of the warmer shades of the color wheel, such as intense yellows, oranges, and scarlets. A vivid yellow-green can also beautifully set off a planting of strong magenta. Think of the yellow-green leaves of some of the hostas, such as *H.* 'Kabitan' and *H.* 'Sum and Substance', with their blooms of lavender and violet.

When you desire a peaceful setting composed of flowers rather than background foliage, creamy whites are an excellent choice;

when planted with vibrant colors, they integrate the bed rather than create separate pockets. For the front of the border, plant *Iberis sempervirens* 'Snowflake' (candytuft), mountain pink, *Geranium sanguineum* 'Album', *Geranium* x *cantabrigiense* 'Biokovo' (a white cranesbill that is washed with palest pink), and *Arabis sturii* (rock cress).

For midsize to taller plantings, consider peonies, daylilies, lilies, garden phlox, the hybrid shrub rose 'Sea Foam', and *Gardenia jasminoides* 'August Beauty'. For a combination of yellow-green leaves and creamy white blooms, *Yucca filamentosa* 'Goldsword' is hard to beat for the back of the border.

An exceptional perennial that blooms nonstop and adds height and long flower heads that droop and mingle with midheight plantings is the shrub *Buddleia davidii* 'White Profusion', with its silvery green leaves. Other

THE UNIFYING POWERS OF SHARED FORM
Brightly colored pink and carmine-rose dianthuses in a Baton Rouge yard (above) combine prettily with purple, yellow, and lavender varieties of Viola x wittrockiana (pansy) because they all share similarly round-shaped flower heads.

small shrubs that have cream or white flowers include *Spiraea japonica* 'Albiflora' (Japanese white spirea) and *Weigela florida* 'Bristol Snowflake', with light green foliage.

Gray Leaves and Pastel Flowers

Corals and oranges planted together will benefit from the tempering values of soft silver or gray-green leaves. They also can be linked with tints of orange, such as salmon or pastel apricot. When stands of the striking 3- to 5-foot-tall *Kniphofia* (torch lily), with its long dense spikes of tubular deep yellow and red-orange flowers, are paired with deep orange daylilies or brilliant yellow *Asclepias tuberosa* (butterfly weed), salmon and apricot yarrows add a harmonious pastel component. An underplanting of silver foaming baby's-breath and fluffy gray wormwood is a fine counterpoint of foliage texture and color.

USING FOLIAGE TO DAMPEN CLASHES
Violet Clematis texensis 'Ville de Lyon' (above) intertwines with apricot-yellow 'Abraham Darby' roses against a foliage background. At left, deep lavender Clematis 'Will Goodwin' coexists happily with yellow-and-scarlet trumpet honeysuckle, their differences eased by the surrounding leaves.

19

From late summer into late fall, some gardens are drenched in lipstick shades of rose-pink, deep pink, red-violet, and violet. There are the thick spires of violet-pink *Physostegia virginiana* (false dragonhead), profuse deep pink blooms of 'Carefree Wonder' roses, and 4- to 6-foot-tall New York aster cultivars in varying tones of violet. These rose-purples will blend well when planted with a backdrop of the tall green leaves and silvery white plumes of flowering ornamental grasses such as the 5- to 6-foot-tall *Cortaderia selloana* 'Pumila' (pampas grass) and an underplanting of the silver-gray velvety mounds of lamb's ears.

Using Form to Marry Colors

A flower's form can also help alleviate the clash of warring colors. This can be seen when you scatter a packet of zinnia seeds for annual display. They bloom in a riot of colors that manage to avoid garishness because the flowers all have the same shape. The daisylike blossoms of the Compositae family—*Echinacea purpurea* (purple coneflower), rudbeckia, chrysanthemum, helianthus, aster, and coreopsis—are other examples of contrasting colors eased into compatibility by their similarly shaped blooms.

The same principle applies to mass plantings of impatiens, where pale pink comfortably rubs elbows with salmon, and mauve with scarlet. You can confidently install an even greater variation with a planting of *Petunia* 'Celebrity Mixed', whose blooms reflect every color on the wheel.

When different plant types share both form and color, combining them sometimes creates a breathtaking display. A stunning example of such a pairing is *Magnolia* x *soulangiana* 'Ann Rosse' underplanted with plum red 'First Lady' tulips. The flowers of both are upright and cup shaped, and the magnolia's rose pink glows in concert with the plum color of the tulips.

Climbing Companions for the Border

Different plant forms can make good companions, especially if you are careful to take into account growth habit and flower color. Vines, among the easiest plants to grow, are excellent for transforming fences and walls, adorning trellises, and disguising tree stumps. Used thus, they become a backdrop for other plantings. They also can be trained to grow up trees, through shrubs, and over sturdy perennials to provide a fascinating intermingling of colors or extend a season of colorful blooms when the supporting plant stops flowering.

Strictly speaking, a vine is a plant that is capable of supporting itself, either by means of tendrils or twining leaves, by a naturally twining stem, or by suckers. Into this category fall plants such as clematis, summer jasmine, *Gelsemium sempervirens* (double Carolina jessamine), Virginia creeper, ivy, trumpet honeysuckle, *Hydrangea anomala* ssp. *petiolaris* (climbing hydrangea), *Vitis* (ornamental grape), wisteria, *Campsis* (trumpet creeper), *Polygonum aubertii* (silver-lace vine), *Trachelospermum jasminoides* (star jasmine), *Aristolochia durior* (Dutchman's-pipe), morning glory, *Thunbergia alata* (black-eyed Susan vine), *Phaseolus coccineus* (scarlet runner bean), sweet pea, nasturtium, and *Datura* (thorn apple).

True climbers require a minimum of training, provided they are given something to climb up, or they can be left to grow horizontally and carpet the ground. Unless you are planting a self-clinging ivy, hydrangea, or Virginia creeper, you will need to erect a grid of plastic-coated wire or a lattice trellis to sup-

port climbers that are to be trained against walls or fences.

You can even grow one vine up another, such as a morning glory or sweet pea up wisteria, trumpet creeper, or hydrangea. In fact, growing several climbers together creates a tapestry effect as well as providing a long season of staggered blooms. This is particularly true of clematis, whose cultivars have staggered bloom times ranging from spring into autumn in colors that span the spectrum.

The thin tendrils of perennial clematis, as well as annual vines such as morning glory, nasturtium, and sweet pea, are lightweight and not overly vigorous; they will not engulf the host plants or the bed. When growing clematis or climbing roses through shrubs, however, make sure that each can be pruned back without disturbing the new growth or blooms of the other.

If you love wisteria, be sure to grow it over a wall, a solid arbor, or a sturdy fence. The woody vining stems grow into a thick vining trunk and branches, and their weight will eventually break all but the strongest trellises and tree branches. Wisteria can take up to 10 years to bloom, but in the meantime its sturdy trunk and resilient branches make it a perfect host for clematis, climbing rose, or any of the annual vines.

The branches of trumpet creeper, star jasmine, and double Carolina jessamine are not as thick or strong as those of wisteria, and these three sturdy perennial vines can be grown up mature trees as long as they are kept under control with some annual trimming. On the other hand, ivy, grape, Virginia creeper, and *Lonicera japonica* 'Halliana' (Hall's Japanese honeysuckle) are notorious stranglers of trees and shrubs and must be tamed by rigorous pruning.

When climbers are planted at the base of trees and shrubs, they will compete fiercely with the host plant for water and nutrients. Ease the struggle by adding compost to the soil and applying mulch several times a year.

THE CLARIFYING POWERS OF PURE WHITE
Bright ribbons of white Chrysanthemum x superbum (Shasta daisy) prevent the muddying of dramatic color contrasts in this New Mexico garden of red bee balm, pink Polemonium caeruleum (Jacob's-ladder), lavender-blue delphinium, and brilliant yellow columbine.

White Flowers for Texture, Light, and Fragrance

Planting masses of creamy white flowers amid a sea of green, gray, and silver foliage will transform a sunny area from a visually hot environment into a cool oasis. In a shady location, the inherent light-reflecting qualities of pure white flowers attract the eye and give relief to dark curves and corners.

At dusk, whites of almost every kind—ivory, pinkish, maroon-flecked, or tinged with a hint of orange or green—take on a glow that transforms the garden into a magic grotto filled with ghostly forms. As reds and oranges, the greens of foliage, and the darker flower colors recede in the fading light, white flowers appear to float in the darkness.

When used as a predominant color in the garden, white teams naturally with gray. Gray foliage can range from pale silver to white-gray to gray-blue to gray-green. As you plan your white garden, however, remember that foliage is not your only source of soft grays and silvers; these colors may be all around you in rocks, weathered wood, statuary, or stone walls, all of which add interest to a monochromatic garden. Variegated leaves with cream or yellow patterns and margins also have their place in a garden of soft whites, silvers, and grays.

Varying Shapes of White Flower Heads

Since white varieties are available of virtually every flowering plant, you can create lovely effects by mixing and matching flowers of different shapes. For example, plants with small, flat flower heads, such as periwinkle, lychnis, and Johnny-jump-up, tend to merge into a solid sheet in brilliant sun when massed together. It is better to separate them with white flowers of strikingly ornamental shape, such as phlox, cleome, liatris, or lupine, which have large round or long heads consisting of many florets. Or team the tiny flowers with the white pompom-shaped heads of garden chrysanthemum, *Paeonia lactiflora* (herbaceous peony), *P. suffruticosa* (tree peony), or *Alcea rosea* 'Powderpuff' (hollyhock).

You can add excitement and texture to your white garden by including some bi- and tricolored whites. Choose a selection that will span the growing season, so that from the first snowdrop to the last *Colchicum autumnale* 'Alboplenum' (autumn crocus) you will enjoy a continuous flow of white.

If you wish to plant white flowers in small pockets to create contrast rather than linkage, icy pure whites make a dazzling statement. Plantings of stark white flowers stand out in the garden—especially when they are partnered with dark green foliage. Some pure whites to consider include *Clematis* 'Duchess of Edinburgh', *Hydrangea arborescens* 'Annabelle', *Narcissus* 'White Ideal' and *N.* 'Ice Wings', *Iris* 'Lacy Snowflake', *Hemerocallis* 'Joan Senior', *Rosa* 'Iceberg', and *Astilbe* x *arendsii* 'Snowdrift'.

White varieties for the sunny border are plentiful; good candidates for a shady woodland garden can be found as well. To create a canopy, plant a few flowering dogwoods and shade-loving shrubs such as *Rhododendron* 'Lodestar', *Kalmia latifolia* 'Elf' (mountain laurel), and *K. l.* 'Olympic Fire'. Fill in with shade-loving white perennials and ground covers—*Galium odoratum* (sweet woodruff), *Convallaria majalis* (lily-of-the-valley), *Bergenia* 'Silberlicht', *Helleborus orientalis* (Lenten rose), *Dicentra eximia* 'Snowdrift', *Cimicifuga simplex* 'White Pearl', *Astilbe* x *hybrida* 'Snowdrift', and *Hosta* 'Patriot.'

A Variety of Scents

White gardens are fragrant. Their flowers are usually more heavily scented than vividly colored flowers, which use color to attract insect pollinators. Pale flowers rely on their perfume for this purpose. And some white flowers release that perfume into the air only as night falls, to attract nocturnal pollinators.

Flower fragrances fall into recognizable categories—for example, heavy, balsamic, spicy, sweet, musky, fruity, violet- or rose-scented. Careful distancing of those flowers that share a common underlying perfumed scent, such

THE CHANGING FACE OF A WHITE GARDEN
Cool and restful by day, softly luminous at twilight or under a full moon, this border blends hostas, dahlias, flowering tobacco, and Shasta daisies in a subtle combination of white flowers. The bright green lawn and green, gray, and variegated foliage contribute an assortment of shapes and lines to this mating of green and white.

Scented Flowers

Daphne
(daphne)
Dianthus
(pink)
Hyacinthus orientalis
(hyacinth)
Jasminum
(jasmine)
Lathyrus odoratus
(sweet pea)
Narcissus jonquilla
(jonquil)
Nicotiana alata
(flowering tobacco)
Paeonia
(peony)
Rosa
(tea and floribunda roses)
Viburnum x *carlcephalum*
(fragrant snowball)
Wisteria floribunda
(wisteria)

Night-Blooming Flowers

Anemone hupehensis var.
japonica
(Japanese anemone)
Chrysanthemum x
morifolium
(garden chrysanthemum)
Clematis montana
'Grandiflora'
(clematis)
Datura
(thorn apple)
Delphinium
(delphinium)
Hosta plantaginea
'Aphrodite'
(double-flowered
hosta)
Ipomoea alba
(moonflower)
Iris ensata 'Great
White Heron'
(Japanese iris)
Lilium 'Casa
Blanca'
(Asiatic lily)
Narcissus
(daffodil)
Nicotiana alata
(flowering tobacco)
Phlox paniculata
'Mount Fuji'
(garden phlox)

as rose and violet, from those that have a balsamic, medicinal smell (wintergreen, camphor) or a spicy odor (nasturtium, chives, garlic) will help to concentrate and unify fragrances that would otherwise clash. And spacing groups of pastel and white flowers in a bed of vivid colors will ensure a thread of fragrance throughout.

To make the most of scented varieties, plant them in well-chosen locations. Place the most fragrant, such as hyacinth, narcissus, freesia, and lily-of-the-valley, in the front of the border close to where you walk. Plant gardenia near the front entrance; grow sweet pea up a trellis outside the garage door. Place tubs of tuberose and flowering tobacco on the deck; surround a patio with rosemary, lavender, and scented geranium. Hang a basket of lemon thyme and mint near the kitchen window. Or grow the thyme near paths or between pavers so that it releases scent when trod upon. Once you experience a season of enchanting fragrances, you will be certain to include aromatic flowers in all your future garden plans.

Datura inoxia ssp.
quinquecuspida
(downy thorn
apple)

Soothing Pastels

A garden planted with a combination of pastels in lemon, apricot, pink, lavender, and blue will be peaceful and serene. And because such color associations are harmonious, you can plant them together without concern and let their flowering times overlap. Some gardeners favor a pastel theme based on gradations of a single color range, such as blue, gray, and silver; or cream, lemon, apricot, and salmon. Such an arrangement will have a range of light shades and pale tints. Because shades are enriched with black, the varying intensities provided by this color scheme may offer more visual appeal than the bed that is planted with several colors all sharing the same pale values.

in direct sunlight. To strengthen a cast of early-season pinks, combine deep pink Grecian windflower with pale pink and pink-lavender garden hyacinths and lilac-striped white crocuses. By midspring, tulips and pansies can offer their own extensive variation on the theme of an all-pink planting.

Early- and midsummer blooms offering a range of pinks and related tints and shades are plentiful. Try an overlapping sequence of deep and pale pink peonies, pale pink and carmine gladiolus; amethyst pink, melon pink, and peachy pink Asiatic and Oriental lilies; and shrub roses such as 'The Fairy', 'Carefree Wonder', and lavender 'Angel Face'.

The Appeal of Pink

To maintain interest, a garden based on pinks needs to include the deeper rose and mauve shades. When used alone, pale pinks get lost

Yellow and Apricot

Choices among pastel yellow and apricot flowers seem almost limitless. The range found within the tulip, narcissus, bearded iris,

daylily, and lily families is so extensive that you could build a sizable monochromatic garden from among these genera alone. But do not overlook some exquisite creamy yellow, lemon yellow, peachy yellow, and apricot roses. In miniatures, clear yellow 'Rise 'n' Shine', apricot 'Ella Mae', and creamy apricot-salmon 'Party Girl' are outstanding.

Add a touch of strong copper with two hybrid tea roses—'Cary Grant' and 'Caramella'. Anchor the color scheme with green-bronze foliage such as that of *Heuchera micrantha* 'Bressingham Bronze' and yellow-green ornamental grasses such as *Carex elata* 'Bowles Golden' (tufted sedge) and *Hakonechloa macra* 'Aureola'.

A Pastel Woodland Nook

If your garden space includes a woodland area, turn it into a peaceful pastel retreat and plant a combination of delicately hued flowers that prefer shade. For early spring blooms, plant bulbs such as *Eranthis* (winter aconite), *Erythronium* (trout lily), and crocuses. For late spring and summer, fill in with perennials such as *Mertensia virginica* (Virginia blue-bell), woodland forget-me-not, *Baptisia* (false indigo), *Tricyrtis* (toad lily), *Dicentra eximia* 'Luxuriant', and the feathery plumes of pale pink and salmon pink astilbe varieties. And for shade-loving plants that flower in summer and fall, choose *Begonia grandis* (hardy begonia), hosta, *Limonium* (sea lavender), and *Valeriana officinalis* (common valerian).

If what you seek is a spectacular show of nonstop blooms from late spring to late fall, annuals are your best bet. The reliable and carefree *Impatiens wallerana* is available in pink, lavender, mauve, salmon, apricot, and white; it is disease and pest free, and does not need deadheading.

A Perception of Spaciousness

Whether in sun or in shade, a garden planted with pastels and whites of virtually any cast gives the illusion of spaciousness, even in a confined area. To strengthen this effect, create a backdrop composed of pale foliage. Or, to reduce the impression of distance in a larger plot and bring it into sharp focus, plant the perimeter with dark green shrubs.

Taming Dominant Colors

Mellowing Out with Magenta

Gardeners either love magenta or hate it. True magenta—like the 'James Walker' bougainvillea, above—is fairly rare among flowers, but a profusion of tints and shades is available, and their misuse in gardens has perhaps contributed to giving the color a bad name.

Magenta is not the least bit unruly when teamed with its own tones or with lavender, blue-violet, or blue tones. Planted in small drifts with gray or silver foliage, or surrounded with pearly white flowers, it brightens without blinding. Placed in front of a dark green hedge, it stands out, and combined with gold, gold-and-green, or yellow-green leaves, it is striking.

If you would like magenta in your garden for several months, choose annuals such as petunia, *Portulaca* (moss rose), *Celosia* (cockscomb), or common geranium. Few perennial magentas can be found, and these bloom only briefly. Look instead for flowering shrubs such as azalea, bougainvillea, and *Rosa rugosa* 'Rubra'.

Although some of the loveliest flowers in the world have strong, rich color, many gardeners are wary of them. Brilliantly colored flowers can create a strident note in a bed or border. Hot, brassy hues of yellow, scarlet, and orange shout for attention; violet and magenta can be powerfully contentious and difficult to fit in. Yet, a planting can be truly spectacular when such eye-catching colors are skillfully introduced. They stimulate the senses and invite the eyes to focus and linger.

One way to handle dominant colors is to isolate them in a separate bed where their brilliance will not overshadow more subdued colors. But if you lack the space to do this, try planting them in partial shade (if they can prosper under these conditions), which will help reduce their impact. When bathed by shadows, these colors are transformed from muscular and garish to luminous and lovely.

You might also place your bold hues in a plot that is sited mainly for viewing either early or late in the day. The flowers will not be as overwhelming when seen in early morning light or in the setting sun. The same principle holds true for the light of early spring or the waning light of fall. Flowers that might clash terribly in the unforgiving light of the summer sun will appear more subdued in pale spring light or in the soft glow cast by the sun as it travels lower on the horizon in the fall. A bed of tulips dressed in flaming orange, carmine, scarlet, and bright yellow, for example, will be a welcome—and well-behaved—burst of warmth in the cool light of spring.

Fighting Fire with Fire

A surprisingly effective way to tone down a bed of brilliant hues is to add a splash of a clashing color. For example, when intense magenta and blue-violet or purple are growing in jangling proximity to each other, a dash of orange will have the paradoxical effect of subduing them. The accent of orange flowers catches the eye first and helps to soften the impact of the larger and more powerful color combination.

Orange is the warmest hue on the color wheel. When planted with other warm colors

such as flame red, bronze, and deep red, it makes a technically harmonious, if bold, combination. You can achieve a less obtrusive effect by planting it with its opposite on the wheel, true blue, or with a split complementary such as blue-green or blue-violet. For a striking combination, team orange lilies or daylilies with the vibrantly rich blue-violet spikes of *Salvia farinacea* 'Victoria'.

Bold colors can also be successfully joined in triads. Try, for example, combining yellow-orange *Kniphofia* 'Ada' with lime-colored *Euphorbia characias* ssp. *wulfenii* (Mediterranean euphorbia) and magenta *Callirhoe involucrata* (poppy mallow) or *Liatris pycnostachya* (Kansas gay-feather).

If a pairing like orange and scarlet seems too gaudy, consider yellow and scarlet. You can produce this rich combination with Oriental poppy or crocosmia planted next to bright yellow coreopsis or *Rudbeckia hirta* 'Marmalade'. Add a backdrop of dark blue delphinium and throw in a few velvet heads of purple bearded iris and you have a winning arrangement of strongly contrasting but compatible colors.

Of course, an uncomplicated, low-key way to tame vividly colored plants is simply to plant fewer of them. Used merely as an accent in the bed, they will not overwhelm the eye.

CHAPTER TWO

Decorating a Garden with Foliage

A garden alive with foliage of varying shapes and colors offers never-ending satisfaction. Foliage not only provides a backdrop for the display of flowers, but it also can stand out as a center of ornamental interest in its own right. Foliage has an architectural quality that gives structure to a garden. The broad canopy of a tree in leaf can scale down the garden's size and create a more intimate atmosphere. An expanse of lawn or other ground cover, by contrast, tends to open up a garden's sightlines. And hedges can divide the garden into compartments with leafy boundaries.

You can deploy foliage in your own garden to achieve a number of different effects, such as the sense of containment and serenity evident in the Bethesda, Maryland, property at left. There, a wall of tree lilac and inula leaves opens a window onto a hidden foliage garden populated with common leadwort, large-leaf coneflower, and a number of ornamental grasses.

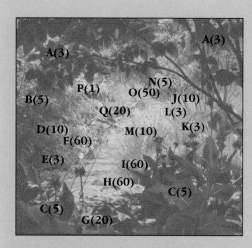

A. *Syringa reticulata (Japanese tree lilac) (6)* B. *Cornus mas (cornelian cherry) (5)* C. *Inula magnifica (inula) (10)* D. *Eupatorium purpureum (green-stemmed Joe-Pye weed) (10)* E. *Aster divaricatus (white wood aster) (3)* F. *Ceratostigma plumbaginoides (common leadwort) (60)* G. *Hosta x 'Honeybells' (plantain lily) (20)* H. *Mazus reptans (creeping mazus) (60)* I. *Coreopsis verticillata 'Zagreb' (threadleaf coreopsis) (60)* J. *Perovskia atriplicifolia (Russian sage) (10)* K. *Stipa gigantea (giant feather grass) (3)* L. *Belamcanda chinensis (blackberry lily) (3)* M. *Pennisetum orientale (Oriental fountain grass) (10)* N. *Mahonia aquifolium 'Compacta' (compact Oregon grape) (5)* O. *Sesleria autumnalis (autumn moor grass) (50)* P. *Artemisia lactiflora (white mugwort) (1)* Q. *Rudbeckia maxima (large-leaf coneflower) (20)*

NOTE: *The key lists each plant type and the total quantity needed to replicate the garden shown. The diagram's letters and numbers refer to the type of plant and the number sited in an area.*

Designing with Foliage

When you first see a garden, your impression of its foliage is generally of loose and shifting curtains of leaves that billow and flutter in the breeze. On closer inspection, however, the garden begins to separate into patterns—curved and straight, vertical, horizontal, and diagonal—traced by the foliage. In the wall of indistinct greenery your eye discerns a fascinating variety of forms—on the ground, at eye level, and up high—that shape and enliven a garden's design and give the site its character.

pose order and dominate portions of a garden. When planted in precise, linear patterns, they establish the sightlines of a garden, defining its focal points and boundaries.

In contrast to that more formal effect, plants whose foliage presents weeping or fountain shapes, such as *Tsuga canadensis* 'Sargentii' (weeping Canada hemlock), *Callicarpa dichotoma,* and many ornamental grasses, soften the garden's appearance as their curves gently lead the eye to plantings at ground level. There, plants with domed shapes, including *Santolina chamaecyparissus* (lavender cotton) and *Buxus sempervirens* (English box), or with horizontal habits like that of *Juniperus horizontalis* 'Wiltonii', tend to cause the eye to linger. For a less static effect, consider fans of irises, with their bladelike leaves; plants with bowl-shaped profiles such as redtwig or yellowtwig dogwood and dwarf pines such as *Pinus strobus* 'Nana';

Establishing the Framework

The leaves of plants—their size, shape, and color, and their collective arrangement and density on the plant—define a garden's spaces. The striking forms of trees and shrubs with ascending foliage, for example, can im-

A POTPOURRI OF GREENERY AND SHAPES
Its branches spread wide, a Persian parrot tree forms a low-hanging ceiling of pale green leaves over fans of widely spaced sword ferns in this foundation planting in Portland, Oregon. The linear contours of a neatly clipped yew hedge add a touch of order to the scene.

and those with airy forms such as *Rhus typhina* (staghorn sumac) and *Spiraea prunifolia* (bridal wreath).

Foliage is also a unifying element in the garden. Highly dramatic foliage forms such as the majestic pyramid of *Picea pungens* 'Glauca' (Colorado blue spruce) or the bright straggly tangle of *Sambucus racemosa* 'Plumosa-aurea' (golden elder) link the house and its terraces, walls, and walkways to understory plants. And because the eye takes in a large expanse of ground cover at a glance, this lowest level of foliage, when well matched with other plantings, unifies disparate garden features.

Considering Foliage and Flowers

Even among commanding displays of foliage, flowers draw the viewer's eye. But when the blossoms fade, long-lasting leaves are what extend a garden's visual appeal. A few plants, such as herbaceous peonies and Siberian irises, have both stunning blooms and distinctive foliage; others, such as New Zealand flax and common tansy, are pleasant enough in bloom but are largely prized for handsome foliage that looks good most of the year. In densely shaded areas, where few flowers bloom after spring, the leaves of plants such as ferns, mountain laurels, privets, and some hydrangeas help keep the garden lively.

An Evergreen and Deciduous Mix

To maintain foliage interest throughout the growing season and into winter, try to strike a balance between evergreen and deciduous plants. Among the evergreens, consider the impact of different leaf shapes. Conifers such as firs, hemlocks, and junipers have dense, narrow-leaved foliage that lends a weighty, formal atmosphere to a garden. Throughout the winter they act as visual anchors amid the skeletons of their deciduous neighbors. Broadleaf evergreens, such as rhododendrons

and camellias, have sparser foliage and contrast nicely with the solid lines of the conifers.

Deciduous foliage, on the other hand, lets a garden change character with the seasons. A hedge of weigela or a stand of dogwoods acts as an opaque screen from bud break to leaf fall, then in winter becomes a tracery of elegant branches. In fall, a climbing hydrangea clinging to a porch drops its large, glossy, dark green serrated leaves and reveals a peeling, reddish tan bark to enliven the winter scene.

Grouping Foliage Plants

Choosing plants for their individual appeal is only one factor in creating a garden; the essence of gardening lies in pairing plants effectively. To assess how a foliage plant will look in a grouping, first consider how the plant grows. Does it have one stem or many? Does its profile have a vertical or horizontal bias? Do leaves cover the whole plant or just the base or the top? Take note of the plant's mature height and spread to ensure its scale is right for your garden. And consider the size, shape, and texture of its leaves *(pages 32-36)*.

A BECKONING SWEEP OF LAWN
A foreground planting of 'Duke's Yellow' coleus, reddish brown perilla, and 'Gold Edger' hosta nestles in an arc of lawn that leads the eye to distant trees and shrubbery. Tall flowering crab apples counter the predominantly horizontal makeup of this Missouri foliage garden.

Discerning the Aspects
of a Single Leaf

The size, shape, and surface texture of a plant's foliage are three features to weigh as you decide where the plant should go in your garden. Some plants have exceptionally attractive attributes in all three categories. *Rheum palmatum* (ornamental rhubarb), for instance, has leaves that are large, incised, and rough textured; rockspray cotoneaster leaves are tiny, oval, and glossy. Many artemisias have leaves with an intricate shape and woolly texture, with the added bonus of a silvery cast. Each plant's unique blend of leaf traits calls for balancing it with neighbors whose traits are complementary. Some plants site well with only a handful of different companions, while others look better when surrounded by a wide variety.

The complex foliage of the ornamental rhubarb, for example, has few compatible mates. It looks best with a neighbor whose leaves appear equally large in proportion to the plant's overall size but are different in shape; both slender-bladed ornamental grasses and ferns, with their lacy fronds, are good complements. The small-leaved cotoneaster,

on the other hand, combines well with a wide selection of plants, often supporting neighbors that have fewer outstanding qualities. The fine detail and fish-bone pattern of the cotoneaster foliage pairs well, for instance, with solid masses of yew foliage or the simple, lancelike leaves of liriope.

The Special Traits of Big-Leaved Plants

Some plants may win their way into your garden for the sheer size of their leaves. Those with the biggest leaves—7 feet across or more—generally are tropical or subtropical plants that need plenty of water and warm temperatures. Yet a number of big-leaved plants are happy in more temperate climates *(list, opposite)*. Leaves are generally considered large if they measure a foot or more across, but size must be seen in relation to the whole plant. *Paulownia tomentosa* (princess tree), which can grow to 40 feet or more, has leaves that are 18 inches wide; the leaves will

SIZE TAKES COMMAND
In this sunny site, the large, robust leaves of an umbrella plant stand out against the smaller and sparser foliage of a Japanese red maple. Placing the round, deeply lobed light green leaves in the foreground ensures that their striking effect will not be diminished.

CONTRAST TO BRIGHTEN SHADY PLACES
In this grouping of shade-loving plants, the simple, smooth-edged leaves of Hosta undulata show up well against the highly complex foliage of Japanese painted fern and the deeply lobed leaves of bloodroot (Sanguinaria canadensis). The fern's tiny leaflets, with their toothed margins, provide a feathery interlude between the two more solid shapes, while its delicate patterns of light and dark are a counterpoint to the hosta's large, splotchy variegations.

grow even larger if the plant is cut to the ground in winter and fed generously as it grows again the following spring. But proportionately speaking, even such grand leaves are smaller than those of the ground-hugging bergenia, which grows only 1 foot high but has leaves 9 inches wide. In comparison to their overall size, both plants have large leaves.

Large leaves are more than just impressive and pleasing to the eye; they are also functional. They smother or shade out weeds and can shelter more delicate plants. As a design element, they soften the geometric lines of architectural features. In a large, informal garden, large leaves emphasize the curves of beds and borders and the sweeping arcs among smaller foliage. In a limited space, plants with huge leaves give you an immediate focal point for your garden design.

Some big-leaved plants make such a bold statement in the garden that the best effects come from using only one kind of plant and very few specimens of it—perhaps no more than one in a small space. *Ligularia dentata* (bigleaf golden-ray), hardy to Zone 5, flaunts crinkled, kidney-shaped leaves that reach almost 2 feet across. Placing it near plants with smaller leaves would emphasize the impact of the more prominent partner and still set off the form and foliage of the smaller-leaved companion plants, even if they are partly hidden. Planting the ligularia at the base of a large tree whose trunk is even wider than the leaves would exaggerate the size of both.

Optical Illusions with Leaf Size

With careful placement, you can also use leaf sizes to alter the visual perception of depth in your garden, creating an illusion of greater or lesser distance. Placing big-leaved plants in the foreground and smaller leaf sizes in the distance makes a garden look larger than it is. For a completely ordered gradation of foliage, diminish leaf sizes by half with each receding planting, so that those at the rear have very tiny leaves. This arrangement is subtler than a

Big-Leaved Plants for Temperate Climates

Acanthus mollis
(bear's-breech)
Agave americana
(century plant)
Alchemilla mollis
(lady's-mantle)
Aloe striata
(coral aloe)
Bergenia cordifolia
(heartleaf bergenia)
Brunnera macrophylla
(Siberian bugloss)
Buddleia davidii
(butterfly bush)
Caladium
(elephant's-ear)
Canna x generalis
(Indian shot)
Cimicifuga racemosa
(black cohosh)
Crambe maritima
(sea kale)
Cynara cardunculus
(cardoon)
Datura metel
(Hindu weed)
Echinops ritro
(globe thistle)
Fatsia japonica
(Japanese fatsia)
*Hosta sieboldiana
'Elegans'*
(plantain lily)
*Hosta 'Sum and
Substance'*
(plantain lily)
Hydrangea macrophylla
(bigleaf hydrangea)
Ligularia macrophylla
(bigleaf ligularia)
Macleaya cordata
(plume poppy)
Mahonia bealei
(leatherleaf mahonia)
Onopordum acanthium
(Scotch thistle)
Phormium tenax
(New Zealand flax)
Pulmonaria angustifolia
(blue lungwort)
Pulmonaria saccharata
(Bethlehem sage)
Rhododendron fortunei
(fortune rhododendron)
Ricinus communis
(castor bean)
Rodgersia podophylla
(bronzeleaf rodgersia)
Rodgersia tabularis
(shieldleaf rodgersia)
Viburnum rhytidophyllum
(leatherleaf viburnum)
Vitis coignetiae
(Japanese crimson
glory vine)
Yucca glauca
(small soapweed)

direct clash of opposing sizes and appeals to gardeners who wish to avoid the obvious contrast of the remarkably big next to the remarkably small.

If you want to foster the illusion of width in a narrow space—say, in an alleylike side yard—play with depth perception by placing a few large-leaved plants at the rear of the site. A grouping of *Fatsia japonica,* which reaches 10 feet in height, easily fills a narrow space with big, hand-shaped leaves as large as a foot across. The sheer breadth of the leaves will seem to expand the confined space. Placing smaller-leaved plants such as a mound of white-variegated winter daphne in front of the fatsia will further exaggerate the broad spread of the evergreen shrub. If your aim is to foreshorten a narrow space, a vigorous grower like *Vitis coignetiae* (crimson glory vine) can quickly cover a back wall or fence with massive, overlapping leaves that seem to leap forward and shrink the distance to them.

Leaf Shapes

Another feature to consider when pairing plants is the configuration of the leaf. Leaf shapes fall into broad groupings. Perhaps the simplest to visualize are the swordlike blades characteristic of ornamental grasses, yucca, iris, and the foliage of the spike-flowered perennial kniphofia. Rounded leaves include those of the huge *Rodgersia tabularis* (shieldleaf rodgersia), the smaller *Asarum europaeum* (European wild ginger), and the heart-shaped leaves of Siberian bugloss and 'Francee' hosta. Other wide shapes include the ovate, as on *Camellia japonica;* and the elliptical, as on many rhododendrons and *Hosta sieboldiana* 'Elegans'.

Some leaves are so intricately detailed that they are best described as ferny or feathery.

SIMILAR, BUT WITH A PLEASING DISSIMILARITY
Different growing angles set off two variations of heart-shaped leaves—those of Hosta 'Northern Halo', at top in the photograph above, and those of lily-of-the-valley; creamy leaf margins accentuate the hosta's flat growing habit. At right, two varieties of heuchera have leaves that are nearly identical in size and shape but offer eye-catching differences in surface texture and color.

Examples include some artemisias, asparagus fern, and fennel. Palmate, or hand-shaped, leaves appear on *Aesculus hippocastanum* (horse chestnut) and Japanese maple.

Leaf margins also come in a variety of characteristic shapes, broadly classified as smooth, toothed, or lobed. Smooth margins, as on epimedium or eucalyptus leaves, are also called entire. Toothed margins vary tremendously: They include serrate, with sawteeth; crenate, with rounded teeth; and sinuate, or ruffled. Another toothed leaf, that of mahonia, has tiny spikes on its margins.

Lobed leaves have margins with deep indentations—cutting at least one-third of the way toward the middle vein of the leaf. These margins can be further defined as rounded or wavy-edged. Another kind of lobed leaf, irregularly incised with narrow, pointed lobes, as on the ornamental rhubarb, is termed laciniate. Finally, leaf tips are simply described as pointed, rounded, squarish, or cleft.

Leaf Shape as a Design Element

When grouping plants on the basis of leaf shape, remember that the larger the leaf and the simpler the shape, the easier it will be for you to anticipate the visual effect. The big, oval leaves of garden hydrangeas, for example, have obvious mates in plants whose leaves are roughly the same shape but slightly smaller. Monarda, with pointed, oval leaves on erect, square stems, offers a casual kinship: While its leaves are similar in shape to those of the hydrangea, the orderly stand of single stems creates a subtle contrast to the unruly mound of hydrangea.

In fact, any setting of different plants that share a common leaf shape often benefits from a contrast of some sort—in habit, scale, or overall form. A tall, arching clump of *Miscanthus sinensis* 'Strictus' (porcupine grass) and a slightly more squat clump of *M. s.* 'Condensatus' (Japanese silver grass) are set off by low, rolling mounds of *Molinia arundinacea* 'Windspiel' (purple moor grass) planted abundantly in front of them. Though all share the same long, graceful lines, the greater mass of the moor grass and the variations in height prevent monotony. You can echo the leaf shapes of these arching grasses with perennials that have swordlike leaves but are more upright—for example, crocosmia or iris.

Because combining plants that vary widely in leaf shape creates an immediate foliage focus, try not to go overboard in juxtaposing contrasting forms. Take care, for example, not to make pairings that seem eccentric, unless that is your personal taste and aim. Also avoid cluttering a foliage garden with too many single plants. Choosing a few varieties and repeating them unifies your composition. In shade, for example, 'Majestic' liriope, 'Regal Splendor' hosta, and Christmas fern provide three contrasting leaf shapes. Six liriope and three each of the hosta and the fern would create a balanced foliage display, but an arrangement of one of each would look spotty. For a sunny setting in northern climates, a patch of bergenia planted in front of the tall, straplike leaves of *Iris*

A PANOPLY OF SHAPES AND SIZES
Fronds of American maidenhair fern share the stage with the arching, pointed spears of Japanese forest grass. Wild dock growing into the scene from the left adds fleshy tongue-shaped leaves, and lobed geranium leaves form a compact mat with bugleweed foliage at bottom right.

35

foetidissima is a classic contrast of shape and scale, but the bergenia must heavily outnumber the iris to offset the strongly upright fans.

Surface Texture

Up close, leaf surfaces exhibit a variety of textures, which are primarily a survival adaptation. Smooth, shiny leaves—such as those on wild ginger—repel rain, permitting quick drying in moist climates. On fuzzy-leaved plants that flourish in full sun and at higher altitudes—lamb's ears, for example—the downy hairs protect the leaf from harsh sunlight.

For the purposes of garden design, it is well to remember that the shinier the surface, the more light it reflects. Certain hollies, for example, have an intensely reflective leaf surface that brightens the space around them. Leaves with a rough, corrugated, ribbed, or pleated surface, such as those of rodgersia or *Viburnum davidii,* tend to absorb light, creating patterns of shade on the leaf itself and thus appearing darker in color. Such foliage is more restful and soothing to the eye.

Combining plants that have different surface textures can highlight otherwise unnoticed details. The leaves of the tall *Verbascum olympicum* (Olympic mullein) are noted for dramatic shape and coloring, but a grouping of three of them with a shiny, evergreen mound of *Skimmia japonica* (Japanese skimmia) brings out both the woolly fleshiness of the verbascum's silvery leaves and the leathery sleekness of the skimmia's. In sunny areas, the matte gray-green leaves of lady's-mantle and silvery artemisia set off the ribbed and shadowy foliage of *Viburnum davidii.*

Highly textured ground covers can do a lot to tame such hardscape features as stone paths, brick terraces, and wooden decking. A border of *Lamium* (dead nettle), with its delicate, fuzzy leaves, blurs the sharp edges of a flagstone walkway. Pots of downy-textured, multicolored sage complement and soften the rigid, gritty look of masonry. The tiny, lustrous leaves of *Teucrium* (germander) provide a foil for rough-hewn wood, and a plush lawn of finely bladed turf grass is a restful counterpoint to the concrete, gravel, and blacktop paths and driveways around many homes.

MULTIPLE CONTRASTS
Flanked by the puckered foliage of 'Palace Purple' heuchera and the curled fronds of Christmas fern, glossy, deep green leaves of wild ginger in this Hamden, Connecticut, garden offer an interesting contrast to the new growth of arborvitae above them.

Leaf Shape and Density

Simple and Compound Leaves

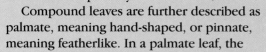

Leaves are broadly classified as either simple or compound, depending on how many distinct units make up an individual leaf. A simple leaf develops as one unit; a compound leaf is made up of smaller units called leaflets. In autumn, a simple deciduous leaf falls in one piece and retains its overall shape. When a compound deciduous leaf falls, its leaflets may come down separately.

Compound leaves are further described as palmate, meaning hand-shaped, or pinnate, meaning featherlike. In a palmate leaf, the leaflets extend like outspread fingers from a common attachment point. A pinnate leaf resembles a bird's feather, with a central rib carrying matched sets of leaflets on either side. Some pinnate leaves branch out doubly or triply into smaller and smaller segments; such leaves are termed bipinnate or tripinnate. The more branching in each leaf, the more feathery the look of the plant's foliage.

Leaflets can be opposite, as in the pinnate leaf illustrated at left, or alternate, with the leaflets on one side sprouting opposite the spaces between the leaflets on the other, as in the bipinnate leaf at right.

At a distance, a plant's overall form is the first thing that strikes the eye, and form is more a matter of foliage density and the plant's growth habit than of leaf traits. Foliage density results from the complexity of the leaves *(left)*, their arrangement on the plant, and their quantity. Growth habit gives the plant its characteristic framework of limbs or stems. Trees, shrubs, and perennials offer a variety of growth habits—upright, layered, pyramidal, domed, mounded, fan-shaped, arching, weeping, bowl-shaped—in varying degrees of symmetry. Each framework may be clothed in different degrees of foliage density. And every combination of growth habit and foliage density adds up to a unique form, with its own visual impact.

Leaf Complexity and Distribution

Seen from afar, foliage may appear coarse or fine, depending on the size and complexity of individual leaves. Plants with big, simple leaves are called coarse-textured, while plants with smaller or more complex leaves

CONTRAST FROM DIFFERING DENSITIES
The fine-textured, sparse foliage of Acer palmatum 'Ever Red' supplies a pleasing contrast to the coarse-textured, dense greenery of Hosta 'Frances Williams'. The slim-fingered maple leaves flutter in the slightest breeze, while the broad, flat hosta leaves rarely move.

are called fine-textured. Regardless of their complexity, leaves can be distributed densely or sparsely; the distribution determines how much of a tree's woody structure can be seen. These four traits—coarse, fine, dense, and sparse—have four permutations: coarse-textured and dense or coarse-textured and sparse, fine-textured and dense or fine-textured and sparse.

Including a plant in your garden on the basis of its distinctive foliage texture allows you to perk up a border when other plants are finished flowering or to highlight particularly splashy blooms. Plants with bold, coarse-textured, sparse foliage, such as *Onopordum acanthium* (Scotch thistle), work well as single specimens within a planting, adding a sense of informality or even a visual jolt. A backdrop of dense, fine foliage of a contrasting color, such as that of *Cotinus coggygria* 'Purpureus' (purple smokebush), sets off such a plant to advantage. Use such pairings sparingly, however; strong contrast can become tiring to the eye if overdone.

Fine-textured plants with small, compound leaves, such as stephanandra or gypsophila, make a garden look more formal. The delicate foliage works well as a background for flowering plants. Try planting *Dictamnus albus,* with glossy, dark green leaflets, next to a clump of double peonies, or *Gillenia trifoliata* (bowman's root), with sharply toothed, narrow leaflets, behind a rolling mound of big, pink-blossomed 'Robin Hill' azaleas.

Combining Foliage Forms

Once you find a plant whose texture and form you like, the next step is to incorporate it with your other plants. Some plants dominate a garden setting. You can see this effect with stately needled evergreens, such as Colorado blue spruce, and with rounded, small-leaved shrubs, such as boxwood. Because their small, densely set leaves cast no inner shadows and reveal no depth, their solid forms seem monolithic, and their stark outlines set them apart from their less austere neighbors.

Such visually heavy shrubs and trees are best used by planting them not in masses but in a repeating pattern. Evenly spaced along a drive or walkway, they create a sequential symmetry leading the eye to a well-defined distant point. As a windbreak or hedge, the broadly pyramidal, steel gray *Juniperus chinensis* 'Ames', for example, forms a 7-foot-high living wall. Spaced along a meandering curve, taller junipers, such as goldtip eastern red cedars, create a rhythmic line that invites strolling.

SHARED TEXTURES AND LEAF SHAPES
The arcing blades of Hemerocallis 'Ed Murray' set off the blue-needled apron of a prostrate spruce and the intricate foliage of Juniperus chinensis 'Hetzii' (upper left) in this Virginia setting. The oval leaves of snapweed and the deeply lobed leaves of a seedling plume poppy add shapely touches of green.

A SUPPORTING CAST FOR A DRAMATIC FORM
Heavy swords of agave dominate this southern California grouping of four contrasting plant forms, silhouetted below. The fluffy ball of mountain marigold and the silvery horizontal mat of snow-in-summer tame the stiff agave, while upright stems of lion's tail (Leonotis) softly echo it.

A FORMAL TRIO
This classic arrangement in an Atlanta garden pairs a cone of Japanese yew with a low mound of American box. The visually dense forms create a triangular configuration, visible in the drawing below, that is enhanced and lightened by the airy, tiered branches of the double file viburnum behind them.

To anchor these vertical forms, consider using smaller, arching shrubs, such as the elegant *Leucothoe fontanesiana* (drooping leucothoe). In a large grouping, you might let the leucothoe and a small, chunky rhododendron offset a heroic column of a yew cultivar such as *Taxus baccata* 'Fastigiata'. A spreading lower layer of woolly-leaved pearly everlasting *(Anaphalis),* whose white flowers last for 3 months, and a clumping mat of the leathery, evergreen *Bergenia* x *schmidtii* 'Jan Schmidt' could complete the picture.

Where you need a focal point, you can use a simple, reliable configuration consisting of three plants of different heights arranged to form a scalene, or unequal-sided, triangle. For the tallest side of the triangle, consider the green-needled dwarf white spruce, which reaches a height of 10 feet. In front of the spruce but off-center, place the semi-evergreen viburnum 'Chesapeake', which seldom grows to more than 6 feet but spreads to at least 10 feet. A line from the tip of the white spruce, along the broad profile of the viburnum, and then to ground will describe a gentle slope. For the base of the triangle, plant a foreground drift of rich yellow tulips, such as *Tulipa batalinii* 'Bronze Charm', to add a color link in spring, and let an underplanting of *Alchemilla mollis* hide the spent tulip leaves with a low cloak of foliage.

The Leaf Color Palette

Foliage color offers surprising variety. With a wide range of greens to choose from, as well as purple, silver-gray, and gold, you'll find a generous palette of foliage possibilities for sitting in sun or shade. Green, the most plentiful, is restful to the eye and soothing to the spirit. An all-green garden tends to look formal, especially if composed of the deeper, richer greens, if only because a one-color design must rely on the more economical elements of plant form and line for visual emphasis. But even here, accents from opposite ends of the green spectrum can enliven the scene. Use the bluish green vine of *Aristolochia durior* (Dutchman's-pipe) and the lime green of *Euphorbia palustris* (cushion spurge), for instance, to introduce distinct shades and tints.

For an informal ambiance, make plant partnerships that afford plenty of contrast—in form and texture as well as in color. Among southeastern natives, two pleasantly contrasting green shrubs are the 15-foot-tall, vase-shaped *Viburnum prunifolium* (black haw), with its petite, smooth midgreen leaves, and *Calycanthus floridus* (sweet shrub), whose shiny green elliptical leaves grow on an open structure that is 6 feet tall and wide.

The Drama of Purple

Pale colors and strong ones benefit equally from a pairing with foliage in the purple range, which takes in anything from maroon to mahogany, deep red to coppery brown, and even near-black. Purple-hued foliage looks splendid next to dark green. For a hedge of muted color throughout the growing season, consider a staggered double row of *Weigela florida* 'Pink Princess' for its dusky green leaves, fronted by an equal number of smaller, bronze-purplish *W. f.* 'Purpurea'.

Use dark foliage judiciously, however; large drifts of it can look gloomy. Climate, too, must be considered. Foliage of the 'Forest Pansy' redbud, for instance, glows a rich purple in full sun in a temperate zone, but tones down to a dark green in the stronger sun of the South. *Berberis thunbergii* 'Crimson Pygmy' (barberry), on the other hand, maintains a wine red cast even in scorching sunlight.

Accents of Silver Foliage

The foliage treasury contains both silver and gold, although not in equal measure; plants in the silver grouping are far more abundant. And these plants, whether their leaves tend toward gray, blue, or bright silver, grow best in full sun. Bright silver foliage is so bold that suitable plant partners are hard to find. *Tanacetum densum* var. *amani* (partridge feather tansy), for instance, looks like a mass of silvery quills. Pair it with grayish foliage for a congenial combination, perhaps using it to encircle a stiff clump of blue-gray ornamental grass such as *Panicum virgatum* 'Heavy Metal'. Finish by fronting it with a planting of low-growing gray-green woolly thyme.

In the gray foliage realm, perhaps the best known and most widely grown is lamb's ears.

A GAMUT OF GREENS
This all-green planting ranges from near-black heart-shaped leaves of white chervil (far left) to yellow-green lances of Bowles' golden grass (lower right), with three types of spurge planted in between. The tiny, pale green leaves of Ballota pseudodictamnus (lower left) provide a gentle foil to the stronger-hued foliage.

The Few True Blue

Cool blue leaves, prized for their beauty and the way they complement other colors around them, are a rarity in the garden. Only a few cultivars have truly blue leaves, and they should be placed with care to preserve their arresting color. Among perennials, two *Hosta* x *tardiana* cultivars, 'Halcyon' *(left)* and 'Hadspen Blue', stay a rich blue throughout the growing season, provided they receive lots of moisture and grow in partial shade; afternoon sun turns them dark green. The grasses *Festuca glauca* 'Blaufuchs' and 'Blauglut' will hold their icy blue if you site them in full sun and poor soil and divide them every 2 to 3 years. *Helictotrichon sempervirens* (oat grass), another sun lover, is taller and even bluer than the festucas.

For year-round blue foliage, try the 'Jackman's Blue' cultivar of garden rue. The bluest Colorado spruces are the pyramidal 'Hoopsii' and the compact 'Moerheimii'. Four junipers offer blue foliage: the ground cover *Juniperus squamata* 'Blue Carpet', the trailing *J. horizontalis* 'Douglasii' and 'Wiltonii', and the upright *J. chinensis* 'Blaauw'.

CONTRASTING COLORS FOR ADDED DEPTH
Bronze-purple and bright yellow varieties of Japanese barberry grown close together stretch the perception of depth in this northern Virginia garden, as the dark foliage seems to recede while the yellow leaps forward. These versatile plants tolerate a wide range of soils and moisture levels.

Its leaves are so greatly admired that its small, round, magenta-to-pale-pink flowers often go unnoticed. But if you interplant lamb's ears with chartreuse-leaved *Origanum vulgare* var. *aureum* (golden oregano) and *Ajuga reptans* 'Bronze Beauty' (purple-flowering ajuga), you can have a handsome display of compatible flower hues amid foliage that ranges from gray to green.

Since gray foliage changes with the light that falls on it, site gray-leaved plants according to the time of day you will view them. The silvery leaves of santolina and senecio sparkle in sunlight, and at dusk they are tinged with a violet cast. If your favorite time in the garden is early evening, surround these plants with the purple flowers of asters, campanulas, and delphiniums for a tranquil display. Plants with frosty leaves and white flowers, such as pearly everlasting and snow-in-summer, glow in moonlight; they, too, are classic specimens to enjoy in the evening hours.

Going for Gold

Brilliant gold foliage is a rarity. In fact, many leaves described as gold—golden oregano and *Hedera helix* 'Buttercup' (buttercup ivy), for instance, as well as *Filipendula ulmaria* 'Aurea' (meadowsweet)—are actually chartreuse. Even so, among the relatively few plants with truly gold-colored leaves, you'll find some that are appropriate for every climate. *Chamaecyparis pisifera* 'Filifera Aurea' (goldthread false cypress) prefers temperate summers, for example, and the shrub *Philadelphus coronarius* 'Aureus' (golden mock orange) is hardy to Zone 4. In full sun in warmer climates, try *Spiraea* x *bumalda* 'Goldflame' (spirea) or the evergreen *Lonicera nitida* 'Baggesen's Gold' (honeysuckle). Unlike silver or gray leaves, most golden foliage scorches in intense sunlight and turns green in dense shade. To bring out the best in gold leaves, site them in partial shade and surround them with mid- to dark green and purplish foliage.

Variegated Leaves

Foliage fanciers prize variegated leaves for their ornamental value. Variegation can take the form of speckles, veins, stripes, blotches of contrasting colors, and colored leaf edges. Although variegation most often appears as yellow or white against the leaf's larger area of green, it may also occur as tones of red, as in the phormium cultivars 'Maori Sunrise' and 'Dazzler'. In a few plants, the green of the leaves is variegated with two colors.

Some variegations occur as a result of random mutation, as in many lungworts. Others are produced by a harmless virus, as in the mottled yellow of *Abutilon pictum* 'Thompsonii' (spotted flowering maple). Most are the product of hybridization, however, which means that the variegations won't grow true from seed but must be propagated from cuttings or by division.

Plants with variegated leaves are particular about the amount of sunlight they receive. It is curious but true, for example, that gold-edged leaves tolerate more sun than those with gold centers and green margins. Leaves with white or cream margins need dappled shade, and white-centered leaves must be sited out of the sunlight.

Despite their horticultural eccentricities, variegated leaves are prominent in many planting schemes. Since they tend to be attention-getters, use them deliberately and sparingly. Place variegated foliage where you need a streak of light or a feeling of movement. You can also bridge the contrasting foliage colors of adjacent plants with variegated foliage that shares their coloration. With hosta, one of the most hybridized of plants, this is a simple matter of progressing from, say,

'Piedmont Gold' to the yellow-margined, green-centered 'Viette's Yellow Edge' to the all-green *Hosta ventricosa*.

For an ornamental grass with stunning markings choose *Miscanthus sinensis* 'Zebrinus', which has bands of yellow across bright green blades. Plant it in sun, with nerines and a lime green nicotiana. For hardy, low-growing plants with white spotting, marbling, and blotching on green leaves, consider the lungworts. Plant them in moist, rich soil and light shade with hostas and the light green *Onoclea sensibilis* (sensitive fern).

A GREEN AND YELLOW SETTING
The cinnamon-colored limbs of a paperbark maple rise in the midst of a garden framed on the left by yellow-green leaves of honeysuckle and the blotched yellow leaves of spotted laurel. Golden marjoram and straplike green leaves of agapanthus front the lemony Achillea x 'Moonshine' at the center.

Garden Artistry

One of the great rewards and joys of gardening is to choose a variety of beautiful plants and arrange them in such a way that the vibrant result is lovelier than any single plant on its own. With the garden bed as a canvas, the gardener artist can compose an outdoor masterpiece, harmonizing and contrasting sizes, textures, shapes, and a host of colors drawn from nature's generous palette. The final work of art—whether designed for seasonal or year-round viewing—may be simple or complex, formal or informal.

A selection of various garden compositions appears on the following pages; for a list of plants and a planting guide for each garden, see pages 54-57.

A STUDY IN CONTRASTS
Gentle mounds of deep green catmint set off the spearlike form of feather reed grass in this Virginia garden, where a violet-blue haze of Russian sage separates swaths of purple and golden coneflower from brightly contrasting lemony common yarrow.

AN INTERPLAY OF COLOR
Masses of blue catmint highlight the vivid red of Jupiter's-beard, used sparingly as a color accent in this low-maintenance New Mexico perennial garden. In the background, the contrasting golden columbine also appears more intense against the cool tone of the catmint. By allowing the bright yellow to leap forward in the mind's eye, this combination and placement of colors makes the garden seem more lushly planted.

**INVITINGLY SOFT FORMS
AND BRIGHT HUES**
White baby's-breath and yellow beggar-ticks spill onto the stone walk in front of an antique fence and gate, softening this formal entryway garden in Seattle. Along with pink petunias and white trumpets of variegated nicotiana, the plants were chosen both for their pleasing color contrasts and their dainty forms, which accent the Victorian setting. Low, deep green mounds of common thrift and other foliage plants unite the composition.

UNEXPECTED VARIETY IN A FOLIAGE BORDER
Set against the lush green backdrop of a tall thuja hedge, a medley of foliage plants supply a breathtaking exhibition of colors, sizes, forms, and textures as they sweep alongside a pebble walk in Washington State. Irregular repetitions of yellow-leaved hakonechloa and arching spires of Chinese silver grass, combined with plantings such as the mounded 'Jackman Blue' rue, add color and textural excitement when the flowering plants are not blooming. When they are, the garden is punctuated by splashes of flowering orange alstroemeria, pink geraniums, and yellow daylilies, a composition tied together by interweaving vines of clematis bearing indigo blossoms.

**CONTRASTING TEXTURES,
HARMONIOUS GREENS**
*Silvery mounds of dusty miller and tall
white orbs of cleome add a luminous
glow to this verdant Pennsylvania
garden. Fan-leafed hyacinth bean, which
covers the rustic fence, and the feathery
foliage of daphne and cleome provide a
beautiful textural backdrop for the
dramatically veined broad leaves of
'Striata' canna and its bold orange
blossom. Touches of yellow marigolds
and purple Brazilian verbena pull the
planting together and spark color interest.*

AN INFORMAL FOLIAGE SCREEN
*Six-foot-tall plume poppies make a
dramatic vertical statement as they
frame the doorway of a timber and
mortar cottage in Virginia. Their huge
but sparse deeply lobed, blue-green leaves
act as a light foliage screen along the
walls, adding interest without obscuring
the architecture. The plume poppy's
invasive growth habit is held in check
by equally aggressive purple coneflower
and pink wild sweet William.*

AN EMPHASIS ON MOVEMENT
Varying heights, textures, and autumn colors help create an impression of movement in this garden near Washington, D.C. Rising behind low-growing light-green spiky lilyturf and rust-colored 'Autumn Joy' stonecrop, dark green leaves of blue flag iris and cotoneaster, gold fountain grass, and plumes of Malepartus silver grass sway and rustle as they arc over a small pool.

**DRAWING THE EYE INTO
THE DISTANCE**
Strong horizontal lines and slight curves make this formal terrace garden in Maryland—shown in the fall—appear larger than it is. Harmonious beds of red-toned New Guinea impatiens, 'Autumn Joy' stonecrop, and scarlet euonymus accentuate the sharp lines of a Hatfield yew hedge, whose dark green complements the other plantings. The garden's formality is eased by white pines and the golden rain tree in the background. In particular, the rain tree's sparse leaves allow its vertical branches to show through, balancing the horizontal thrust of the yew.

A Guide to the Gardens

A STUDY IN CONTRASTS
pages 44-45

A. *Calamagrostis acutiflora 'Karl Foerster'* (50)
B. *Nepeta sibirica* (30)
C. *Echinacea purpurea* (50)

D. *Rudbeckia fulgida 'Goldsturm'* (30)
E. *Perovskia atriplicifolia* (100)
F. *Aster lateriflorus 'Horizontalis'* (50)

G. *Achillea millefolium 'Hoffnung'* (100)
H. *Pennisetum alopecuroides* (50)
I. *Sedum x 'Autumn Joy'* (100)
J. *Miscanthus sinensis 'Rotsilber'* (1)

AN INTERPLAY OF COLOR
page 46
A. *Nepeta x faassenii* (8)
B. *Centranthus ruber* (5)
C. *Aquilegia chrysantha* (9)
D. *Pinus edulis* (1)
E. *Hemerocallis 'September Gold'* (4)
F. *Aronia melanocarpa* (4)
G. *Populus tremuloides* (4)

NOTE: The key lists each plant type and the total quantity needed to replicate the garden shown. The diagram's letters and numbers refer to the type of plant and the number sited in an area.

INVITINGLY SOFT FORMS AND BRIGHT HUES
pages 46-47

A. *Nicotiana langsdorffii 'Variegata'* (2)
B. *Tagetes x 'Striped Marvel'* (2)
C. *Tagetes 'Lemon Gem'* (2)
D. *Petunia integrifolia* (3)

E. *Gypsophila paniculata* (1)
F. *Chamaecyparis pisifera 'Plumosa Compacta'* (2)
G. *Armeria maritima 'Sea Thrift'* (2)
H. *Fuchsia x 'Checkerboard'* (1)

I. *Bidens ferulifolia 'Variegata'* (1)
J. *Fragaria x 'Pink Panda'* (1)
K. *Liatris spicata* (1)
L. *Hibiscus moscheutos 'Lady Baltimore'* (1)

UNEXPECTED VARIETY IN A FOLIAGE BORDER
pages 48-49

A. *Cotinus 'Velvet Cloak'* (1)
B. *Clematis x durandii* (2)
C. *Agapanthus 'Bressingham White'* (3)
D. *Sedum spectabile 'Meteor'* (1)
E. *Helleborus x sternii 'Blackthorn Hybrids'* (1)
F. *Onosma alboroseum* (1)

G. *Hakonechloa 'Aureola'* (3)
H. *Ruta 'Jackman's Blue'* (2)
I. *Artemisia x 'Huntington Botanic'* (1)
J. *Alstroemeria Ligtu Hybrids* (3)
K. *Hemerocallis 'Happy Returns'* (6)
L. *Achillea 'W. B. Child'* (1)
M. *Geranium x 'Mavis Simpson'* (1)

N. *Stachys byzantina 'Silver Carpet'* (1)
O. *Miscanthus sinensis 'Variegatus'* (2)
P. *Salvia guaranitica* (1)
Q. *Thuja 'Pyramidalis'*
R. *Hydrangea anomala ssp. petiolaris* (1)

CONTRASTING TEXTURES, HARMONIOUS GREENS
pages 50-51

A. *Verbena bonariensis* (many)
B. *Senecio vira-vira* (10)
C. *Daphne x 'Carol Mackie'* (2)
D. *Cleome 'Helen Campbell'* (many)

E. *Dolichos lablab* (3)
F. *Elymus glaucus* (2)
G. *Calendula officinalis*
(volunteer seedlings)

H. *Dahlia 'David Howard'* (2)
I. *Canna x generalis 'Striata'* (3)
J. *Dahlia 'My Love'* (3)
K. *Pyrus* (1)

AN INFORMAL FOLIAGE SCREEN
page 51

A. *Macleaya cordata* (9)
B. *Echinacea purpurea*
'Bright Star' (5)

C. *Liatris spicata* (2)
D. *Phlox maculata*
'Alpha' (6)

NOTE: The key lists each plant type and the total quantity needed to replicate the garden shown. The diagram's letters and numbers refer to the type of plant and the number sited in an area.

AN EMPHASIS ON MOVEMENT
page 52

A. *Iris versicolor* (3)
B. *Liriope muscari 'Big Blue'* (10)
C. *Sedum x 'Autumn Joy'* (10)

D. *Molinia litoralis 'Windspiel'* (1)
E. *Cotoneaster salicifolius 'Scarlet Leader'* (30)

F. *Pennisetum alopecuroides* (50)
G. *Miscanthus sinensis 'Malepartus'* (20)

DRAWING THE EYE INTO THE DISTANCE
pages 52-53

A. *Euonymus alata 'Compacta'* (5)
B. *Taxus x media 'Hatfieldii'* (12)

C. *Sedum x 'Autumn Joy'* (18)
D. *Spiraea japonica 'Little Princess'* (10)

E. *Impatiens hawkeri 'Aglia'* (14)
F. *Pinus strobus* (4)
G. *Koelreuteria paniculata* (1)

CHAPTER THREE

Color for the Cold Seasons

Once the warm months have gone, taking with them the extravagant hues of spring and summer, the cool of autumn nurtures a new color scheme, heralded by the emerging reds, yellows, and oranges of deciduous foliage. In the Vermont garden at left, flowers that bloom in the fall—rosy sedum and golden potentilla—pick up the warm palette of the nearby trees and shrubs. Here and there in the garden, brilliant vermilion rose hips and purple-leaf sand cherry add points of color, while the magnificent Nicotiana sylvestris dangles scented white trumpets that pick up the cool cream-striped leaves of a white willow.

Come winter, gardens like this one will open up. Frost will mute the colors, and snow will provide a backdrop for barren trees and shrubs, highlighting their shapes, barks, and berries. Evergreens will relieve the bleakness with color and texture. And then will come the cold-blooming plants—witch hazel, hellebores, and scores of bulbs—whose pretty faces will enliven the winter landscape and lead the garden into spring.

A. *Nicotiana sylvestris (flowering tobacco) (6)* B. *Potentilla fruticosa (shrubby cinquefoil) (1)* C. *Prunus x cistena (purple-leaf sand cherry) (1)* D. *Hypericum forrestii 'Hidcote' (St.-John's-wort) (1)* E. *Sedum x 'Autumn Joy' (stonecrop) (3)* F. *Geranium macrorrhizum (bigroot geranium) (15)* G. *Pinus sylvestris 'Nana' (dwarf Scotch pine) (1)* H. *Prunus serotina (wild black cherry) (1)* I. *Salix alba var. sericea (silver willow) (1)*

The key lists each plant type and the total quantity needed to replicate the garden shown. The diagram's letters and numbers refer to the type of plant and the number sited in an area.

Flowers and Shrubs for Fall and Winter Color

As summer's soft days shorten into fall, the flower border in your garden may look somewhat woebegone. The once-lush foliage is now worn, the old blooms spent. Yet the sun still shines bright, and the soil retains warmth already gone from the air above. With care and planning, your garden will continue to reward you with bouquets of color. Some late-summer varieties can be encouraged to keep blooming into fall, while many others just naturally wait for the change of season to put on a floral display that lasts until hard frost.

As the coldest months descend, the garden can remain satisfying. A number of perennials and shrubs flower in late winter and earliest spring. The hues tend to be paler than those of their brilliant summer counterparts, but they are no less welcome for providing splashes of color against the winter gray and snow.

Perennials to Take the Garden into Fall

A kind of rampant abundance can characterize a garden of robust fall perennials. Warm colors—hot pinks, plums, and purples, burnt orange, and every tint of yellow—dominate the ornamental border. Summer-flowering acanthus, coreopsis, dianthus, and salvia keep on blooming valiantly, while Japanese anemone, sunflower, goldenrod, sedum, and chrysanthemum are just coming into flower.

In northern zones, where forests and wood lots are fiery with color, the best approach to planning a fall garden is to seek out flowers that pair up well with the surrounding trees and shrubs. Look for yellow, gold, bronze, pink, and wine red chrysanthemums. Add the yellow of sneezeweed and goldenrod and the contrasting blue and lavender of Michaelmas daisies for a long-lasting autumn display.

A Glory of Grasses

Ornamental grasses are a splendid complement to fall-blooming perennials. Prized in the summer garden for their blade-shaped leaves and sweeps of subtle color, many grasses are in full flowering glory by September. Texturally, the blooms make an interesting contrast to the grass itself. Soft and feathery—in the form of foxtails, bottle brushes, open fans, or upright sheaves—the flowers and the seed heads that follow them glow in the autumn sunlight.

The majestic maiden grass grows to 5 feet and taller, and its many cultivars take on different hues, from silver to taupe to rusty brown, with fan-shaped plumes that range from silver-white to brown. On the smaller side, *Helictotrichon sempervirens* (blue oat grass) forms compact 2-foot mounds with erect, straw-colored panicles. Cultivars of fountain grass bloom in black, purple, or rose pink. And when the grasses are finished blooming, you can let them dry in place over the winter. They keep their shape handsomely, the feathery seed heads nodding gently in the wind.

Fall Fanfares of Shrubs and Trees

Many deciduous shrubs and small trees also bloom as the season cools, offering virtually every color but blue. The delicately flowered *Camellia sasanqua* bears blooms ranging from white to dark pink, beginning in early autumn and continuing until hard frost. *Hamamelis virginiana* (common witch hazel) has threadlike lemon yellow flowers that burst forth as its foliage turns deep gold. *Buddleia davidii* (butterfly bush) bears clusters of honey-scented, deep violet-purple tubular flowers from summer into the fall. And the vigorous summer- and fall-blooming vine *Clematis maximowicziana* resembles nothing so much as a thick blanket of tiny, fragrant white blooms.

Among the trees, *Franklinia alatamaha* (franklinia), which grows to a height of 15 feet or more, produces 3-inch camellia-like white blossoms in striking contrast to its bright red fall foliage; the flower petals unfurl from knobby buds resembling large pearls. Late-

blooming crape myrtles have intricate crinkled flowers that range from hot pink
through lavender to white. And the branches
of Higan cherry are covered with masses of
lavender-pink buds that open on warm days
throughout the fall and winter.

Planning for Winter Blooms

Compared with the fall landscape, the winter
garden is somewhat austere, but it need not
be barren. Late-winter-blooming perennials,
though less showy than their warm-weather
relatives, can nevertheless lift the spirits on a
bleak afternoon.

Among the first and most welcome are the
hellebores, whose colorful roselike flowers
offer as much style and substance as any summer beauty *(overleaf)*. Slightly later come

Frost-Defying Hellebores

Members of the buttercup family, hellebores develop buds in late autumn and bring forth waxy, long-lasting flowers to enliven the garden from midwinter until early spring. Their downward-facing blossoms sit on stems 15 to 20 inches tall nodding over mounds of glossy gray-green leaves leaves that remain evergreen to 10°F.

Unhappily named for the scent of its root—not its flower—*Helleborus foetidus* (stinking hellebore), shown above set against spiky bramble canes, is but one of several attractive varieties: *H. niger* (Christmas rose), with shell pink cups and yellow stamens; *H. orientalis* (Lenten rose), which ranges from greenish white to green-stained purple; and *H. argutifolius* (Corsican hellebore), whose lime green flowers become canary yellow at their centers.

Hardy to Zones 3 and 4, hellebores need a moist, humus-rich soil and do best in partial shade with some protection. When dividing the plants in late summer, take care not to damage the brittle roots. In the fall, mulch with leaves and cover with evergreen boughs or an overturned fruit basket to keep off the worst of the ice and snow.

yellow or satin white Amur adonis; *Doronicum* (leopard's-bane), with its daisylike yellow flowers; *Primula denticulata* (drumstick primrose), bearing flowers in lilac, purple, or pink; and the exotic-looking *Pulmonaria* (lungwort), its white-speckled green foliage setting off small pink flowers that eventually turn blue. These hardy plants are shade tolerant and look natural clumped beneath shrubs and trees.

Hamamelis vernalis (vernal witch hazel) is the earliest of a long list of winter-blooming shrubs; it bursts into flower in February in Zone 4. Golden yellow to slightly reddish on bare branches, the blossoms glow against the dark green of surrounding rhododendrons, and the sweet fragrance is a delight to the senses on a cold, crisp morning. Higan cherry continues its show, blooming lavender-pink on sunny days through the coldest months. And in earliest spring *Rhododendron mucronulatum* produces flowers that range from rosy purple to white.

If your garden has moist conditions and acid soil, try planting a bed of assorted *Erica* (heath) and *Calluna* (heather). Their pink, lavender, and white flowers are set against fine, needlelike foliage that turns red or gold in winter. Most of these winter-blooming shrubs have a pleasing fragrance as well. Sprigs of daphne, winter jasmine, or witch hazel brought indoors and placed in water will perfume a room nicely.

Mimicking Early Spring

Many plants can be stimulated to bloom early if you mimic the warmth of early spring. Situate your shrubs and perennials against south-facing walls or rocks that absorb the sun's heat and offer shelter from winter winds. Warmth and protection are crucial, because frost will damage blooms that arrive prematurely. This is a recurrent problem with the lovely star magnolia, whose delicately petaled blossoms will not survive even a moderate freeze, although the tree itself is satisfactorily hardy.

Bulbs That Brave the Coldest Months

Bulbs can be wonderful transitional plants, taking the garden into fall and winter with brief but delightful bursts of color. Bulbs fall into two categories—tender and hardy. Tender bulbs cannot withstand hard frost, and must be moved inside before temperatures turn frigid. Hardy bulbs are impervious to frost. Properly planted and then left to fend for themselves, they reappear year after year as if by magic, offering vivid hues against the warm tones of autumn and the browns and grays of the dormant season.

black-green leaves, pairs beautifully with red-wine-colored *Berberis* 'Rosy Glow' (barberry) or purple-leaved *Cotinus coggygria* 'Purpurea' (smoke tree). Canna, dahlia, and other tender fall bulbs such as wavy-petaled pink or red nerine and scented white-trumpeted *Amaryllis belladonna* (belladonna lily) must be brought inside to survive the winter. However, one plant, *Lycoris radiata* (spider lily), with its feathery red blossoms, does not like to be moved, and thus should be grown only in the South and on the West Coast.

EARLIEST OF THE SNOW CROCUSES
Fragile species crocuses push through the protective ground cover of Juniperus x media 'Daub's Frosted' into the February sun. The chalice-shaped blooms are easily knocked over by snow and wind, but more buds and flowers emerge from each corm.

Autumn and Winter Bulbs

Fall-blooming bulbs begin to emerge when many perennials are still in flower and the colors that signal the changing season are just beginning. Because autumn bulbs come in a great range of colors, it is easy to find a niche for them in the late-season garden.

Hardy fall bulbs are standards in beds and borders and also naturalize well. Lavender colchicums dotting a green lawn appear to glow from within. White *Crocus speciosus* 'Albus' poking out of a bed of variegated *Catharanthus* (periwinkle) will pick up the stripes in the surrounding foliage. And hardy cyclamen, with its pink, red, or white upswept flowers and mottled foliage, looks best nestled among fallen leaves at the base of a tree.

The foliage of these hardy bulbs emerges at unusual times. The tall, coarse leaves of fall crocuses and colchicums appear in spring and slowly die off before the blooms appear. Hardy cyclamen foliage begins to grow in the summer and remains even after the flowers have come and gone in the fall. Of the tender bulbs, cannas are the most spectacular, with their greenish maroon leaves and huge flower trusses in shades of yellow, pink, orange, and red. Dahlias, in hues of yellow, apricot, orange, maroon, and scarlet, expand the palette, providing an enormous range from which to make pleasing combinations.

For a tropical note, try matching cannas with ornamental grasses. The 'Japanese Bishop' dahlia, with its scarlet flowers and rich

Winter bulbs are available in a wide spectrum of colors—except brilliant red. The earliest to appear is *Galanthus* (snowdrop). It is followed closely by bright yellow winter aconites, blue, lavender, or yellow dwarf irises, crocuses in white, lavender, cream, yellow, burgundy, and purple, and *Chionodoxa* (glory-of-the-snow), with bright blue star-shaped flowers. Then, on the cusp of spring, come squills with small bell-shaped flowers in blue to lavender, pink, and white, and early daffodils in varying tints of yellow.

In the colder zones, you can create contrasting combinations of brilliant yellow winter aconite with lavender crocus or blue chionodoxa, tempered by creamy snowdrops. Or combine early-blooming species of bulbous iris, such as the bright yellow *Iris danfordiae* or the blue or purple *Iris bakerana*, with snowdrops or cream to yellow *Narcissus cyclamineus*. In warmer climates (Zones 9 and 10), interplant snowdrops among *Cyclamen coum,* notable for its crimson-rose flowers and mottled gray-green heart-shaped leaves. In Zones 7 to 9, the giant snowdrop, a 10-inch version, makes a good match with cyclamen.

Daffodils generally bloom in early spring, but several miniature types can be counted on to appear in late winter. The hoop-petti-coat narcissus *(Narcissus bulbocodium)* is a wild species with an oddly shaped corolla-less gold flower. It and several other small varieties of daffodil grow vigorously in moist conditions and full sun. They do well accompanied by winter heath or in a complementary blue-yellow color scheme with scillas and some bluish white striped squill.

Bugleweed, periwinkle, and English ivy are all good evergreen ground covers for this purpose. Their foliage also provides a good canvas for the bright flowers.

Designing for Impact

You can plant for a blaze of simultaneous bloom or choose species and varieties with staggered flowering times for a continual show of color. Many gardeners plant large numbers of crocuses and snowdrops; both will naturalize easily in humus-rich soil, as will chionodoxa.

Some people like a sprinkling of crocuses in a lawn; however, because lawns will likely need their first cut before the crocus leaves have had time to absorb enough energy for the next season's growth, you may prefer to plant these bulbs amid perennials or ground covers that will conceal the foliage as it fades.

Treating Bulbs with Care

To encourage your bulbs to return year after year, give them a good start. Put them in the ground as soon as they arrive, so the roots will have time to develop before the ground freezes. The exceptions are the dahlias and cannas of autumn, which you should delay planting until mid-June to prevent their blooming too early. Work in a little bone meal or 10-10-10 fertilizer, and add lime if your soil is acid; bulbs like alkaline conditions.

Dig individual holes for each bulb and place the growing end up; look for the remains of roots, then for the beginnings of growing points. If you are unsure about which end should go up, plant the bulb sideways; the growing tip will find its way. A rule of thumb is to bury a bulb three times as deep as its diameter: 6 to 12 inches for large bulbs such as daffodils, 2 to 3 inches for tiny crocuses. Space the bulbs according to size and how close together you want the blooms.

Once your colchicums, crocuses, and hardy cyclamens are in the ground, you can more or less sit back and watch them expand their colonies year after year. Cannas, dahlias, and other tender bulbs are another matter, however. Immediately after the first frost, cut back the blackened foliage to 6 inches. Then, before a hard frost, carefully loosen the soil around the dahlia tubers or the canna rhizomes, and lift them out of the ground with a garden fork. Gently brush away the surplus soil and dry the plants for about 2 weeks, placing them upside down in a box of sand or peat moss to preserve the new growth around the old stems. Then store them in a cool, dry place away from drafts. Check through the winter for disease and shriveling. Shriveled tubers can be revived overnight in a bucket of water, then dried before being stored again.

BULBS FOR FALL AND WINTER FLOWERS

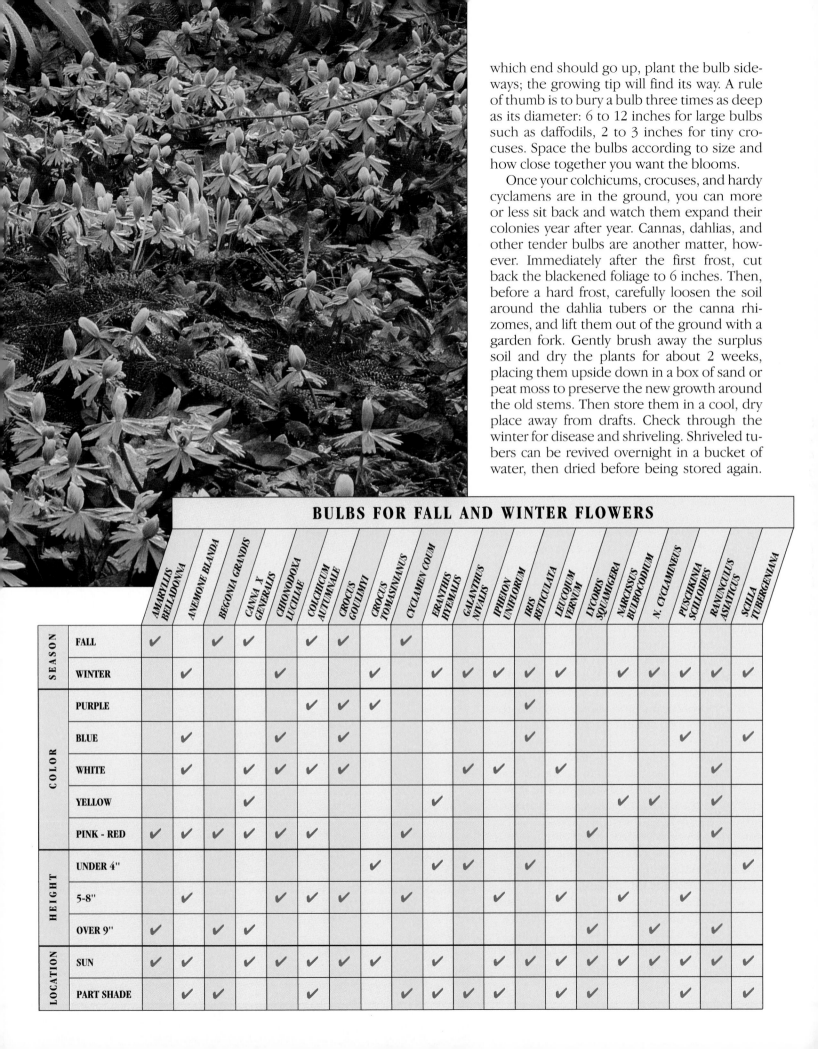

		AMARYLLIS BELLADONNA	ANEMONE BLANDA	BEGONIA GRANDIS	CANNA X GENERALIS	CHIONODOXA LUCILIAE	COLCHICUM AUTUMNALE	CROCUS GOULIMYI	CROCUS TOMASINIANUS	CYCLAMEN COUM	ERANTHIS HYEMALIS	GALANTHUS NIVALIS	IPHEION UNIFLORUM	IRIS RETICULATA	LEUCOJUM VERNUM	LYCORIS SQUAMIGERA	NARCISSUS BULBOCODIUM	N. CYCLAMINEUS	PUSCHKINIA SCILLOIDES	RANUNCULUS ASIATICUS	SCILLA TUBERGENIANA
SEASON	**FALL**	✓		✓	✓		✓	✓		✓											
	WINTER		✓			✓			✓		✓	✓	✓	✓	✓		✓	✓	✓	✓	✓
COLOR	**PURPLE**						✓	✓	✓					✓							
	BLUE		✓			✓			✓					✓					✓		✓
	WHITE		✓			✓	✓	✓				✓	✓		✓					✓	
	YELLOW				✓						✓						✓	✓		✓	
	PINK - RED	✓	✓	✓	✓	✓	✓			✓						✓				✓	
HEIGHT	**UNDER 4"**								✓		✓	✓		✓							✓
	5-8"		✓			✓	✓	✓		✓			✓		✓		✓		✓		
	OVER 9"	✓		✓	✓											✓		✓		✓	
LOCATION	**SUN**	✓	✓		✓	✓	✓	✓	✓	✓		✓		✓	✓	✓	✓	✓	✓	✓	✓
	PART SHADE		✓	✓			✓			✓	✓	✓	✓	✓	✓		✓		✓		✓

Mother Nature's Fall Fireworks

For all the splendors of autumn bloom, it is foliage that defines the season. The onset of cool weather signals dramatic color changes, and the most dazzling displays occur where the nights are cool and the days dry. In addition, there must be a genetic predisposition for a plant to take on the rich hues of autumn. These two requirements are most readily to be found in New England, but every region across North America enjoys some fall color.

Autumn's Blazing Pageant

Nearly every plant exhibits autumn color. Certain evergreens deepen from green to a rich purplish burgundy or bronze, especially when sited in full sun. The winged euonymus, a favorite shrub for autumn foliage also known as the burning bush, turns a deep, saturated red. Varieties of rhododendron and viburnum become red or yellow, depending on the cultivar. *Aronia arbutifolia* (chokeberry) and barberry turn pumpkin orange.

Ornamental grasses change to burgundy or gold in the period before they die off to tawny brown. Some clinging vines, among them Virginia creeper and Boston ivy, become an autumn red, as does the ground cover leadwort. Bittersweet and wisteria turn buttery yellow. The foliage of certain perennials also changes color in fall.

But the deciduous shrubs and trees are the headliners of the autumn garden, flashing the season's hottest, brightest colors—deep orange and gold, lemon yellow, scarlet red, lush purple, and a rich, almost black mahogany. And nothing quite matches the magnificence of maples. The colors of sugar-maple leaves can range from a startling red on the outside of the tree, where they are exposed to the sun, to glowing orange and yellow in the shaded interior. Not to be outdone, the small, graceful Japanese maples add fascinating leaf shapes to the pageant of color.

You can maximize fall color by planting trees and shrubs where they will get at least 6 hours of sun a day; a west- or south-facing location with afternoon sun is best. Remember

**GLOWING HOT IN
COOL TEMPERATURES**
The large, coarse leaves of the hybrid witch hazel Hamamelis x intermedia *'Diane' (above) blaze red and gold against the soft pink-and-white-marbled foliage of a barberry. Later, the witch hazel will bear masses of fragrant orange flowers.*

A MARVEL OF FALL COLOR
*Standing over a carpet of shining leaves and a base of cool western sword ferns (*Polystichum munitum*), the foliage of Persian parrotia flares yellow, orange, and reddish purple in flamboyant harmony with the emerging crimson of winged euonymus.*

that plants growing in low spots will color earliest because cold air moves downhill. Also, be sure to water your plants during summer or autumn dry spells to preserve the leaves for the best color.

Foliage as a Foil

The masses of foliage color provide an excellent foil for contrasting or harmonizing colors in the foreground. The multitoned trees and shrubs combine beautifully with late-flowering perennials, particularly chrysanthemums. Such late-blooming border plants and bulbs as azure monkshood, New England aster, and crocus, with their lavenders and blues, offer cooling complementary alternatives to the hot foliage hues.

For a mix of contrasting shapes and textures, combine rose pink Japanese anemones with white *Aster* 'Niobe' and *Sedum* x 'Autumn Joy'. Place these in front of oakleaf hydrangea with leaves turned rusty red, and pick up the white of the aster in the variegated leaves of a red-stemmed Tartarian dogwood *(Cornus alba* 'Elegantissima').

If you'd like to explore combinations of hot and tranquil colors, fall is the perfect time. Try pairing Japanese maple with Colorado blue spruce. The warm, dark maple foliage will appear to recede, while the cooler, stabilizing blue-gray spruce will advance. Similarly, wine red staghorn sumac or orange-yellow Japanese barberry will glow above a planting of gray-green blue fescue, catmint, or lavender.

The graceful arches of ornamental grasses in yellows, greens, reds, purples, and gray-blue combine beautifully together and with other autumn foliage. Two cultivars of *Miscanthus,* 'Arabesque' and 'Morning Light', have quite different plumed flower heads, although their graceful curling foliage is similar. Combine the grasses with broadleaf shrubs for textural variation, and with the pink-bronze flowers of *Sedum* x 'Autumn Joy' to bring out the golden brown in the plumes.

Color and Shape
after Leaf Fall

In the end, autumn leaves will drift away, revealing the structures of deciduous trees and shrubs. Unfiltered winter light will play over the surface of the bark, highlighting colors

from the pure, bluish white of *Betula papyrifera* (paper birch) to the metallic mahogany of *Prunus serrula* (paperbark cherry). On some trees, the bark peels and exfoliates, allowing bright underbark to peek through and create interesting patterns.

Some shrubs come into their own in the winter, after their leaves have fallen. New growth on the red-stemmed Tartarian dogwood is bright vermilion. To best manage this shrub and its yellow variety *Cornus sericea* 'Flaviramea', you should cut it back to the ground in early spring. Other shrubs with beautifully colored twigs include *Rubus cockburnianus*, a type of bramble bearing edible berries and powdery white canes; the willow *Salix purpurea*, with purple winter shoots; *S. alba*, with orange-red shoots; and *S.* x *rubens*, with orange-yellow shoots.

Last, but certainly not least, consider the sculptural element that bare trees and shrubs bring to your winter garden. And watch how, in the pale, low sunlight, they cast their complex shadows along the snowy ground—some pendulous, others standing valiantly upright, marching in horizontal tiers or twisting into ornate arabesques.

DRAMATIC WINTER SHAPES

	PENDULOUS	BROAD-HEADED	UPRIGHT AND COLUMNAR	HORIZONTALLY TIERED STEMS	TWISTED BRANCHES	SMALL (5'-15')	MEDIUM (15'-30')	LARGE (OVER 30')
ACER PLATANOIDES 'COLUMNARE' *NORWAY MAPLE*			✔					✔
ACER SPECIES *MAPLE*		✔				✔	✔	✔
BETULA PENDULA *EUROPEAN WHITE BIRCH*	✔							✔
CORNUS FLORIDA *FLOWERING DOGWOOD*				✔		✔		
CORYLUS AVELLANA 'CONTORTA' *HARRY LAUDER'S WALKING STICK*					✔	✔		
CRATAEGUS *HAWTHORN*		✔				✔	✔	
LIGUSTRUM VULGARE 'PYRAMIDALE' *UPRIGHT PRIVET*			✔			✔		
MALUS *CRAB APPLE*		✔				✔		
PRUNUS *FLOWERING CHERRY*		✔				✔		
PRUNUS LAUROCERASUS *CHERRY LAUREL*			✔			✔		
PRUNUS SUBHIRTELLA *HIGAN CHERRY*	✔					✔		
SALIX MATSUDANA 'TORTUOSA' *CORKSCREW WILLOW*					✔			✔
SALIX REPENS *CREEPING WILLOW*				✔		✔		
SYRINGA VULGARIS *LILAC*			✔			✔	✔	

A Harvest of Color from Winter Fruits and Berries

For certain trees and shrubs, the culmination of the annual reproductive cycle is the emergence of a brilliantly colored crop of fruits and berries. Some appear in fall and mature with the season, gaining color as the air chills. Others emerge and ripen in the summer, hidden from view by leaves; winter draws aside the curtain of foliage to reveal bright splashes of red, orange, yellow, blue, lilac, gray, black, or white, vivid against the bare branches.

A Preponderance of Red

Of all the fruit and berry colors, red appears most often. Two common examples of shrubs with red berries are the evergreen *Ilex opaca* (American holly) and *Pyracantha* (firethorn). Indeed, glossy green holly leaves dotted with bright red berries have become the symbol of the Christmas holiday season. Firethorn's graceful arching branches, laden in winter with clusters of crimson berries, are particularly well suited to formal espalier culture in full sun against a wall. The plant is equally attractive grown free-form or as a thick hedge.

Fiery red berries also appear on such deciduous trees as hawthorn, dogwood, crab apple, and *Sorbus aucuparia* (mountain ash). Among the shrubs whose berries appear later in the season, after the foliage has departed, are *Ilex verticillata* (winterberry), which boasts great masses of coral red berries, and *Viburnum trilobum* (American cranberry bush), with large red berries that resemble those of its namesake. The fruits of barberries hang like tiny ruby earrings on spiny branches throughout the winter. And the Kousa dogwood has an interesting dark pink, dangling strawberry-shaped fruit that contrasts with its scarlet autumn foliage and decorative bark.

Flowering crab apples generally produce red fruits that last into winter. Certain varieties, however, such as *Malus hupehensis* (tea crab apple) and *M. floribunda* (Japanese flowering crab apple), yield a pretty lemon yellow fruit. Some cultivars of holly, viburnum, and firethorn also produce a range of yellow, pale orange, and red-orange berries.

The Far Spectrum

Less brilliant than the reds but treasured for their intense colors are the blue berries. Mahonias bear large clusters of bright blue berries that are spectacular against their mahogany autumn foliage. *Callicarpa* (beautyberry), with its gleaming lavender-blue berries, lasts well into winter, and several ivies also develop blue berries. *Parthenocissus tricuspidata* 'Green Showers' (Boston ivy) has profuse bunches of icy blue berries set against foliage that takes on a rich burgundy color. Its relative Virginia creeper *(Parthenocissus quinquefolia)* brings forth berries that

A PAIRING OF SPOTS AND POLKA DOTS
The striking red-stemmed fruit of white baneberry (Actaea pachypoda)—so named for its extreme toxicity—is echoed in the white-speckled leaves of the leopard plant (Ligularia tussilaginea 'Aureomaculata'). Both plants like moist conditions and grow to about 2 feet in height.

are dark blue in color; they resemble small blueberries but are poisonous to humans. (While garden berries may be favorites of wildlife, humans should sample only those known to be edible.)

Several cultivars of holly and viburnum offer striking black berries in winter, but the most spectacular effect of all is produced by the shrub *Symphoricarpos albus* (snowberry), bearing its clusters of marble-size opaque white fruits. The waxy blue-gray berries of the native bayberry are drab by comparison. However, bayberries have a favored place in history: The early American colonists melted down these leathery, rough-textured orbs to make fragrant bayberry candles, and some New Englanders still practice the old tradition.

A MIX OF BERRIES AND BLOOMS
The pinkish purple fruit of the beautyberry marries well with the soft pink blossoms of a musk rose. The shrub will eventually tower over the rose and should be sharply pruned in early spring, both for size and to encourage flower production.

Cultivating the Best Crop

Whatever berry-bearing species or cultivar you favor for your garden, be sure to plant it in a sunny location. The amount of sun a plant gets determines how abundantly it will flower and thus the size of your berry crop. In addition, some plants are dioecious, which means that the female specimen bears the berries and must be pollinated by a separate male specimen to flower and fruit. Most hollies are dioecious, so you should plant a male holly bush in an inconspicuous spot within about 100 feet of the female if a male does not already exist in the vicinity. But it is not a one-for-one situation. A single male plant is sufficient to pollinate a number of female plants of the same type.

And you should prepare to share your bounty of berries with the birds that will flock to your garden. Indeed, some people plant berry- and fruit-bearing trees and shrubs especially to attract birds *(opposite),* which are particularly fond of red berries. But if you want to preserve the ornamental fruit for your own enjoyment, locate your plants near the house, where foot traffic will discourage feeding birds.

As a further deterrent, you can put in plants that produce yellow or golden fruits, which are less attractive to birds than are red berries. Finally, keep a bird feeder filled with sunflower seed for hungry cardinals, chickadees, and tufted titmice, and perhaps a second containing thistle seed for the smaller goldfinches and siskins.

Berries in the Garden Color Scheme

Berries naturally set themselves off against the surrounding color scheme. Large scarlet clusters of cockspur hawthorn berries look stunning against the cool, bluish needles of a neighboring Scotch pine. The same holds for blue-gray bayberry set among the purple-tipped foliage of a *Thuja orientalis* 'Compacta' and a red-stemmed dogwood. For a pleasing combination of warm colors, try placing a yellow-berried viburnum next to the bright red hips of a rugosa rose; or introduce the classic pairing of red and white by matching the white fruits of snowberry next to dangling red barberries.

Attracting Birds with Winter Berries

Birds enliven the garden with beauty, song, and motion—to say nothing of their effectiveness against noxious insects. But to encourage them to stay you must provide food, water, and shelter.

Berries and fruits make an ideal fall and winter forage for birds, as is proven by the flock of cedar waxwings above, swarming over the red berries of a Korean mountain ash. The juicy berries of mountain ash, dogwood, autumn olive, Virginia creeper, and firethorn are excellent sources of quick energy. Birds eat those first, saving the drier berries until later, when cold weather softens and ferments the mealier produce of hollies, hawthorns, and viburnums.

To attract birds, select plants whose fruits and berries last well into winter. You will also need to provide a safe place for birds to nest when spring arrives. Offer a diversity of cover plants—shrubs with branching structures for nesting and thorns for protection. Try for an equal mix of thick evergreen and the more-open deciduous plants, such as spruce and viburnum, or willow and cotoneaster. Thorny roses and barberry are always good bets to fend off prowling cats and provide food at the same time.

You can also make interesting combinations by pairing similar plants in contrasting colors. Combine two varieties of crab apple, such as 'Red Sentinel' and 'Butterball', which produce splendid red and yellow apples. Or match red- and yellow-berried viburnums, firethorns, and hollies, or orange- and yellow-berried mountain ash.

To achieve the best effect, situate your fruit-bearing plants in masses against a uniform background—a wall or a fence, an evergreen hedge, or even the open sky, so that the fruit stands out. As a rule, the color of orange-red berries projects better at a distance than the darker red or blue. And, as is the case with light-colored flowers, lighter-colored berries stand out better in shaded than in sunny locations.

Plants with Colorful Berries

RED

Aronia arbutifolia
(red chokeberry)
Berberis thunbergii
(Japanese barberry)
***Cotoneaster* spp.**
(cotoneaster)
***Crataegus* spp.**
(hawthorn)
Ilex aquifolium
(English holly)
Malus cultivars
(crab apple)
Pyracantha coccinea
(scarlet firethorn)
***Rhus* spp.**
(sumac)
Rosa rubrifolia
(redleaf rose)
Rosa rugosa
(rugosa rose)
Sorbus alnifolia
(Korean mountain ash)
Viburnum opulus
(cranberry bush)
Viburnum trilobum
(American cranberry bush)

YELLOW TO GOLD

***Ilex opaca* 'Xanthocarpa'**
(yellow-berried American holly)
***Pyracantha* 'Shawnee'**
(firethorn)
Sorbus aucuparia
(European mountain ash)
***Viburnum opulus* 'Xanthocarpum'**
(yellow-fruited cranberry bush)

ORANGE

***Ilex verticillata* 'Aurantiaca'**
(orange-berried winterberry)
***Pyracantha* 'Mohave'**
(firethorn)
Sorbus aucuparia
(European mountain ash)
***Viburnum setigerum* 'Aurantiacum'**
(orange-fruited tea viburnum)

BLUE TO PURPLE

Callicarpa americana
(American beautyberry)
Viburnum tinus
(laurustinus)

BLACK

Aronia melanocarpa
(black chokeberry)
***Viburnum* spp.**
(viburnum)

WHITE

***Ilex glabra* 'Ivory Queen'**
(white inkberry)
Ilex serrata* var. *leucocarpa
(white-berried Japanese winterberry)
Symphoricarpos
(snowberry)

Note: The abbreviation "spp." stands for the plural of "species"; where used in lists it means that many, but not all, of the species in a genus meet the criterion of the list.

Evergreens for the Winter Garden

The evergreens in your garden serve nobly year round as screens against undesirable views and as verdant backdrops for other favored plants. But most of all, the cold months are theirs to soften and beautify. By this time, the annuals and perennials have largely vanished, and the deciduous trees and shrubs reveal only their skeletal outlines. It is up to the evergreens to supply shape and color, height and mass—indeed to serve as the structure of the winter garden.

Evergreens fall into two groups: broadleaf and needled, and are available in full-size and dwarf varieties. Like deciduous plants, they produce flowers and bear fruit. Some also take on winter color. Standing alone or in clumps, ranged along walls or planted as hedges, evergreens can be breathtaking in their dark, dense majesty. And all are wonderfully adaptable, combined either with each other or with other types of plants.

The fine texture of a short-needled spruce or a long-needled pine contrasts nicely with the glossy, broad leaves of a rhododendron or holly. And consider the fascinating contrasts when you combine either or both of these needled evergreens with the bare twiggy branches of a lilac and the dried arching fronds of an ornamental grass.

Broadleaf Evergreens

Among the broader-leaved plants are magnolia, holly, and rhododendron, with their coarse, shiny green leaves and magnificent blooms or berries; they are often grouped by themselves or with a specimen conifer. Finer-leaved dark green evergreens, such as boxwood, cotoneaster, and various barberries, make excellent hedges to set off brighter-colored plants in the foreground.

Many broadleaf evergreens have variegated foliage that contrasts splendidly with that of less showy plants. Silver-edged winter creeper, English holly, golden euonymus, *Leucothoe fontanesiana* (drooping leucothoe), and *Pieris japonica* 'Variegata' have whitish or yellowish leaf margins that pick up the smoky blue-white colors of Colorado blue spruce, for example.

Aside from its fragrant cascades of white blossoms in late winter, andromeda also develops a bright burgundy red new growth, and is among several broadleaf evergreens that have reddish foliage in winter. It reaches a height of about 12 feet at maturity. Oregon grape holly grows only to about half that size, but is equally impressive when in bloom, carrying fragrant yellow flowers among its blue-red spiny leaves. These mahogany-colored shrubs also combine well with blue-green conifers.

Several broadleaf evergreen ground covers turn bronze in fall, including *Arctostaphylos uva-ursi* 'Massachusetts' (Massachusetts bearberry), purple-leaf winter creeper, and the low-mounding coast leucothoe. Evergreen *Cotoneaster dammeri,* with its bright red berries and ground-hugging habit, turns

EVERGREENS IN WINTER GARB
Golden bronze American arborvitae 'Rheingold' shines in the sun next to a white cedar 'Heather Bun' (Chamaecyparis thyoides) resplendent in seasonal maroon tones. Both members of the cypress family, the shrubs express their winter color in time to contrast with the spiked crimson branches of a red-stemmed dogwood.

orange-red in the fall. Interplanted late-winter bulbs look stunning among these reddish ground covers, which complement the green of the bulb foliage while harmonizing with the violet-purple and yellow-gold of the flowers. The ground covers also discreetly conceal the ripening bulb foliage later in the season.

Needled Evergreens

Nothing epitomizes the winter landscape like the profile of a snow-laden pine, spruce, or hemlock. It projects an air of permanence and dignity, of unquenchable life on even the coldest, most numbing day. In addition, many needled evergreens produce interesting cones, fruits, or berries. And in their shrubby forms—notably false cypress, juniper, yew, and arborvitae—they make excellent hedges and foundation plantings.

In the roaring gales and heavy snows of deep winter, evergreens are vulnerable to windburn and broken limbs. You can take a few simple steps to protect them.

Plant evergreens in sheltered locations and give them plenty of moisture before the first hard freeze to counter the drying effects of wind. In addition, spray the leaves with an antidesiccant to give them a waxy coating that will slow evaporation.

In particularly harsh climates, shield plants against the wind with a screen of burlap, or wrap shrubs in burlap tied with twine. This procedure has the added benefit of supporting the limbs against heavy snow. Shrubs planted near the house may need to be shielded against snow and ice sliding from the roof. Dwarf and ground-cover evergreens can be protected by a layer of cut evergreen boughs. However, snow itself provides an effective blanket for ground cover against the bitter cold.

Because of their dense, fine-textured shapes, needled evergreens also make impressive accent specimens. Different cultivars of the same variety of conifer may have different characteristics. For example, the branches of *Pinus densiflora* 'Pendula' (weeping Japanese red pine) droop to the ground, whereas *P. d.* 'Umbraculifera' (Japanese umbrella pine) has a flat-topped, parasol-shaped head. And different species can share the same attributes: *Thuja* 'Filiformis' (weeping threadleaf arborvitae) has lacy, drooping branches, as does *Juniperus scopulorum* 'Tolleson's Weeping Juniper'.

Using Form to Make a Statement

Geometrical figures contribute effectively to the design and mood of a garden. Strong forms, such as the upright columns of false cypress or red cedar, carry the eye aloft in a kind of visual exclamation point. They create a severer, more formal statement than the conical or pyramidal shapes of spruce and fir trees. But, because they are so striking, all three should be used sparingly as accents rather than as mass plantings.

Rounded plants, such as winged euonymus, are relatively neutral and make good fillers. The horizontal spreading shapes of the many prostrate junipers and cotoneasters are

Colorful Winter Evergreens

TREES AND SHRUBS WITH VARIEGATED FOLIAGE

Daphne x burkwoodii 'Carol Mackie'
(Burkwood daphne)

Daphne odora 'Aureo-marginata'
(variegated winter daphne)

Euonymus japonica 'Gold Spot'
(Japanese euonymus)

Ilex aquifolium 'Argenteo-marginata'
(silver-edge English holly)

Gold-Needled Shrubs

Chamaecyparis obtusa 'Golden Drop', 'Golden Sprite'
(golden hinoki false cypress)

Chamaecyparis pisifera 'Filifera Aurea'
(goldthread false cypress)

Juniperus chinensis 'Pfitzeriana Aurea'
(golden Pfitzer juniper)

Picea orientalis 'Aurea Compacta'
(compact golden Oriental spruce)

Taxus baccata 'Aurea'
(golden English yew)

Golden Broadleaf Shrubs

Ilex crenata 'Golden Gem'
(Japanese holly)

Blue or Blue-Gray Needled Shrubs

Chamaecyparis pisifera 'Boulevard'
(blue moss Sawara false cypress)

Juniperus horizontalis 'Wiltonii'
(blue rug juniper)

Picea pungens 'Fat Albert', 'Montgomery'
(dwarf blue spruce)

Purplish, Red, or Bronze Shrubs and Ground Covers

Juniperus horizontalis 'Livida'
(creeping juniper)

Leucothoe fontanesiana 'Scarletta'
(leucothoe)

Mahonia aquifolium
(Oregon grape)

Pieris japonica 'Variegata'
(variegated Japanese pieris)

Rhododendron 'P.J.M.'
(rhododendron)

Thuja orientalis 'Juniperoides'
(Oriental arborvitae)

TRUE BLUE SPLASHED WITH YELLOW
The cool tones of a dwarf Colorado blue spruce offer a soothing visual underpinning for the saturated yellow of fallen sugar-maple leaves (below). The low-growing spruce is also an excellent foil for the pastel tints of early-blooming bulbs.

---

appropriate for the edge of a path or for carrying the eye across a design. Vase-shaped plants, notably *Zelkova serrata* (Japanese zelkova) and *Prunus serrulata* (Japanese flowering cherry), allow space beneath their high branches and are excellent for walks and driveways. You might try weeping forms such as *Cedrus libani* 'Pendula' (weeping cedar-of-Lebanon) and *Pseudotsuga menziesii* 'Pendula' (weeping Douglas fir) on hillsides where they can spill down the slopes.

Some pines and spruces are notable for dramatically irregular branching patterns and leaning trunks, as if they had been shaped by the winds scouring a coastal headland or mountain crag. They are marvelously well suited to naturalistic sites, silhouetted starkly against the sky.

Variations on a Theme of Green

To shape can be added color variations that enliven the winter palette. Many hues exist within the green spectrum itself, with color from yellow- to gray-green and blue-green, and tones from dark to light.

Two other important needled evergreen colors are warm yellow-gold and cool blue-gray. Juniper, false cypress, and spruce stand out among the conifers for their range of gold and blue cultivars. The gold-tipped Pfitzer juniper combines two colors in its foliage, gray-green splashed with golden yellow. 'Crippsii' hinoki false cypress (*Chamaecyparis obtusa* 'Crippsii') boasts a golden fernlike foliage all

A DIALOGUE IN COLOR AND TEXTURE
The fine, needlelike leaves of winter-blooming ever-green heathers nestle against the stiff bottle-brush bristles of a Colorado blue spruce (above).

year and is particularly luminous against the snow. Goldthread false cypress *(Chamaecyparis pisifera* 'Filifera Sungold') is similar, but its interior foliage remains bright green. American arborvitae turns a warm yellow-bronze, which combines well with either redtwig or yellowtwig dogwood.

False cypress, juniper, and spruce can all be found in blue varieties. Perhaps the best known is Colorado blue spruce, with its dense, branching upright form. Blue moss Sawara false cypress *(Chamaecyparis pisifera)* is a dwarf evergreen with finely textured feathery foliage. And two types of *Juniperus horizontalis* make excellent ground covers: Bar Harbor juniper and blue rug juniper, whose short side branches grow up and away from the ground.

The Accommodating Miniatures

Dwarf shrubs, of which there are more than a thousand varieties of conifers alone, retain the virtues of their larger cousins but require far less space and attention. They grow at half the rate (1 inch per year is considered vigorous) and achieve only half the bulk. Besides these advantages, they rarely need pruning and thrive on less fertilizer and water.

These mighty miniatures can be used to soften the harsh lines along the front of a house or fence, help disguise the base of taller shrubs, and enliven the dormant flower border. As hedges, they provide year-round accents to a walkway or boundary line. Weeping or ground-hugging forms make valuable ground covers on steep banks, where they fight erosion.

Chamaecyparis lawsoniana 'Aurea Densa' (Port Orford cedar)

CHAPTER FOUR

A Sampling of Garden Plans

A beautiful yard exemplifying all the design principles discussed in the preceding chapters is every gardener's dream. But unless you have a garden plan to provide the transition from your imagination to actually putting plants into the ground, that dream could dissolve in chaos.

A garden plan is a detailed drawing of your planting scheme as viewed from overhead. The eight simple plans shown on the following pages were created by either professional landscape architects or homeowners. Each design is expressed in a watercolor rendering of the garden, a schematic drawing to identify the plants, and an overhead planting plan.

The plans illustrate a variety of imaginative schemes—from a rock garden to an island bed of ornamental grasses to the perennial border at right. Use the plans to recreate these gardens in toto or in part, making sure to adapt them to your particular climate and tastes, or use them as a starting place for your own creative designs.

A. *Achillea x 'Moonshine' (yarrow)
(1)* **B.** *Dianthus armeria (pink) (3)*
C. *Stokesia laevis 'Blue Danube'
(Stokes' aster) (1)* **D.** *Stachys officinalis (betony) (1)* **E.** *Geranium
sanguineum var. striatum (bloody
cranesbill) (1)* **F.** *Rosa 'Gruss an
Aachen' (1)* **G.** *Alstroemeria Ligtu Hybrids (Peruvian lily) (1)* **H.** *Phlomis
lanata (Jerusalem sage) (1)* **I.** *Anemone coronaria (6)* **J.** *Chrysanthemum
parthenium (feverfew) (1)* **K.** *Centaurea dealbata (knapweed) (1)*
L. *Lavandula dentata (lavender) (2)*
M. *Dietes vegeta (African iris) (1)*
N. *Daucus carota (Queen Anne's lace)
(2)* **O.** *Verbena bonariensis (Brazilian verbena) (4)* **P.** *Rosa 'Iceberg' (1)*
Q. *Salvia greggii (autumn sage) (1)*

A Perennial Border for Sunny, Dry Conditions

A neat white fence sets off a profusion of pastels in this sunny front border, created jointly by the homeowner and her landscape architect in La Jolla, California. Designed to capture the chaotic charm of an English cottage garden, the blending of soft colors evokes a cool mood in this hot region located near the ocean.

Although the temperature here is tropical, it is not accompanied by tropical moisture levels. In fact, since rainfall normally occurs only in brief periods in the fall and spring, salt tends to build up in the adobe clay soil. To improve this unpromising earth, the homeowner amends it with compost and mulches the garden frequently with fir bark and rotted horse manure.

Adaptable, drought-tolerant flowers such as *Salvia greggii* fill the border. The plants grow rapidly and to a good size, and the garden is almost constantly in flower. Alstroemeria blooms not only in spring but again in fall, while *Verbena bonariensis*, *Achillea* x 'Moonshine', and roses show their colors nearly year round. The mounded shapes of the plants, occasionally punctuated by tall, flower-topped stems of verbena, echo the undulating horizontal line of the fence.

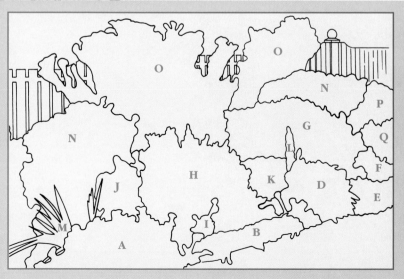

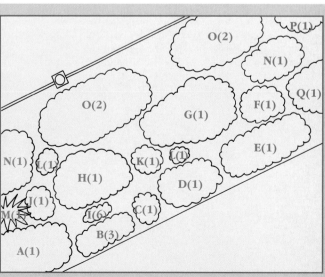

A Terraced Suburban Hillside

This garden plan was chosen to solve a number of problems on a property in a Maryland suburb of Washington, D.C. First, the land sloped and was subject to erosion. In addition, the site lay partly in shade, and the roots of two large Norway spruce trees obtruded on the area. The most obvious solution would have been a simple ground cover. Instead, the homeowners built a series of terraces and raised beds—eight in all. These not only put a stop to the erosion while improving drainage, but the terraces also allowed the homeowners to experiment with different light and moisture conditions. No longer constrained by the site, they could indulge their desire to combine different kinds of plants.

The garden blends subtle foliage colors and textures such as the fuzziness of gray lamb's ears *(Stachys byzantina)* and the silver of dusty-miller *(Senecio cineraria)* with the lacy greenery of Christmas fern *(Polystichum acrostichoides)* and the broad, flat foliage of hosta. By interspersing these plants with brightly flowering perennials such as geranium, begonia, and iris, the design invites the eye to linger. And a brick walkway rising with the terraces creates leisurely opportunities for a visitor to pause and enjoy the view.

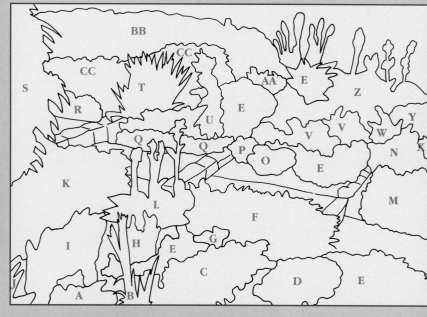

A. *Viola 'Royal Robe'* (6) **B.** *Mentha x 'Grapefruit Mint'* (1) **C.** *Senecio cineraria* (6) **D.** *Asteromoea mongolica* (5) **E.** *Catharanthus roseus (many)* **F.** *Stachys byzantina* (8) **G.** *Asarum canadense* (5) **H.** *Dianthus* (10) **I.** *Nepeta faassenii* (3) **J.** *Polystichum acrostichoides* (11) **K.** *Geranium* (7) **L.** *Hosta decorata* (1) **M.** *Begonia grandis* (10) **N.** *Allium senescens* (12) **O.** *Artemisia schmidtiana 'Silver Mound'* (3) **P.** *Spiraea japonica* (5) **Q.** *Sedum spurium 'Dragon's Blood'* (6) **R.** *Aquilegia flabellata 'Pumila'* (3) **S.** *Vernonia noveboracensis* (5) **T.** *Iris x germanica* (4) **U.** *Lilium auratum* (3) **V.** *Spiraea japonica 'Little Princess'* (6) **W.** *Artemisia ludoviciana 'Silver King'* (3) **X.** *Calamintha grandiflora 'Bert's Beauty'* (3) **Y.** *Aquilegia canadensis* (8) **Z.** *Hosta elegans* (7) **AA.** *Impatiens x New Guinea* (9) **BB.** *Polygonatum odoratum var. thunbergii 'Variegatum'* (4) **CC.** *Hypericum* (12)

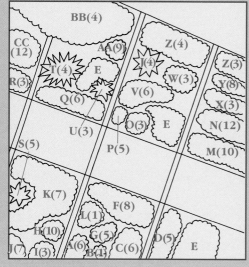

A Lakeside Grass Garden

Designed by a landscape architect for the owner of an inland lakeshore site near Milwaukee, Wisconsin, this island bed of ornamental grasses sways delicately with every passing breeze, adding motion to the more usual garden attractions of plant color and form. The clump-forming, noninvasive grasses, chosen primarily for their color, textural appeal, and adaptability, are virtually maintenance free, needing only to be cut back to about 2 inches high in early spring.

Throughout the year the grasses present an ever-changing but consistently beautiful appearance, which is particularly valuable in a region where winter is 6 months long. The 'Haense Herms' switch grass, for example, produces showy red seeds in autumn, then turns a soft, tawny beige for the winter. The fountain grass keeps much of its mass year round, becoming a lovely bright almond color in the coldest months.

The height and growing habit of each plant also played a role in the garden's design. Graceful maiden grass, the tallest of the grasses chosen, was placed in the center of the bed. Surrounding it are feather reed grass, standing bold and upright; dwarf fountain grass, which is pendulous and arching; and switch grass, whose form is delicate, light, and airy.

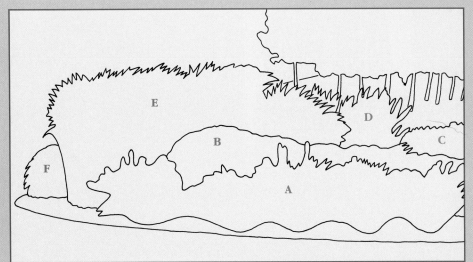

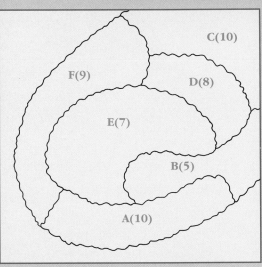

A. *Pennisetum alopecuroides 'Hameln' (dwarf fountain grass) (10)*
B. *Panicum virgatum 'Strictum' (switch grass) (5)*
C. *Schizachyrium scoparium (bluestem) (10)*
D. *Calamagrostis acutiflora 'Stricta' (reed grass) (8)*
E. *Miscanthus sinensis 'Gracillimus' (maiden grass) (7)*
F. *Panicum virgatum 'Haense Herms' (red switch grass) (9)*

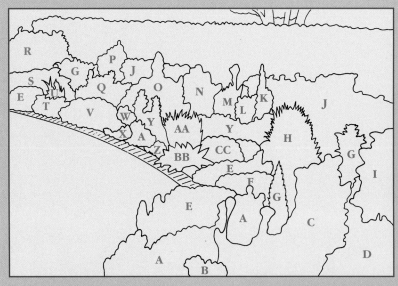

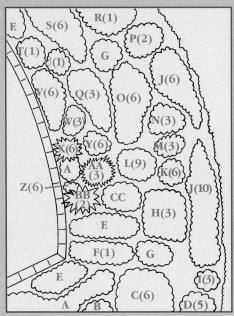

A. *Viola (many)* B. *Papaver pilosum (many)* C. *Dianthus barbatus (6)* D. *Campanula glomerata 'Superba' (5)* E. *Dianthus (many)* F. *Sedum x 'Autumn Joy' (1)* G. *Lilium (many)* H. *Adenophora liliifolia (3)* I. *Alcea rosea (3)* J. *Chrysanthemum leucanthemum (16)* K. *Digitalis purpurea cultivars (6)* L. *Aquilegia x 'Biedermeier Strain' (9)* M. *Iris x germanica (3)* N. *Paeonia cultivars (3)* O. *Delphinium hybrids (6)* P. *Rosa 'Betty Prior' (2)* Q. *Amsonia (3)* R. *Rosa 'Gruss an Aachen' (1)* S. *Nicotiana sylvestris; N. 'Domino' (6)* T. *Dianthus gratianopolitanus 'Bath's Pink' (1)* U. *Anemone japonica (1)* V. *Chrysanthemum pacificum (6)* W. *Geranium 'Johnson's Blue' (3)* X. *Stachys byzantina (6)* Y. *Aquilegia x 'Maxistar' (6)* Z. *Erysimum 'Bowles' Mauve' (6)* AA. *Iris sibirica (3)* BB. *Limonium latifolium (2)* CC. *Viola (many)*

Vivid Color against a Hedge

The owner of this Atlanta, Georgia, garden achieved the lush effect of a traditional English border by planting a mixture of annuals and perennials in very close proximity. Shown at its spring peak, the border is all the more striking for being set against the dark backdrop of a stately holly hedge.

The garden teems with harmonious color combinations of pinks, pale yellows, whites, blues, purples, and grays, with occasional accents of red poppies. The owner's planting philosophy was simply to fill the garden with her favorite flowers in pairings she found

pleasing. To lengthen the border's blooming season, she included summer- and fall-flowering perennials, such as Japanese anemone and stonecrop (*Sedum* x 'Autumn Joy'). Although she has to amend the heavy Georgia clay with composted manure, pine bark, and granite sand, she does not mulch her plants because they are placed so closely together. In the hot, humid Georgia summers, mulch touching plant crowns could promote rot; moreover, what little bare ground remains is already well shielded from sun and heat by the dense foliage.

From Tanzania

The Saintpaulia, or as it is more commonly known, the African violet, was first discovered in the hills of Tanzania in east Africa by Herr Von Saint Paulliare. Its botanical name comes from its finder, and its popular name from the place where it was found.

America was the first country to take this little flower to its heart, although it is now popular throughout the world. Even though its natural environment is in the tropics, it has adapted itself well to many different growing conditions. It is an evergreen plant which can flower for most of the year, but there are, of course, short rest periods between each flowering. The leaves are hairy and succulent, with long, fragile stems, and grow in a rosette. The flowers grow from the center of the rosette in groups of 4-8, in loose clusters. The flower itself is not unlike the violet. The petals are broad, flat and round which set off the two stamens with button-like yellow anthers.

Many different varieties

The species African violet, *Saintpaulia ionantha*, once had only small, deep-purple flowers, but as soon as the plant became well-known in America, fanciers started breeding new hybrids, and today we have a whole range of colors to choose from. There are purple, white, pink, blue, bi-colored or mottled flowers, which can be both single and double, and have either smooth or fringed petals.

Pink and white African violets in a small basket make a pretty center-piece or a lovely gift.

Propagation

The easiest way to start new plants is to take leaf cuttings, although you can plant seeds. Seed propagation is, however, a long and difficult process since the small plants must be moved and 'pricked out' several times, and growth is extremely slow. This method is mostly used when new varieties are brought on from seed by a plant breeder.

Propagating with seed

The seeds are tiny and should be sown in seed trays in January. Water the soil well before you sow. Don't cover the seeds, but press them lightly into the surface of the soil. Put the trays in a warm spot (70°-75°F) and cover with a sheet of glass or plastic. You can put the trays over the top of a radiator if you wish. It is important that the soil is kept warm during germination.

The first leaves will appear after 10-14 days. Wait another 14 days and prick the seedlings out into a new tray of sandy compost. Repeat this process once or twice again at one month intervals, and increase the distance between the plants each time. Wait until the plants are about 4 inches across before you put them into pots of their own. The temperature must be kept at about 72°F all through this period, while the "final" potted plant can be kept at about 65°F.

Leaf cuttings

You can take leaf cuttings from a healthy plant at any time of year, and it will take about 8 months from the first cutting to a new, adult plant. Take the leaf from the parent plant together with its stem, and plant the leaf in soil with about half the stem covered. After a month at 72°F you will find that this leaf has grown roots, and after a further 8-14 days the new plant will appear. Once the plant has reached a diameter of about 4 inches it can be put in a pot of its own. Water with liquid plant food every 14 days. High humidity is important.

Plant Doctor

African violets are basically healthy plants but they can suffer from neglect.

☐ **Brown spots/ scorched leaves** can appear if the sun has been shining directly on the leaves or if you have spilled cold water on them. Do not expose the plant to strong sunlight between March and October and water carefully.

☐ **Crown rot fungus** is a major problem. Discard plants and clean area thoroughly.

☐ **Mildew** can appear if the surrounding air is too dry. Prevent this by maintaining a high humidity around the plant.

☐ Thrips or Cyclamen mites will cause **sunken, brown spots on the leaves,** especially underneath. Plants under severe attack should be discarded.

African Violet

Saintpaulia ionantha

SAMPLE

African violets have been greatly improved over the years. They are more reliable growers and bloomers now, and the range of both color and form has been widened.

A blue-purple African violet — a semi-double.

A cerise African violet — clearly red.

A rich purple variety with white fringed edges.

The miniature variety. Sold in 2-3 inch pots.

Buying Tips

Make sure that there are no brown patches, and that there are plenty of buds.

Lifespan: With the right care the African violet will grow for many years.

Difficulty quotient: Easy to look after. It will reward you with flowers all year round.

Other names: The African violet is sometimes also known by its generic name of Saintpaulia.

In Brief

Size and growth rate
The African violet can be 4-6 inches high and up to 8 inches or more across. The miniature varieties are about half this size.

Flowering and fragrance
Although the African violet can bloom at any time of year, the flowers are rather sparse between November and February/March. Once the days are longer flowering increases again.

Light and temperature
Although it loves the light, the African violet cannot take hot sunlight, especially from March to October. The best growth and the best flowers are achieved if the plant has a constant summer and winter temperature of 70°-77°F.

Watering and feeding
The African violet cannot tolerate cold water on its leaves or crown. It should be watered in the saucer, and surplus water should be poured off after half an hour. Give liquid fertilizer once every 14 days during the growth period.

Soil and transplanting
The soil should be light and rich. Peat, mixed with a little sand and compost is fine. Transplant every spring or summer when the roots have filled the pot. Split plants into multiple crowns at this time.

Grooming
Pick off old leaves to maintain only 4 to 5 whorls on plants.

Propagating
Easiest with cuttings from healthy parent plants (see middle pages).

Environment
The African violet likes company. The more plants there are, the higher the humidity, and the happier it is. It can also be grown as a solitary plant. Just watch the humidity.

For further information on Success With House Plants write to:
Success With House Plants
444 Liberty Ave.
Pittsburgh, PA 15222
1-800-586-7774

Spider Plant—perfect for hanging baskets

Spider Plant is a decorative rosette plant with long hanging foliage and flower stems. It is one of the best choices for an indoor hanging basket, and is extremely easy to grow. This plant is ideal for beginners, since it can survive for several days without water and can grow in varied temperatures, as long as it isn't exposed to freezing conditions.

Variegated varieties are popular

Botanically, Spider Plant is *Chlorophytum comosum,* and is a native of South Africa. *Chlorophytum* means "green color" and refers to the fresh green shade of the leaves. The most popular Spider Plants, however, are variegated varieties with white- or yellow-striped leaves.

Blooms in summer

Spider Plant has its main flowering season in summer, although it can bloom at other

times of the year. The small white flowers are star-shaped and grow along an arching flower stalk that can reach a height of 40 inches. Young plants also develop on these long flower stems, which has led to such unusual plant names as "Throw the Children Out the Window."

The most popular varieties of Spider Plant are variegated varieties with white- or yellow-striped leaves.

Spider Plant is a decorative rosette plant with long hanging foliage and flower stems.

Growing Spider Plants

Spider Plants can survive for several days without water. They can grow in varied temperatures, as long as they are not subjected to freezing conditions. Although the plant thrives in bright, shady environments, markings on variegated leaves will not be as prominent in excessive shade.

The thick roots— a good reserve

Spider Plants do not need repotting each year — only when the roots start to creep out of the pot. The leaves should be misted with lukewarm water in summer and the plant should be watered well when the soil is dry. Feed once every 14 days from spring through fall with a balanced fertilizer. Water less in winter.

Increase by division or plantlets

Spider Plant is easy to increase by division during spring repotting. Separate small plantlets from the parent, pot them in three-inch pots of rich, porous soil and place them at about 66°F in light shade. Keep soil and air moist until growth is established.

Plant Doctor

☐ The leaves develop **brown tips** when they are too dry or have been exposed to direct sunlight in summer. Water more and move the plant to a less-sunny location.

☐ The markings on variegated leaves will become **less clear** if the plant grows in shady conditions. Move it to a brighter spot.

Spider Plant

Chlorophytum comosum 'Vittatum'

SAMPLE

Spider Plant is the ideal plant for beginners who have not yet developed their "green thumbs." It needs no special room temperature and can grow in both light and shade.

New plants grow along the flower stalk.

Buying Tips

Can be bought at any time of year. Check that all leaves are unbroken and without brown tips.

Lifespan: Can be grown almost indefinitely when not exposed to frost.

Season: All year.

Difficulty quotient: A very easy and tolerant plant.

In Brief

Size and growth rate

Spider Plant is a perennial rosette plant with green-, yellow- or white-striped narrow leaves that may curve to a length of 20 inches. The thick roots can store food. The young plants, which grow from the flower stems of the parent plants, have short, thick side roots.

Flowering and fragrance

The plant blooms through most of summer with small, white, scentless flowers.

Light and temperature

Spider Plant can grow in sun or shade. The leaves can be scorched by strong sun and lose their markings in deep shade. Plants thrive at around 66°F (less in winter) and can't stand much frost.

Watering and feeding

Plants will do best in summer if watered well and often, although soil should be allowed to dry between waterings. Leaves should be sprayed with lukewarm water several times a week in warmer months, while the plants can tolerate drier conditions in winter. Feed once every 14 days in summer. Do not feed in fall or winter.

Soil and transplanting

Repot when roots fill pot entirely. Use ordinary potting soil.

Grooming

Cut off long flower stems when withered or unattractive.

Propagating

Best with plantlets separated from parent. They should establish and grow in about three months. Spider Plants can be divided, or propagated from seed, but new seed plants will be plain green.

Environment

Young plants are suitable for green plant arrangements. Older plants make attractive hanging baskets.

For further information on Success With House Plants write to:
Success With House Plants
444 Liberty Ave.
Pittsburgh, PA 15222
1-800-586-7774

Bulb Planting Basics

Bulbs let you create beautiful shows of multicolored blooms in stunning masses, and will flower year after year.

WHAT ARE BULBS?

Bulbs are "storage tanks". They help a plant to survive dormant periods, when it is too cold or hot for it to flower, and they nourish the plant during the growing and flowering season.

There are three major types of bulbs, including true bulbs, such as Hyacinths, Daffodils, and Tulips; tubers, such as Dahlias and some Begonias; and corms, such as Crocuses and Gladioli. All vary in shape as well as size.

Bulbs are sold when they are in a dormant state. You can order bulbs during the planting season from local garden centers and nurseries, or earlier from mail-order catalogs. Plant your bulbs as soon as possible to ensure that they grow.

Bulbs, such as these Irises, can make a spectacular border

HOW TO PLANT BULBS CORRECTLY

Teardrop-shaped bulbs, including large bulbs, such as Daffodils and Hyacinths, should be planted with their tips facing up. If their tips face down, they waste their energy trying to grow in the opposite direction.

Some bulbs, such as Irises, are flat or have "claws". If a bulb has an obviously flat side, plant this side facing up. Plant all bulbs that have appendages or roots facing down. If you are unsure, plant the bulb sideways.

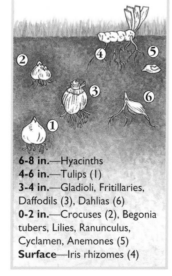

BEST PLANTING DEPTHS

6-8 in.—Hyacinths
4-6 in.—Tulips (1)
3-4 in.—Gladioli, Fritillaries, Daffodils (3), Dahlias (6)
0-2 in.—Crocuses (2), Begonia tubers, Lilies, Ranunculus, Cyclamen, Anemones (5)
Surface—Iris rhizomes (4)

PLANTING A SHOW OF BULBS

YOU WILL NEED:
- ❏ Kneeling mat
- ❏ Garden spade, trowel, or bulb planting tool
- ❏ Plastic sheet

Tip

Create a dramatic effect by planting bulbs in large masses. Since bulbs are sold by color, you can choose vivid, contrasting colors, or more subtle combinations. Lay bulbs out on the ground before planting to get a sense of your color scheme.

1 **To plant a full bed** or wide border of bulbs, dig a trench, placing the soil on the side on a plastic sheet.

2 **Place bulbs** in trench according to your design. Plant close together for impact, but do not let them touch.

3 **Replace the soil,** being careful not to disturb the positioning of the bulbs. Firm soil once all bulbs are covered.

4 **Water thoroughly** if soil is dry, and then add a thick layer of mulch, such as pine bark, to keep bulbs moist.

PLANTING SINGLE BULBS

If you are planting a few bulbs or just one bulb in your garden, there is no need to dig out a tray bed. An easier way to plant a small number of bulbs is with a special bulb planting tool. Excellent bulbs for small plantings include:

- ● Emperor Tulips
- ● Irises
- ● Daffodils
- ● Crown Imperial Fritillaries
- ● Hyacinths

1 **Sink bulb planting tool** straight down into the soil. Pull up tool and squeeze its handle to remove soil plug.

2 **Place bulb** in the hole, making sure that it faces the right way up. Replace soil and water planting well.

A Basic Guide to
Planting Bulbs SAMPLE

Planting your bulbs in the right conditions will ensure a glorious show of colorful blooms.

Seasonal Tips

FALL
Planting bulbs for spring
Plant spring-flowering bulbs in the fall. Plant earlier in cold areas to avoid attack by frost.

SPRING
Planting bulbs for summer
Plant summer-flowering bulbs in a cool but frost-free place.

EARLY SUMMER
Cleaning up
Pinch the heads off faded flowers before they set seed. Let the leaves die naturally. Dig up spring-blooming bulbs (and some summer-blooming bulbs in cold climates) and store them in a dry, dark place for replanting the next year.

SUMMER
Planting bulbs for fall
Plant fall-flowering bulbs over the summer months.

Weather Watch

In warmer areas, give bulbs an artificial cold period to simulate winter. Place bulbs in a refrigerator for about eight weeks to trick them into dormancy, so they can store energy for new growth. Keep fruit out of the refrigerator, as ripening fruit produces ethylene, a gas that will stop bulbs from flowering.

AFTERCARE

Cut faded blooms before the flowers have started to set seed. This will ensure that the bulb conserves and stores up all its energy, ready to produce new blooms in the next season.

Bulbs can be left in the ground. Some will, in time, spread out from their planting position and form new bulbs. This is called "naturalizing". After a few years, dig up and divide overcrowded bulbs.

Bulbs need to be dry. To store them, clean and keep them in a cool, dry place, such as a garage. Plant or replant them in well-drained soil. Dig in a gritty draining material, such as sand, if the soil is very wet.

For further information: Gardening Made Easy, International Masters Publishers, 444 Liberty Ave., Pittsburgh, PA 15222-1207   1-800-954-5210

Printed in U.S.A.   ©MCMXCV IMP AB/IMP Inc.   Gardening Made Easy™ International Masters Publishers AB, produced under license

Packet 00

123-708-209

Juicy Salad Fruits

Tomatoes come in a wide range of sizes, shapes and colors, each offering its own unique taste.

There are four basic types of Tomatoes available, distinguished according to their size: Cherry, Medium, Plum, and Beefsteak. Cherry Tomatoes are small, round fruits, perfect for tossing whole into salads. Plums are rather oblong and good for sauces, while Medium and Beefsteak are quite meaty, large, and good for slicing.

Some Tomato varieties can be grown in pots or hanging baskets. Water containers well, as they tend to quickly dry out.

Stake Tomatoes with sticks, wire cages, or twine strung from an overhead pole. Supporting their stems helps flower and fruit production, while also keeping Tomatoes off the ground and away from insects.

TYPE	VARIETY	DESCRIPTION	TIME TO MATURE
CHERRY	Sweet 100	Large Tomato clusters; vigorous vine growth needing cage or stake; very sweet, 1 in. fruits	70 days
	Gardener's Delight	Bright red, bite-sized Tomatoes; produces clusters of very sweet, 1 in. fruits	65 days
	Small Fry	Strong taste; disease resistant; good for growing in 5-gallon containers; 1 in. fruits	65 days
MEDIUM	Early Girl Improved	Smooth, meaty, and firm Tomatoes; disease resistant; 4-6 oz. fruits	52 days
	Better Boy	Full, semi-firm Tomatoes; very tasty; perfect for slicing; 8-16 oz. fruits	72 days
	Sunray	Yellow and firm Tomatoes; mild flavor; grown more for appearance than taste; 6 oz. fruits	80 days
	Golden Boy	Yellow and firm Tomatoes; low-acid fruit that has a mild flavor; 6 oz. fruits	70 days
PLUM	Roma	Thick-walled Tomatoes with few seeds; bland taste; good for sauces; 3-4 oz. fruits	76 days
	Chico III	Curvaceous, firm, and tasty; excellent for juice or slicing; 3-4 oz. fruits	75 days
BEEFSTEAK	Burpee's Supersteak	Meaty and firm Tomatoes; oblate shape; ideal for slicing; up to 2 lb. fruits	80 days
	Beefmaster	Large, thick-walled, juicy; resistant to fusarium and verticulum wilt; up to 2 lb. fruits	80 days
	Bush Beefsteak	Firm, deep red Tomatoes; will grow under even adverse conditions; 8 oz. fruits	62 days

Troubleshooter

Split skins are a common problem for Tomatoes caused by irregular watering habits. Give plants a steady supply of water rather than watering heavily after letting them go dry.

Skin imperfections are a normal sign of changes in temperature. They do not affect the taste. Keep plants at an even temperature and protect them from excessive heat or strong wind.

PLANTING & AFTERCARE

YOU WILL NEED: ❏ Tomato plant ❏ Trowel ❏ Stake or wire cage ❏ Compost ❏ Fertilizer ❏ Mulch

1 **After the last frost,** plant your Tomato in a large hole with a support. Mulch and supply plants with 2 gal. of water per week.

2 **Carefully tie** Tomato plant to the stake or wire cage for support as it grows taller. Fix stake to a wall for heavy-fruiting plants.

3 **Check regularly** for little sideshoots in the leaf axles. Pinch out between fingers and thumb when they are about ¾ in. long.

4 **Pinch out the** top of the plant once it has grown four flower bunches. Now the plant can ripen its fruit instead of growing taller.

5 **Harvest fruit until** temperatures fall. Green Tomatoes will ripen off the vine if they are mature: their skin should look glossy.

Tip

Helpful partners, such as Nasturtiums, Poppies, and Marigolds, attract insects that eat aphids and other pests.

Tomatoes

SAMPLE

A delicious vegetable straight off the vine

Season

 A **Annual**

 Fruits early summer to early fall

Special Features

 Average yield: 4 lb. per plant

Best Conditions

 All zones

Full sun

Shelter from wind

← Height: 1-4 ft. →
← Spread: 2-3 ft. →

Secrets of Success

✓ ✗
BUYING HINTS

SUN & SOIL

SPECIAL ADVICE

● **Buy young plants.** Look for pot-grown Tomatoes with healthy green leaves and no flower bunches. Tomato plants should be about 8 in. tall, and their roots should be white.
● **Avoid Tomato plants** that have been stuck in their pots for too long. Do not buy those with yellow, thin, scraggly stems.

● **Plentiful sunshine.** Tomato plants thrive when given an abundance of sun. Keep them in a warm and sheltered position, but protect them from blazing heat or gusting winds.
● **Humus-rich soil.** Enrich your Tomatoes' soil with compost or well-rotted manure before planting and fertilize the plants regularly.

● **For easier watering,** bury a bottomless coffee can next to the Tomato and pour the water into the can. This will allow water to go straight down to the roots.
● **Ripen green Tomatoes** at the end of the season by placing them indoors next to ripe Apples or Bananas. They contain ripening agents that will redden the Tomatoes.

Seasonal Tips

EARLY SPRING
Sowing
Sow indoors eight to ten weeks before last frost date. Repot when plants are 3-4 in. tall, thin and harden them off.

LATE SPRING
Planting
Transplant Tomatoes into the garden after last frost. Stop plants from growing taller after four flower bunches have grown.

Plant Doctor

Blight can destroy your plants during a wet summer, turning the leaves brown, then the stems black. To prevent damage, clean debris off the plant. Avoid planting Tomatoes in the same position the following year.

Holes in the fruits may indicate the presence of Tomato hornworms. These huge caterpillars feed on fruit and leaves. Handpick them as soon as you spot them.

Blossom end rot *(below)* turns the bottom of fruits brown and leathery. It is a common problem, caused by calcium deficiency and moisture fluctuation. Water regularly and apply calcium.

For further information: Gardening Made Easy, International Masters Publishers, 444 Liberty Ave., Pittsburgh, PA 15222-1207 1-800-954-5210

Printed in U.S.A. ©MCMXCV IMP AB/IMP Inc. Gardening Made Easy™ International Masters Publishers AB, produced under license

Packet 00

A. *Geranium macrorrhizum (bigroot geranium) (1)*

B. *Carex (sedge) (2)*

C. *Alyssum (madwort) (12)*

D. *Erodium chamaedryoides (stork's-bill) (many)*

E. *Laurentia fluviatilis (blue star creeper) (many)*

F. *Sedum spathulifolium 'Cape Blanco' (stonecrop) (1)*

G. *Hypericum (St.-John's-wort) (1)*

H. *Thymus (thyme) (many)*

I. *Sedum (stonecrop) (many)*

J. *Iberis (candytuft) (12)*

K. *Myrtus communis 'Compacta' (dwarf myrtle) (1)*

L. *Armeria maritima (thrift) (many)*

M. *Achillea (yarrow) (9)*

N. *Geranium dalmaticum (cranesbill) (2*

O. *Erigeron karvinskianus (Mexican daisy) (many)*

P. *Geranium sanguineum (bloody cranesbill) (many)*

Q. *Arrhenatherum elatius var. bulbosum 'Variegatum' (variegated oat grass) (*

A Unique Setting for a Rock Garden

By tucking sturdy, low-growing plants like sedum, armeria, and hypericum into small pockets in steps made of chunks of broken sidewalk, the creator of this unusual plan has built a rock garden that leads up to a home in Pasadena, California. The plants, which can withstand light foot traffic, have been allowed to spread, producing a delightful wandering effect.

The designer selected plants with a variety of foliage textures and flower colors. Purple *Geranium sanguineum* cascades over the top step, leading down to the rose-colored *Armeria maritima,* with its narrow, grasslike leaves. Yellow-flowering sedum backs a mass of white iberis flowing over the bottom step, where a topiary of dwarf Greek myrtle adds vertical interest on the right. Although the garden's peak blooming season runs from March through May, the plants have been chosen so that something is in bloom every day of the year. And many plants, including the armeria, the sedum, and the Mexican daisy, have evergreen foliage.

The site needs little maintenance beyond removing dead flowers, cutting back when plants spread too much, and watering regularly. The plants grow in a mixture of peat moss and sand, with a top dressing of finely textured "bird shot" gravel to promote good drainage.

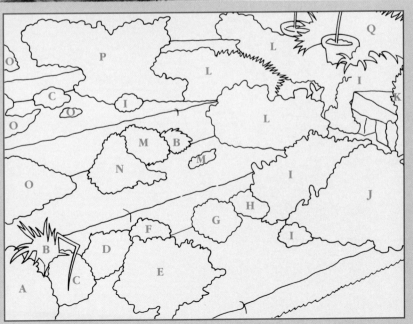

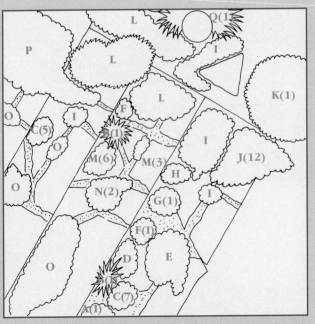

Whimsy on a Formal Garden Path

Purple verbena and waving stems of white *Cleome hasslerana* edge a meandering pathway—the essence of informality—as it makes its way through the heart of a neatly formal garden rectangle cut out of a sloping side yard at this garden designer's Virginia home.

Planted to display a seasonal variety of color combinations, the garden changes personality throughout the year. A visitor to the gazebo in early spring would look out on yellow and white narcissus blooms; later in the season, purple allium would follow. In summer the pastel-hued annuals illustrated here predominate, and pineapple-scented sage provides sparks of red in fall. During winter, the boxwood hedge stands out against the distinctive white path, composed of equal parts mortar, stone dust, and oyster shells.

A. *Salvia elegans (pineapple-scented sage) (4)* **B.** *Hibiscus 'Red Shield' (purple hibiscus) (4)* **C.** *Eupatorium fistulosum (hollow Joe-Pye weed) (4)* **D.** *Nicotiana sylvestris (flowering tobacco) (many)* **E.** *Sophora japonica (Japanese pagoda tree) (4)* **F.** *Verbena tenuisecta 'Edith' (moss verbena) (many)* **G.** *Buxus sempervirens 'Graham Blandy' (boxwood) (4)* **H.** *Cleome basslerana (spider flower) (many)* **I.** *Verbena tenuisecta 'Alba' (white verbena) (many)* **J.** *Buxus sempervirens 'Suffruticosa' (boxwood) (3)* **K.** *Miscanthus sinensis 'Variegatus' (variegated maiden grass) (6)* **L.** *Prunus spinosa 'Purpurea' (purple-leaf plum) (5)*

A. *Trachelospermum asiaticum (Asiatic jasmine)* (4) **B.** *Lantana 'New Gold' (shrub verbena)* (9) **C.** *Lantana montevidensis (shrub verbena)* (6) **D.** *Rosemarinus officinalis (rosemary)* (2) **E.** *Dasylirion wheeleri (Wheeler's sotol)* (2) **F.** *Salvia greggii (autumn sage)* (2) **G.** *Hesperaloe parviflora (red yucca)* (1) **H.** *Raphiolepis indica 'Clara' (dwarf indian hawthorn)* (3) **I.** *Leucophyllum frutescens 'Compactum' (compact Texas sage)* (2) **J.** *Yucca recurvifolia (yucca)* (3) **K.** *Muhlenbergia capillaris (muhly grass)* (1) **L.** *Sophora secundiflora (mescal bean)* (2) **M.** *Plumbago auriculata (Cape leadwort)* (1)

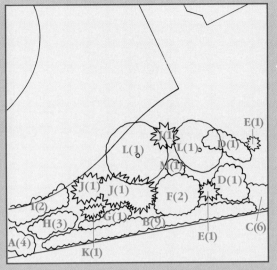

A Lush Curbside Planting

A design philosophy calling for a mixture of sedate plantings and something a bit on the wild side guided the landscape architect who created this curbside garden in San Antonio, Texas. The designer achieved the effect by combining, for example, the manicured look of Asiatic jasmine ground cover with billowy and untrimmed golden and purple trailing lantanas and pink and purple salvias.

To guarantee a continuous flow of color through the seasons, the designer included native plants like Texas muhly grass, which changes from a beige-brown in summer to a heathery pink in the fall. For variety in texture and growth habit, he included such bold plants as the cactuslike *Yucca recurvifolia,* with its towering plumes of white blossoms, and the spiky desert sotol, which he contrasted with soft, silvery Texas sage and fine-textured rosemary.

Meant primarily to add beauty to this highly visible house on a corner lot, the tall, dense plantings in this garden have the added purpose of totally concealing a front driveway, which can be seen in the overhead planting diagram, above.

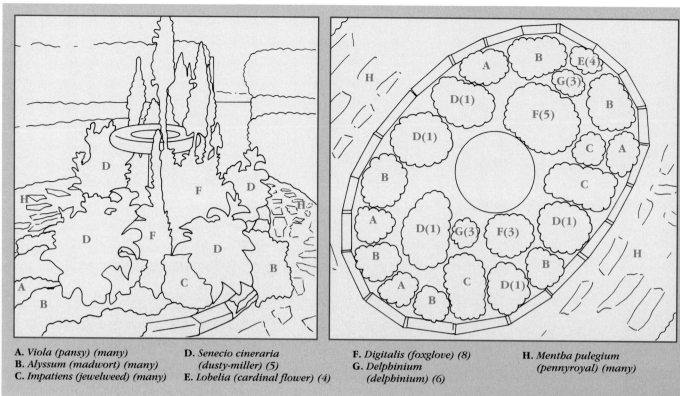

A. *Viola (pansy) (many)*
B. *Alyssum (madwort) (many)*
C. *Impatiens (jewelweed) (many)*
D. *Senecio cineraria (dusty-miller) (5)*
E. *Lobelia (cardinal flower) (4)*
F. *Digitalis (foxglove) (8)*
G. *Delphinium (delphinium) (6)*
H. *Mentha pulegium (pennyroyal) (many)*

Island Flower Bed

The colorful display in this oval-shaped island bed, which measures 6 feet at its widest point by 11 feet long, is produced by surprisingly few varieties of flowers. Towering spires of foxglove in pink and white surround a small stone birdbath at the bed's center, making a strong vertical statement. The feathery silver foliage of dusty-miller draws the eye toward the base of the bed, where impatiens of varying pastel hues, dainty white alyssum, and violet-colored pansies spill over the stone edging. Except for a few lobelia plants and a single small clump of delphiniums *(garden plan, above right),* the bed includes no other plant types.

The homeowner, who lives in Del Mar, California, designed this island to be almost constantly in bloom. She achieves this by varying her plantings with the seasons, mixing annuals with perennials. The island floats in a sea of creeping pennyroyal, planted between circles of steppingstones.

91

Answers to Common Questions

I've tried lots of plant combinations but am still not satisfied that I've hit on one with exquisite beauty. How do I get beyond pretty to truly beautiful?

The foremost quality of any exquisite plant combination is simplicity. You may be using too many different plants or arranging them in a way that makes them hard to read visually. Some of the best ways to achieve simplicity are to limit your palette to just two or three kinds of plants (although you may use several of each kind in a massed effect), to limit your flower colors to variations on a single color theme, and to plant them so that there is open space around or between them, even when they grow to full, mature size. Simple, beautiful combinations possess restraint, yet enough contrast in form, foliage, and color to stir the viewer's interest.

Which characteristic of a plant should I start with when choosing material for a combination—soil requirements, light requirements, shape, foliage, or flower color?

Start with the physical features of the site where you'll put the garden. Will it be next to a walkway, against a fence, on a berm? Once you've chosen the site, you'll have a good idea what size plants you'll want. Then identify the soil type and the amount of light the site receives each day. Those parameters will help you narrow down the candidates. Start choosing plants first by their shapes, then by foliage texture and color, finally working toward features like flower color. Repeat several plants of the same type if it looks good in masses, or plant a single specimen if it's a dramatic plant.

I try to put together perennials and annuals with matched flower colors, but the effect is rather haphazard. What's the secret to making good-looking color combinations?

The problem you describe is usually caused by too few plants in the combination. Single plants tend to recede to mere points of color when viewed from even a short distance. Try using drifts rather than just one, two, or three plants. A drift is a group of five to nine plants, all of the same variety, usually arranged in a shape with tapered ends. Drifts will give you broad swaths of color that can be combined by weaving their tapered ends into one another. These generous areas of color will have much more impact than the spotty color afforded by single plants.

What looks better—lots of different colors in a flower bed or just a few?

The answer depends, of course, on your aesthetic sense, but a limited palette usually gives a more integrated and visually pleasing look than a sheer riot of color. Try limiting your color scheme to one-third of the color wheel, such as yellow-orange through red, and add a little contrasting color—in this case blue—as an accent. Use enough plants of the same type to give a true color impression. If you use too few plants of varying colors the human brain (through the eye) will blend these colors. A garden of mixed dots of red and blue flowers, for instance, will appear at a distance to be violet overall.

I want to do an all-red combination because I just love red flowers. Will this kind of combination work?

You can try it, but if all the reds are of a similar hue and value, your flower bed may look as if it were covered by a red snow. Consider varying the reds by hue (crimson, brick red, red-violet) and tones (deep red, medium red, pink). Also, experiment first with annuals to get an idea of combinations that appeal to you. The same advice holds for a garden of any single color except white. In a white garden, the purer the whites, the prettier and cooler it all looks.

Most days I get to enjoy my garden only in the evening, after work, when the light is low and failing. Are there any plants that I can combine to add interest to the evening garden?

As daylight fails, the cones, or color-sensing cells in the eye, begin to stop functioning in favor of the rods, or light-sensing cells. Colors on the red end of the spectrum appear to darken first, and eventually red looks black. The violet- and lavender-sensing cones are the last to lose their function in the dimming light. Thus, planting lavender or violet flowers will give you a startlingly fluorescent display as this shift occurs in the eye. Among perennials, a combination of *Platycodon grandiflorus* 'Blue' (balloon flower), *Adenophora confusa* (ladybells), and *Linum perenne* (blue flax) will fairly glow in the gloaming.

My perennial combinations look good in flower but dull when their blooming periods are over. What can I do to keep them attractive all season?

Since most of the perennial garden is solely green for most of the growing season, begin planning your beds by considering combinations of foliage that will look good whether or not there is bloom on them. Use eye-catching foliage plants such as those with unusual leaf colors for accents or contrasts. Foliage in shades of gray, gray-green, black, white, silver, gold, red, and cream will maintain interest when bloom is gone. For continuous color through the season, you might also add some annuals.

I like color in my gardens, and for years have planted red salvia with multicolored zinnias. This year, though, I'm tired of this combination. It seems too garish and unplanned. How can I keep lots of color in my garden without it looking so awkward?

Focus on the pastel form of a favorite color. If you like the deep, rich, saturated red of the salvia, think in terms of a light, clear pink pastel. Then choose a flower that will give you this color, and plant it in masses and drifts to form the color basis of the garden. Accent it with the pure red of the salvia or with another saturated color, such as rich violet-blue. This kind of arrangement will be much more elegant and eye-pleasing than large amounts of intense, mixed colors.

FORM, SIZE, AND TEXTURE

I planted a border of perennials and mixed shrubs, and it looked good for the first few years. But now, 5 years later, the shrubs are too large for the perennials and it looks out of proportion. Should I tear everything out and start again?

Don't tear everything out. Instead, move the perennials out of the bed, and plant other shrubs or grasses that will grow into proportion with the existing shrubs, which are now reaching their mature size. In general, when planning combinations of shrubs and perennials, either choose shrubs that stay small and in proportion with their associated perennials, or figure on replacing the perennials when the garden is a few years old.

Along the foundation of my house I have combinations of evergreens, both needled and broadleaf, that tend to look like big lumps of green rather than a designed grouping. How can I create a more dramatic effect?

Select the most interesting evergreens as the basis for a revamped design—that is, the ones with the most distinct shape, the most distinct foliage texture, or the most distinct colors—and transplant to other areas the shrubs that have less character. If the open space is appealing, either keep it open and cover it with a mulch or plant it with a low ground cover whose color contrasts with the evergreens around it. If the open space calls for a plant, consider a deciduous one with twisting, sinuous trunks or branches, or one whose form or texture strongly contrasts with the plants around it.

When making combinations, is it a good idea to use plants of different heights, or should they all be about the same?

Variation makes for interest. Plants that are all the same height create a blob in the landscape, but if you vary heights—and especially if you vary shapes as well—you create the highs and lows reminiscent of a city's skyline. When creating a combination, choose the tallest plant first, and position it off-center rather than in the precise middle of the garden to give motion to the picture. Combine plants so that the low-growing varieties are toward the outside of the bed, building them in height toward the tallest plant. Such a bed not only looks more interesting but also allows the viewer to "read" the combination because the individual plants stand out from one another.

How do I choose a combination of plants that will mature nicely together?

It's always best to choose plant combinations with their full form in mind since they'll spend most of their time together in maturity. You can figure that most perennials will reach maturity and need division after 3 years. It usually takes woody shrubs and vines 5 to 7 years to achieve full height and width; small trees take about 10 to 12 years, while large shade trees can grow for decades before reaching maturity. Plants—like people—tend to grow fast when young, then slow down. Hold pruning and thinning to a minimum when the plants are putting on their youthful growth spurts, then shape them up after they reach maturity.

DISTINCTIVE TREATMENTS AND EFFECTS

I want to make a featured group of three woody shrubs that I think are beautiful together, and I want them to stand out from the background. How can I achieve this effect?

First, you can plant them in a group as stand-alone specimens—that is, provide them a stage in the garden by themselves, without interference from other plants. You might find a spot like this where a fence touches a building wall, by the front steps, or where patio paving is removed to produce a space for planting. Second, you can place such a featured group in the garden bed or border, but use mulches, rocks, and dark evergreens like mugo pine, rhododendron, or yew as a backdrop. The darker the backdrop, the more your featured group will stand out.

How can I combine striking plants like crinum and gladiolus with other plants for good effect?

Specimen plants need to be given their due, so combine them with plants that let them take center stage. For instance, surround them with small-leaved ground covers or airy plants like baby's-breath. Also, note the shape of your specimen plants and try to find companions that echo their shape in some way. An upright, urn-shaped plant like a succulent aloe, for instance, might be echoed by the hanging bells of *Campanula medium.* Gladiolus, because of their strong vertical shape and bright colors, are not easy companions but can be associated with horizontal junipers and other evergreens.

I would like to plant a combination of different ground covers. How can I make them look really interesting?

Plant them in free-form masses 6 to 8 feet across, and alternate light ground covers like *Lamium maculatum* 'Beacon Silver' or *Achillea tomentosa* with dark ones like *Pachysandra terminalis* or *Ajuga reptans.* Succulents make nice pools of light leaves. Small areas of Corsican mint or dark green *Sagina subulata* create dark mats. By alternating these, you will give the ground a dappled look. Most of these ground covers do well in partial shade, which will add to the light-dark tapestry effect.

I have a spot on a rise where the sun sets—a perfect place for backlighting plants with the late afternoon sun. What plants would look good together in backlight?

The Japanese maple *Acer palmatum* with *Imperata cylindrica* 'Rubra' (Japanese blood grass) in front makes a great combination for backlighting, especially in fall, when the maple is turning color. Grapevines, black locust, and many other thin-leaved plants are also beautiful when the sun shines through them.

CULTIVATION AND MAINTENANCE

I want to plant lilacs together with mountain laurel, but I have read that lilacs like full sun while mountain laurel prefers partial shade. Does this mean I can't plant them together? How hard-and-fast are these recommendations for sun exposure?

Recommendations for sun and shade should be followed when possible, but they are not always engraved in stone. Roses, for instance, are listed for full sun, but many thrive and bloom prolifically with less light. On the other hand, some plants demand the conditions listed—such as full shade for certain Japanese maples. As for your suggested pairing of lilacs and mountain laurel, lilacs need sun to develop profuse flowering but do quite well mixed in a shrub border. Plant your mountain laurel on the northern side of the lilacs so that the taller lilacs throw shade on the laurel for most of the day. You might flank the laurel on either side with taller leafy shrubs or evergreens that add shade and serve as a backdrop for the lilacs.

I have a good loamy soil with a pH of 6.2. Will it be adequate for all my plant combinations, or will I have to amend it to account for the plants' different pH needs?

A good loamy soil amended with compost and somewhere in the 6 to 7 pH range is fine for almost all ornamental plants. Most nutrients are optimally available to plants when the pH is in this slightly acid range. While it is true that some plants, such as rhododendrons and azaleas, like a more acid soil and some prefer a more alkaline soil, they will probably do well enough in your garden. If you like, though, you can purchase soil amendments at a garden center to place around your acid-loving plants, or dig in a shovelful of ordinary wood ashes around grasses and plants that thrive in an alkaline soil.

I am putting together a combination of plants for my Zone 8 garden. One of the plants I want to use is listed for Zone 4, another as hardy to Zone 9. Must I only use plants listed for Zone 8, or can I grow these others?

The USDA zones delineate regions with similar average winter minimum temperatures. Zone information is provided so that gardeners don't put in a plant that is too tender for their climate. Plants listed as hardy only to Zone 9 (winter minimums average 20° above 0°F), for instance, will probably sustain winter freezing damage in colder zones—even in your Zone 8. On the other hand, most plants hardy to Zone 4 (where winter minimums average about 30° below 0°F) will do fine in warmer zones, although in the warmest zones they may not get enough winter chilling. Lilacs and peonies, for instance, need more cold winter dormancy than they usually get in Zones 9 through 11.

I've chosen three plants for my garden, but my books tell me that two of them like a moist, well-drained, humusy soil while the third likes a dry, sandy soil. Does this mean that I can't successfully grow them together?

Almost all plants will thrive in a well-drained, humusy soil, except for desert plants such as cacti, which can rot if given constantly moist soil. Your choices can probably be planted together without fear, as long as the one that likes a dry, sandy soil is given excellent drainage. Consider mixing a scoop or two of sand in its hole. Generally, plants that like dry, sandy soil, such as Mediterranean herbs like yarrow and lavender, won't stop growing if the soil is rich and moist. In fact, just the opposite will happen: They'll grow long and leggy. Plants that prefer a dry, sandy medium grow more thriftily and compactly in such soils. Your plant will probably become quite luxuriant, though it will be less sturdy and may need staking that it otherwise wouldn't require.

Troubleshooting Guide

Even the best-tended gardens can fall prey to pests and diseases. To keep them in check, regularly inspect your plants for warning signs, remembering that lack of nutrients, improper pH levels, and other environmental conditions can cause symptoms like those that are typical of some diseases. If wilting or yellowing appears on neighboring plants, the source is probably environmental; damage caused by pests and diseases is usually more random.

This guide is intended to help you identify and solve most of your pest and disease problems. In general, good drainage and air circulation will help prevent infection, and the many insects, such as ladybugs and lacewings, that prey on pests should be encouraged. Natural solutions to garden problems are best, but if you must use chemicals, treat only the affected plant. Try to use horticultural oils, insecticidal soaps, and the botanical insecticide *neem;* these products are the least disruptive to beneficial insects and will not destroy the soil balance that is the foundation of a healthy garden.

PESTS

PROBLEM: Leaves curl, are distorted in shape, and may be sticky and have a black, sooty appearance. A clear, sticky substance often appears on stems and leaves. Buds and flowers are deformed, new growth is stunted, and leaves and flowers may drop.

CAUSE: Aphids are pear-shaped, semi-transparent, wingless sucking insects, about ⅛ inch long and ranging in color from green to red, pink, black, or gray. Infestations are severest in spring and early summer, when pests cluster on tender new shoots, on undersides of leaves, and around flower buds. Winged forms appear when colonies become overcrowded. Aphids secrete honeydew, a sticky substance that fosters the growth of a black fungus called sooty mold.

SOLUTION: Spray plants frequently with a steady stream of water from a garden hose to knock aphids off plants and discourage them from returning. Ladybugs or lacewings, which eat aphids, may be introduced into the garden. In severe cases, prune off infested areas and use a diluted insecticidal soap solution or a recommended insecticide.
SUSCEPTIBLE PLANTS: VIRTUALLY ANY PLANT.

PROBLEM: Small round or oblong holes are eaten into leaves, leaf edges, and flowers. Leaves may be reduced to skeletons with only veins remaining.

CAUSE: Japanese beetles, iridescent blue-green with bronze wing covers, are the most destructive of a large family of hard-shelled chewing insects ranging in size from ¼ to ¾ inch long. Other genera include Asiatic garden and rose chafer, as well as blister and flea beetles. Adult beetles are voracious in the summer. Larvae, the white grubs, feed on the roots of plants and are present from midsummer through the following spring, when they emerge as adults.

SOLUTION: Handpick small colonies *(Caution: Use gloves when picking blister beetles),* placing them in a can filled with soapy water. Japanese beetles can be caught in baited traps. The larval stage can be controlled with milky spore disease. For heavy infestations, contact your local Cooperative Extension Service for information on registered pesticides and the best times to apply them in your region.
SUSCEPTIBLE PLANTS: MANY ANNUALS AND PERENNIALS; ROSES, ESPECIALLY THOSE WITH LIGHT-COLORED BLOSSOMS; BULBS; SHRUBS; TREES.

PROBLEM: Holes appear in leaves, buds, and flowers; entire leaf or blossom may be eaten. Stems may be chewed or broken; whole plant may be stripped. Weblike nests that resemble tents appear in the crotches of trees.

CAUSE: Caterpillars, the wormlike larvae of moths, butterflies, and sawflies, range in size from less than 1 inch to several inches long. They come in a variety of shapes and colors and can be smooth, hairy, or spiny. These voracious pests are found in gardens primarily during the spring.

SOLUTION: Handpick and destroy to control small populations. *Bacillus thuringiensis* (Bt) kills many species without harming plants. Several species are susceptible to insecticidal soap; spray it directly on the caterpillar. Keep garden clean. Deep spading in early spring can destroy many species that pupate underground. Destroy all cocoons and nests. *SUSCEPTIBLE PLANTS: MANY ANNUALS AND PERENNIALS; BULBS; ALL ROSES AND SHRUBS, ESPECIALLY EUONYMUS; MANY TREES.*

PROBLEM: White or light green tunnels appear in leaves; older tunnels turn black. Leaves may die. Leaf tips of conifers turn yellow, then brown. Boxwood leaves have yellow spots that enlarge to blisterlike patches and turn brown; holly leaves, yellowish or brown serpentine trails.

CAUSE: Leaf miners—minute (1/16 to 1/8 inch long), translucent, pale green larvae of certain flies, moths, or beetles—are hatched from white, cylindrical eggs laid in clusters on the leaves of plants. During spring and summer, the larvae eat the tender interior below the surface of the leaf, leaving behind serpentine trails of blistered tissue called mines.

SOLUTION: Damage is usually not lethal. Pick off and destroy infested leaves. In fall, cut the plant to the ground and discard stalks; for trees and shrubs, severely prune branch tips and leaves. Keep the garden well weeded and free of plant debris. Use a systemic insecticide before leaf mining becomes extensive. *SUSCEPTIBLE PLANTS: MANY ANNUALS AND PERENNIALS; SHRUBS, INCLUDING AMERICAN HOLLY AND BOXWOOD; CONIFERS; MANY TREES.*

PROBLEM: Leaves become stippled or flecked, then discolor, curl, and wither. Webbing may appear, particularly on undersides of leaves and on the branches of shrubs and trees.

CAUSE: Mites are pinhead-size, spiderlike sucking pests that can be reddish, pale green, or yellow. A major problem in hot, dry weather, several generations of mites may occur in a single season. Adults of some species hibernate over the winter in sod and bark and on weeds and plants that retain foliage.

SOLUTION: Damage is worst in full sunlight and hot areas. Keep plants watered and mulched, especially during hot, dry periods. Regularly spray the undersides of leaves, where mites feed and lay eggs, with a strong stream of water or a diluted insecticidal soap solution, which controls nymphs and adults but not eggs. Horticultural oils can be applied. Introduce predators such as ladybugs and green lacewing larvae. For severe cases, use a miticide. *SUSCEPTIBLE PLANTS: ALL TYPES OF PLANTS.*

PROBLEM: Plants or leaves discolor, leaves drop, and plants eventually die. Growth is stunted. With shrubs, the growing tips of many branches may die, and flowers are not produced. Branches, twigs, or leaves are covered with small white cottony patches or rounded or oval shells that may be black, brown, gray, or white.

CAUSE: Scale insects have hard or soft shells, ranging in size from 1/10 to 3/8 inch long, that may be white, yellow, green, red, brown, or black. They usually appear in clusters. Adult females appear on stems or leaves as bumps. Males are minute flying insects with yellow wings. The insects suck plant juices. White patches are egg sacs.

SOLUTION: Destroy severely infested stems or branches. Scrub off the shells with a plastic scouring pad. Spray trees, shrubs, and roses with horticultural oil in early spring before plant growth begins to smother eggs. If insects appear in summer, control with insecticidal soap or spray with a chemical insecticide. *SUSCEPTIBLE PLANTS: MANY ANNUALS; MOST PERENNIALS; ROSES, ESPECIALLY CLIMBERS THAT ARE NOT PRUNED YEARLY; SHRUBS; MANY TREES.*

PROBLEM: Ragged holes appear on leaves, especially those near the ground. New leaves and entire young seedlings may be eaten. Telltale shiny silver streaks appear on leaves and garden paths.

CAUSE: Slugs and snails hide during the day and feed on low-hanging leaves at night or on overcast or rainy days. They prefer damp soil in a shady location and are most damaging in summer, especially in wet regions or during rainy years.

SOLUTION: Keep garden clean to minimize hiding places. Handpick or trap slugs and snails by placing saucers of beer near plants. Slugs will also collect under grapefruit halves or melon rinds. Salt kills slugs and snails but may damage plants. Poison bait is available at garden centers and can be applied at dusk; reapply after rain or watering. Spading in spring destroys dormant slugs and eggs. *SUSCEPTIBLE PLANTS: VIRTUALLY ANY PLANT, ESPECIALLY WITH YOUNG OR TENDER FOLIAGE. HOSTA IS HIGHLY SUSCEPTIBLE.*

DISEASES

PROBLEM: A brownish gray, moldy growth appears on flowers and foliage. Stalks are weak, flowers droop. Buds may not open. Discolored blotches appear on leaves, stems, and flowers. Stem bases rot. Plant parts eventually turn brown and dry up. Flowering plants are most affected.

CAUSE: Botrytis blight, also known as gray mold, is a fungus disease that thrives in moist air and cool temperatures. The blight survives the winter as hard, black lumps in the soil or on dead plant parts.

SOLUTION: Water early in the day and avoid overhead watering. Place plants in well-drained soil. Thin out plants so they get more light and air circulation, or transplant them to a dry, sunny location. Cut off and destroy all infected plant parts. *SUSCEPTIBLE PLANTS: MANY ANNUALS AND PERENNIALS; BULBS; ROSES; SHRUBS; TREES.*

PROBLEM: Leaves develop small yellow, brown, or black spots that are surrounded by a rim of discolored tissue. Spots often join to produce large, irregular blotches. Entire leaf may turn yellow, wilt, and drop. Spotting usually starts on lower leaves and moves upward.

CAUSE: The many leaf-spot diseases are caused by a number of fungi or bacteria. All are particularly severe in wet weather because they are spread by splashing water.

SOLUTION: Clean up all fallen leaves before winter. Water overhead only in the morning, as damp foliage in cool night air encourages spreading of the diseases. Prune and destroy infected leaves of perennials and shrubs. A fungicide can protect healthy foliage but will not destroy fungus on infected leaves. *SUSCEPTIBLE PLANTS: ALL TYPES OF PLANTS.*

PROBLEM: Leaves are covered with spots or a thin layer of grayish white powdery matter. Infected parts may distort and curl, then turn yellow or purplish; leaves may finally drop off. Badly infected buds will not open properly.

CAUSE: Powdery mildews are fungus diseases that thrive when nights are cool and days are hot and humid. The diseases are most noticeable in late summer and fall.

SOLUTION: Plant mildew-resistant varieties. Susceptible plants should receive full sun with good air circulation. Water overhead only in the early morning. In the fall, cut infected perennials to the ground and discard. Fungicides may be used to prevent spreading. Also effective are summer oil sprays and antitranspirants, which decrease the amount of water lost through leaves. *SUSCEPTIBLE PLANTS: ANY TYPE OF PLANT.*

PROBLEM: Leaves turn yellow, red, or brown and are stunted and wilted; the entire plant may wilt and die. Flowers may not develop. Roots are discolored dark brown or black, are soft and wet, and carry a mushroomlike odor. Trees have rotting bark at the base, followed by a white, fibrous fungus.

CAUSE: Root rot is caused by a variety of fungi, many of which thrive in heavy, wet soil conditions.

SOLUTION: Remove and destroy infected plant parts; if infection is severe, remove plant and the surrounding soil. Improve soil drainage. Water early in the day and allow the soil to dry between waterings. A fungicide can be applied to the soil before replanting.
SUSCEPTIBLE PLANTS: ALL TYPES OF PLANTS.

PROBLEM: Upper leaf surfaces have yellow or white spots, and undersides are covered with orange or yellow pustules. Leaves hang down along the stem. Pustules may become more numerous, destroying leaves and occasionally the entire plant. Plants may be stunted.

CAUSE: Rust, a fungus disease, is a problem in the late summer and early fall and is most prevalent when nights are cool and humid. The orange or brown powder, which consists of fungus spores, spreads easily by wind.

SOLUTION: Buy rust-resistant varieties whenever possible. Water early in the day so plants can dry before nightfall. Avoid wetting leaves. Remove and destroy all infected leaves, including those on the ground. To prevent the disease, spray with a fungicide in cool, wet weather, especially in the late spring.
SUSCEPTIBLE PLANTS: MANY ANNUALS AND PERENNIALS; ROSES; SHRUBS; MANY TREES.

PROBLEM: Plants suddenly lose their color, turn yellow, and wilt. Entire branches may die back. Roots are damaged or deformed and have small, knotty growths and swellings.

CAUSE: Soil nematodes—colorless, microscopic worms that live in the soil and feed on roots—inhibit a plant's intake of nitrogen. Damage is at its worst in warm, sunlit, sandy soils that are moist.

SOLUTION: Only a laboratory test will confirm the presence of nematodes. Be suspicious if roots are swollen or stunted. There are no chemical controls; dispose of infected plants and the soil that surrounds them, or solarize the soil. Grow resistant species or cultivars. Add nitrogen fertilizer.
SUSCEPTIBLE PLANTS: VIRTUALLY ANY PLANT.

PROBLEM: One side or one branch of the plant typically wilts. Leaves turn yellow, then brown, and finally wilt and die. Wilt progresses up from the bottom of the plant and out toward branch tips. A cross section of a tree branch reveals a dark ring or rings.

CAUSE: Verticillium wilt is a fungal disease that can be confirmed only by a laboratory test. The fungus thrives in cool, moist soil but usually does not reveal its presence until warm, dry weather has stressed the plants.

SOLUTION: There are no organic or chemical controls. Once soil is infected, plant only resistant varieties. If infection on a tree is detected early, fertilize and water to encourage natural recovery, and remove damaged parts. If infection is severe, the tree cannot be saved. Do not replant the same species, as soil remains contaminated.
SUSCEPTIBLE PLANTS: MANY ANNUALS; SOME PERENNIALS, SUCH AS ASTER AND CHRYSANTHEMUM; ROSES; SHRUBS; TREES, ESPECIALLY ELMS AND JAPANESE AND OTHER MAPLES.

Color Guide to Herbaceous Plants

Organized by flower color, this chart provides information needed to select species and varieties that will thrive in the particular conditions of your garden. For additional information on each plant, refer to the Encyclopedia that begins on page 108.

Color	Plant	Zone 3	Zone 4	Zone 5	Zone 6	Zone 7	Zone 8	Zone 9	Zone 10	Dry	Well-Drained	Moist	Full Sun	Partial Shade	Shade	Spring	Summer	Fall	Winter	Under 1 ft.	1-3 ft.	Over 3 ft.	Form	Foliage	Fragrance	Flowers	Fruit/Seeds	Winter Interest
WHITE	ACANTHUS SPINOSUS			✓	✓	✓	✓	✓		✓	✓		✓	✓			✓					✓	✓	✓		✓		
	ACONITUM NAPELLUS 'SNOW WHITE'	✓	✓	✓	✓	✓					✓	✓					✓	✓				✓	✓	✓		✓		
	AGERATUM HOUSTONIANUM 'HAWAII WHITE' [1]										✓	✓	✓					✓	✓		✓			✓	✓		✓		
	ARTEMISIA LACTIFLORA		✓	✓	✓	✓	✓	✓			✓		✓	✓				✓				✓		✓		✓		
	ASTILBE X ARENDSII 'PROFESSOR VAN DER WIELAN'		✓	✓	✓	✓					✓	✓			✓			✓				✓		✓	✓		✓		
	CAMPANULA PERSICIFOLIA 'ALBA'	✓	✓	✓	✓	✓	✓	✓			✓	✓	✓	✓	✓						✓					✓		
	CHRYSANTHEMUM X SUPERBUM	✓	✓	✓	✓	✓	✓					✓	✓					✓	✓		✓					✓		
	CIMICIFUGA SIMPLEX 'WHITE PEARL'		✓	✓	✓	✓						✓		✓				✓	✓			✓	✓		✓		✓		
	CLEMATIS PANICULATA		✓	✓	✓	✓	✓	✓			✓		✓	✓	✓			✓	✓			✓			✓		✓	✓
	CRAMBE CORDIFOLIA		✓	✓	✓	✓					✓		✓					✓				✓		✓		✓		
	DELPHINIUM ELATUM PACIFIC HYBRIDS	✓	✓	✓	✓	✓					✓	✓	✓					✓				✓				✓		
	HELIANTHUS ANNUUS 'ITALIAN WHITE' [3]						✓	✓			✓		✓					✓	✓			✓				✓		
	HOSTA PLANTAGINEA 'APHRODITE'	✓	✓	✓	✓	✓	✓					✓		✓	✓	✓		✓			✓			✓	✓	✓		
	HYACINTHUS ORIENTALIS 'CARNEGIE'			✓	✓	✓	✓				✓	✓	✓		✓		✓			✓					✓	✓		
	IRIS CRISTATA 'ALBA'	✓	✓	✓	✓	✓	✓	✓				✓		✓		✓				✓				✓		✓		
	LATHYRUS ODORATUS [2]										✓		✓	✓		✓	✓	✓				✓			✓	✓		
	LILIUM CANDIDUM		✓	✓	✓	✓	✓	✓				✓		✓	✓		✓	✓				✓			✓	✓		
	MACLEAYA CORDATA	✓	✓	✓	✓	✓	✓				✓	✓	✓					✓				✓		✓		✓		
	NARCISSUS TRUMPET DAFFODILS 'WHITE IRON'		✓	✓	✓	✓	✓				✓		✓			✓					✓					✓		
	PAEONIA HYBRIDS	✓	✓	✓	✓	✓					✓	✓	✓	✓		✓					✓				✓	✓		
	RICINUS COMMUNIS [1]										✓		✓					✓				✓		✓		✓		
	RODGERSIA TABULARIS		✓	✓	✓							✓		✓	✓			✓				✓		✓	✓	✓		✓
	YUCCA FILAMENTOSA		✓	✓	✓	✓	✓	✓		✓		✓										✓		✓	✓	✓		
YELLOW	ACHILLEA 'CORONATION GOLD'	✓	✓	✓	✓	✓	✓	✓	✓	✓		✓					✓	✓			✓				✓		✓	
	ALCHEMILLA MOLLIS		✓	✓	✓	✓					✓	✓	✓	✓		✓	✓				✓			✓	✓	✓		
	CANNA X GENERALIS 'CONESTOGA'			✓	✓	✓	✓			✓	✓	✓	✓				✓	✓				✓				✓		
	CHRYSANTHEMUM X MORIFOLIUM		✓	✓	✓	✓	✓				✓	✓						✓	✓			✓			✓	✓		
	COREOPSIS LANCEOLATA 'GOLDFINK'		✓	✓	✓	✓				✓	✓		✓					✓			✓			✓		✓		

[1] TENDER ANNUAL   [2] HALF-HARDY ANNUAL   [3] HARDY ANNUAL

	Plant	Zone 3	Zone 4	Zone 5	Zone 6	Zone 7	Zone 8	Zone 9	Zone 10	Dry	Well-Drained	Moist	Full Sun	Partial Shade	Shade	Spring	Summer	Fall	Winter	Under 1 Ft.	1-3 Ft.	Over 3 Ft.	Form	Foliage	Fragrance	Flowers	Fruit/Seeds	Winter Interest
YELLOW	HELIANTHUS SALICIFOLIUS	✓	✓	✓	✓	✓	✓	✓		✓	✓	✓	✓				✓	✓				✓				✓		
	HEMEROCALLIS 'HYPERION'	✓	✓	✓	✓	✓	✓	✓			✓		✓	✓		✓					✓				✓	✓	✓	
	LIGULARIA PRZEWALSKII 'THE ROCKET'			✓	✓	✓	✓				✓	✓		✓			✓					✓		✓		✓		
	LIGULARIA TUSSILAGINEA 'ARGENTEA'			✓	✓	✓	✓				✓	✓		✓			✓	✓			✓			✓		✓		
	NARCISSUS BULBOCODIUM VAR. CONSPICUUS			✓	✓	✓	✓				✓	✓	✓	✓		✓				✓						✓		
	RUDBECKIA FULGIDA 'GOLDSTURM'		✓	✓	✓	✓	✓	✓			✓		✓	✓			✓				✓					✓		
	RUDBECKIA HIRTA 'GOLDILOCKS' [3]										✓		✓				✓				✓					✓		
	TULIPA HYBRIDS 'BELLONA'	✓	✓	✓	✓	✓	✓				✓		✓			✓					✓					✓		
ORANGE	ALOE STRIATA						✓	✓	✓	✓	✓		✓			✓		✓			✓		✓	✓				
	CANNA X GENERALIS 'MOHAWK'				✓	✓	✓	✓		✓	✓	✓	✓				✓	✓				✓				✓		
	HEMEROCALLIS HYBRIDS	✓	✓	✓	✓	✓	✓	✓			✓		✓	✓		✓	✓	✓			✓				✓	✓		
	IMPATIENS X NEW GUINEA 'TANGO' [1]										✓	✓	✓	✓	✓	✓	✓				✓					✓		
	LILIUM TIGRINUM		✓	✓	✓	✓	✓	✓			✓	✓	✓	✓			✓	✓				✓				✓		
	PAPAVER ORIENTALE 'DOUBLOON'	✓	✓	✓	✓	✓					✓		✓			✓						✓				✓		
	SEDUM X 'WEIHENSTEPHANER GOLD'	✓	✓	✓	✓	✓	✓	✓			✓		✓				✓	✓	✓					✓		✓		✓
	ZINNIA ANGUSTIFOLIA [3]										✓		✓				✓	✓		✓						✓		
RED	ACHILLEA X GALAXY HYBRIDS 'PAPRIKA'	✓	✓	✓	✓	✓	✓	✓	✓	✓		✓	✓				✓	✓			✓			✓		✓		
	DIANTHUS DELTOIDES 'FLASHING LIGHT'		✓	✓	✓	✓	✓	✓			✓		✓	✓			✓		✓				✓			✓		
	DICENTRA 'LUXURIANT'	✓	✓	✓	✓	✓	✓				✓			✓		✓	✓				✓					✓		
	HEUCHERA 'PLUIE DE FEU'	✓	✓	✓	✓	✓	✓				✓		✓	✓	✓	✓	✓				✓					✓		
	PAEONIA HYBRIDS	✓	✓	✓	✓	✓	✓				✓	✓	✓	✓		✓	✓				✓				✓	✓		
	PAPAVER ORIENTALE 'GLOWING ROSE'	✓	✓	✓	✓	✓					✓		✓	✓		✓						✓				✓		
	PHORMIUM TENAX 'ATROPURPUREUM'						✓	✓			✓	✓	✓				✓					✓	✓	✓				✓
	SALVIA COCCINEA 'LADY IN RED' [1]						✓	✓			✓	✓	✓				✓				✓					✓		
	SEDUM X 'AUTUMN JOY'	✓	✓	✓	✓	✓	✓	✓			✓		✓				✓	✓			✓					✓		✓
	TULIPA HYBRIDS 'ELECTRA'	✓	✓	✓	✓	✓	✓				✓		✓			✓					✓					✓		
PINK	ANEMONE X HYBRIDA 'QUEEN CHARLOTTE'		✓	✓	✓	✓	✓	✓			✓	✓	✓	✓				✓			✓			✓		✓		
	ASTILBE X ARENDSII 'ERICA'		✓	✓	✓	✓	✓					✓	✓	✓			✓				✓		✓			✓		
	BERGENIA CORDIFOLIA		✓	✓	✓	✓	✓	✓		✓	✓		✓	✓		✓			✓					✓		✓		
	CALADIUM X HORTULANUM						✓	✓	✓		✓	✓	✓	✓	✓		✓				✓			✓				
	CHRYSANTHEMUM WEYRICHII 'PINK BOMB'	✓	✓	✓	✓	✓	✓	✓			✓	✓	✓	✓			✓	✓		✓				✓		✓		
	CLEOME HASSLERANA 'ROSE QUEEN' [1]									✓	✓		✓	✓			✓	✓				✓				✓		

[1] TENDER ANNUAL   [2] HALF-HARDY ANNUAL   [3] HARDY ANNUAL

Color	Plant	Zone 3	Zone 4	Zone 5	Zone 6	Zone 7	Zone 8	Zone 9	Zone 10	Dry	Well-Drained	Moist	Full Sun	Partial Shade	Shade	Spring	Summer	Fall	Winter	Under 1 Ft.	1-3 Ft.	Over 3 Ft.	Form	Foliage	Fragrance	Flowers	Fruit/Seeds	Winter Interest
PINK	COSMOS BIPINNATUS 'SEASHELLS' [3]									✓	✓		✓	✓			✓	✓				✓				✓		
PINK	DIANTHUS GRATIANOPOLITANUS 'TINY RUBIES'	✓	✓	✓	✓	✓	✓	✓			✓		✓				✓			✓						✓		
PINK	GERANIUM SANGUINEUM VAR. STRIATUM	✓	✓	✓	✓	✓	✓				✓	✓	✓	✓		✓	✓			✓						✓		
PINK	HEUCHERA MICRANTHA 'PALACE PURPLE'	✓	✓	✓	✓	✓	✓				✓		✓	✓		✓	✓				✓			✓		✓		
PINK	MISCANTHUS SINENSIS 'MALEPARTUS'		✓	✓	✓	✓	✓				✓		✓					✓				✓	✓			✓		✓
PINK	PAEONIA HYBRIDS	✓	✓	✓	✓	✓	✓				✓	✓	✓	✓		✓	✓				✓				✓	✓		
PINK	PANICUM VIRGATUM 'HAENSE HERMS'		✓	✓	✓	✓	✓					✓	✓				✓	✓			✓		✓	✓		✓	✓	✓
PINK	PENNISETUM ALOPECUROIDES 'HAMELN'		✓	✓	✓	✓	✓				✓		✓				✓				✓		✓					✓
PINK	STACHYS BYZANTINA		✓	✓	✓	✓	✓				✓		✓				✓			✓				✓				
PURPLE	ASTER AMELLUS		✓	✓	✓	✓	✓	✓			✓		✓				✓	✓		✓				✓		✓		
PURPLE	ASTER LATERIFLORUS		✓	✓	✓	✓	✓	✓			✓		✓					✓			✓			✓		✓		
PURPLE	ASTILBE TAQUETII 'SUPERBA'		✓	✓	✓	✓	✓				✓	✓		✓	✓		✓				✓	✓		✓		✓		
PURPLE	CLEMATIS X JACKMANII	✓	✓	✓	✓	✓	✓	✓			✓	✓	✓	✓		✓	✓	✓			✓	✓				✓		✓
PURPLE	COSMOS ATROSANGUINEUS [3]									✓	✓		✓	✓			✓	✓			✓					✓		
PURPLE	DIGITALIS PURPUREA		✓	✓	✓	✓	✓	✓			✓			✓		✓	✓				✓					✓		
PURPLE	ECHINACEA PURPUREA 'MAGNUS'	✓	✓	✓	✓	✓	✓	✓	✓		✓		✓				✓				✓			✓		✓		
PURPLE	EUPATORIUM FISTULOSUM	✓	✓	✓	✓	✓	✓	✓				✓	✓				✓	✓			✓					✓		
PURPLE	HELENIUM AUTUMNALE 'BRILLIANT'	✓	✓	✓	✓	✓	✓				✓	✓	✓					✓			✓					✓		
PURPLE	LAVANDULA ANGUSTIFOLIA		✓	✓	✓	✓	✓				✓		✓				✓			✓				✓	✓	✓	✓	
PURPLE	ONOPORDUM ACANTHIUM [3]									✓	✓		✓			✓	✓					✓	✓	✓		✓		
PURPLE	VERBENA TENUISECTA [1]							✓	✓		✓	✓	✓				✓	✓		✓			✓	✓		✓		
BLUE	AGAPANTHUS PRAECOX					✓	✓	✓	✓		✓	✓	✓				✓				✓			✓		✓		✓
BLUE	AGERATUM HOUSTONIANUM [1]										✓	✓	✓				✓	✓		✓			✓	✓		✓		
BLUE	BRUNNERA MACROPHYLLA 'LANGTREES'		✓	✓	✓	✓	✓	✓				✓	✓	✓	✓						✓			✓		✓		
BLUE	CAMPANULA CARPATICA 'BLUE CHIPS'	✓	✓	✓	✓	✓	✓	✓			✓		✓			✓	✓			✓						✓		
BLUE	CERATOSTIGMA PLUMBAGINOIDES			✓	✓	✓	✓	✓			✓		✓	✓			✓	✓		✓				✓				✓
BLUE	CLEMATIS HERACLEIFOLIA VAR. DAVIDIANA	✓	✓	✓	✓	✓	✓	✓			✓	✓	✓	✓			✓						✓	✓	✓	✓		✓
BLUE	CYNARA CARDUNCULUS					✓	✓				✓		✓				✓	✓				✓	✓	✓		✓		
BLUE	DELPHINIUM 'BLUE FOUNTAINS'	✓	✓	✓	✓	✓					✓	✓	✓				✓				✓					✓		
BLUE	ECHINOPS RITRO 'TAPLOW BLUE'	✓	✓	✓	✓	✓	✓				✓		✓				✓				✓		✓			✓		
BLUE	ERYNGIUM GIGANTEUM		✓	✓	✓	✓	✓			✓	✓		✓				✓				✓		✓	✓		✓		
BLUE	HOSTA X 'HONEYBELLS'	✓	✓	✓	✓	✓	✓				✓	✓		✓	✓		✓				✓			✓		✓		

[1] TENDER ANNUAL   [2] HALF-HARDY ANNUAL   [3] HARDY ANNUAL

Color	Plant	Zone 3	Zone 4	Zone 5	Zone 6	Zone 7	Zone 8	Zone 9	Zone 10	Dry	Well-Drained	Moist	Full Sun	Partial Shade	Shade	Spring	Summer	Fall	Winter	Under 1 Ft.	1-3 Ft.	Over 3 Ft.	Form	Foliage	Fragrance	Flowers	Fruit/Seeds	Winter Interest
BLUE	HYACINTHUS ORIENTALIS 'DELFT BLUE'			✔	✔	✔	✔				✔	✔	✔			✔				✔					✔	✔		
	IRIS ENSATA 'ELEANOR PERRY'	✔	✔	✔	✔	✔	✔	✔				✔	✔	✔			✔				✔	✔				✔		
	LATHYRUS VERNUS		✔	✔	✔	✔	✔				✔	✔	✔	✔		✔	✔			✔						✔		
	LIRIOPE MUSCARI 'MAJESTIC'		✔	✔	✔	✔	✔	✔	✔		✔	✔		✔			✔				✔		✔	✔		✔		
	MYOSOTIS SYLVATICA 'ROYAL BLUE' [3]										✔	✔	✔	✔	✔		✔	✔			✔		✔			✔		
	NEPETA MUSSINII 'BLUE WONDER'	✔	✔	✔	✔	✔	✔			✔			✔			✔	✔			✔				✔		✔		
	PEROVSKIA ATRIPLICIFOLIA		✔	✔	✔	✔	✔	✔		✔			✔									✔	✔	✔	✔	✔		✔
	PHLOX STOLONIFERA 'BLUE RIDGE'		✔	✔	✔	✔	✔					✔	✔	✔	✔	✔				✔						✔		✔
	PLATYCODON GRANDIFLORUS VAR. MARIESII	✔	✔	✔	✔	✔					✔		✔	✔			✔				✔					✔		
	PULMONARIA ANGUSTIFOLIA	✔	✔	✔	✔	✔					✔			✔	✔	✔				✔				✔		✔		
	SALVIA AZUREA VAR. GRANDIFLORA		✔	✔	✔	✔	✔	✔			✔		✔				✔				✔			✔		✔		
	VERONICA SPICATA 'BLUE FOX'		✔	✔	✔	✔	✔				✔		✔	✔		✔	✔				✔					✔		
MULTI-COLORED	ACONITUM 'BICOLOR'	✔	✔	✔	✔						✔	✔					✔	✔			✔	✔	✔		✔		
	AQUILEGIA CANADENSIS	✔	✔	✔	✔	✔	✔	✔			✔			✔		✔					✔					✔		
	DATURA METEL [1]						✔	✔			✔	✔	✔	✔			✔				✔					✔		
	IPOMOEA TRICOLOR 'HEAVENLY BLUE' [1]										✔		✔				✔					✔	✔	✔		✔		
	IRIS 'BRIDE'S HALO'	✔	✔	✔	✔	✔	✔	✔	✔		✔	✔	✔			✔					✔		✔			✔		
	LILIUM ASIATIC HYBRIDS		✔	✔	✔	✔	✔	✔			✔		✔	✔			✔	✔			✔					✔		
	LUPINUS 'RUSSELL HYBRIDS'		✔	✔	✔						✔	✔	✔	✔			✔				✔					✔		
	NARCISSUS POETICUS 'ACTAEA'		✔	✔	✔	✔	✔				✔	✔	✔			✔					✔					✔		
	PAPAVER ORIENTALE 'PINNACLE'	✔	✔	✔	✔	✔					✔		✔	✔		✔					✔					✔		
	PETUNIA X HYBRIDA [2]										✔		✔				✔	✔		✔						✔		
	PHLOX PANICULATA 'FAIREST ONE'		✔	✔	✔	✔	✔					✔	✔	✔			✔	✔				✔			✔	✔		
	TULIPA CLUSIANA VAR. CHRYSANTHA	✔	✔	✔	✔	✔	✔				✔		✔			✔				✔						✔		
	TULIPA HYBRIDS	✔	✔	✔	✔	✔	✔				✔		✔			✔					✔					✔		
	ZINNIA HAAGEANA 'PERSIAN CARPET' [3]										✔		✔				✔	✔			✔					✔		
GREEN	AGAVE ATTENUATA							✔	✔	✔	✔		✔				✔					✔	✔	✔				
	ALCHEMILLA CONJUNCTA		✔	✔	✔	✔					✔	✔	✔	✔		✔	✔			✔				✔		✔		
	CHASMANTHIUM LATIFOLIUM			✔	✔	✔	✔	✔			✔	✔	✔	✔			✔					✔		✔		✔		✔
	HAKONECHLOA MACRA 'AUREOLA'			✔	✔	✔	✔					✔		✔			✔					✔		✔		✔		✔
	IMPERATA CYLINDRICA RUBRA			✔	✔	✔	✔	✔			✔	✔	✔				✔			✔				✔				
	NICOTIANA ALATA 'LIME GREEN' [1]										✔	✔	✔	✔			✔	✔			✔				✔	✔		

[1] TENDER ANNUAL [2] HALF-HARDY ANNUAL [3] HARDY ANNUAL

Guide to Woody Plants

Organized by plant type, this chart provides information needed to select species and varieties that will thrive in the particular conditions of your garden. For additional information on each plant, refer to the Encyclopedia that begins on page 108.

		ZONES								SOIL		LIGHT			BLOOM TIME				HEIGHT					NOTED FOR				
		Zone 3	Zone 4	Zone 5	Zone 6	Zone 7	Zone 8	Zone 9	Zone 10	Dry	Moist	Full Sun	Partial Shade	Shade	Spring	Summer	Fall	Winter	Under 3 ft.	3-6 ft.	6-10 ft.	10-20 ft.	Over 20 ft.	Form	Foliage	Flowers	Fruit/Seeds	Bark/Twigs
GROUND COVERS	COTONEASTER ADPRESSUS		✓	✓	✓	✓					✓	✓			✓				✓					✓	✓			
	COTONEASTER DAMMERI 'SKOGHOLMEN'		✓	✓	✓						✓	✓			✓				✓					✓	✓			
	EUONYMUS FORTUNEI 'LONGWOOD'		✓	✓	✓						✓		✓		✓				✓						✓			
	EUONYMUS FORTUNEI VAR. RADICANS		✓	✓	✓	✓					✓		✓		✓				✓						✓			
	JUNIPERUS CHINENSIS 'GOLD COAST'	✓	✓	✓	✓	✓	✓			✓		✓							✓					✓	✓			✓
	JUNIPERUS HORIZONTALIS 'BAR HARBOR'	✓	✓	✓	✓	✓				✓		✓							✓					✓	✓			✓
	JUNIPERUS PROCUMBENS 'NANA'	✓	✓	✓	✓	✓	✓			✓		✓							✓					✓	✓			✓
	MAHONIA REPENS		✓	✓	✓	✓					✓		✓		✓				✓					✓	✓	✓	✓	
	RHODODENDRON NORTH TISBURY AZALEAS		✓	✓	✓	✓	✓			✓	✓		✓	✓	✓				✓					✓	✓	✓		
SHRUBS	ARONIA ARBUTIFOLIA 'BRILLIANTISSIMA'	✓	✓	✓	✓	✓	✓			✓	✓	✓			✓						✓					✓	✓	
	AUCUBA JAPONICA 'VARIEGATA'			✓	✓	✓	✓	✓			✓		✓	✓	✓						✓				✓	✓		
	BUDDLEIA ALTERNIFOLIA 'ARGENTEA'		✓	✓	✓	✓	✓	✓		✓		✓			✓	✓						✓		✓	✓	✓		
	CALLICARPA JAPONICA		✓	✓	✓	✓				✓	✓	✓				✓				✓							✓	
	CAMELLIA JAPONICA			✓	✓	✓					✓		✓	✓	✓							✓				✓		
	CHAMAECYPARIS OBTUSA 'NANA'		✓	✓	✓	✓	✓				✓	✓						✓						✓	✓			
	CORNUS ALBA	✓	✓	✓	✓	✓				✓	✓	✓	✓		✓						✓				✓	✓		✓
	COTONEASTER HORIZONTALIS		✓	✓	✓	✓					✓	✓			✓				✓						✓			
	DAPHNE CNEORUM 'RUBY GLOW'		✓	✓	✓	✓	✓			✓	✓	✓			✓				✓					✓	✓	✓		
	EUONYMUS ALATA 'COMPACTA'		✓	✓	✓	✓				✓		✓			✓					✓					✓			✓
	FATSIA JAPONICA					✓	✓	✓		✓				✓			✓	✓			✓			✓	✓	✓		
	FOTHERGILLA MAJOR		✓	✓	✓	✓	✓			✓	✓	✓	✓		✓						✓				✓	✓		
	HAMAMELIS X INTERMEDIA 'JELENA'		✓	✓	✓	✓				✓	✓	✓	✓					✓				✓		✓		✓		
	HYDRANGEA ARBORESCENS 'GRANDIFLORA'		✓	✓	✓	✓	✓				✓		✓			✓	✓			✓						✓		✓
	ILEX CRENATA 'CONVEXA'			✓	✓	✓					✓	✓	✓									✓			✓		✓	
	JASMINUM NUDIFLORUM			✓	✓	✓	✓	✓	✓	✓	✓	✓						✓		✓				✓		✓	✓	
	JUNIPERUS SCOPULORUM 'SKYROCKET'	✓	✓	✓	✓	✓	✓	✓		✓		✓										✓		✓	✓		✓	
	LAGERSTROEMIA INDICA 'POTOMAC'				✓	✓	✓			✓	✓	✓				✓						✓		✓		✓	✓	
	NANDINA DOMESTICA 'MOYERS RED'			✓	✓	✓				✓	✓	✓	✓		✓					✓				✓	✓	✓	✓	

Category	Plant	Zone 3	Zone 4	Zone 5	Zone 6	Zone 7	Zone 8	Zone 9	Zone 10	Dry	Moist	Full Sun	Partial Shade	Shade	Spring	Summer	Fall	Winter	Under 3 ft.	3-6 ft.	6-10 ft.	10-20 ft.	Over 20 ft.	Form	Foliage	Flowers	Fruit/Seeds	Bark/Twigs
SHRUBS	PARROTIA PERSICA		✓	✓	✓	✓	✓			✓		✓			✓								✓	✓	✓	✓		✓
SHRUBS	PIERIS JAPONICA 'VALLEY VALENTINE'	✓	✓	✓	✓	✓	✓			✓	✓	✓	✓		✓					✓				✓	✓	✓		
SHRUBS	PYRACANTHA COCCINEA 'MOHAVE'			✓	✓	✓	✓	✓		✓		✓			✓						✓					✓	✓	
SHRUBS	RHODODENDRON CATAWBIENSE		✓	✓	✓	✓	✓			✓	✓	✓	✓	✓	✓						✓					✓	✓	
SHRUBS	RHODODENDRON EXBURY AZALEAS			✓	✓	✓	✓			✓	✓	✓	✓	✓	✓					✓					✓	✓		
SHRUBS	RHODODENDRON GLENN DALE AZALEAS			✓	✓	✓	✓			✓	✓	✓	✓	✓	✓				✓	✓	✓					✓		
SHRUBS	ROSA HYBRIDS - CLIMBING ROSES	✓	✓	✓	✓	✓				✓	✓	✓				✓	✓		✓							✓		
SHRUBS	ROSA HYBRIDS - TEA ROSES	✓	✓	✓	✓	✓				✓	✓	✓				✓	✓			✓						✓		
SHRUBS	TAXUS BACCATA 'REPANDENS'		✓	✓	✓					✓	✓	✓								✓				✓	✓		✓	
SHRUBS	TAXUS CUSPIDATA 'THAYERAE'		✓	✓	✓					✓	✓	✓								✓				✓	✓			
SHRUBS	THUJA OCCIDENTALIS 'RHEINGOLD'	✓	✓	✓	✓	✓				✓		✓	✓									✓		✓	✓			
SHRUBS	THUJA ORIENTALIS		✓	✓	✓	✓				✓		✓	✓							✓				✓	✓			
SHRUBS	VIBURNUM PLICATUM VAR. TOMENTOSUM 'SHASTA'		✓	✓	✓					✓	✓	✓	✓		✓					✓				✓	✓	✓	✓	
TREES	ACER GRISEUM	✓	✓	✓	✓	✓				✓		✓	✓		✓								✓	✓	✓			✓
TREES	ACER PALMATUM 'SENKAKI'	✓	✓	✓	✓	✓	✓			✓		✓	✓		✓							✓		✓	✓			✓
TREES	CERCIS CANADENSIS	✓	✓	✓	✓	✓	✓	✓		✓		✓	✓		✓								✓	✓		✓	✓	
TREES	CHAMAECYPARIS LAWSONIANA			✓	✓	✓						✓	✓										✓	✓	✓			✓
TREES	CHAMAECYPARIS PISIFERA 'FILIFERA AUREA'		✓	✓	✓	✓						✓	✓										✓	✓	✓			
TREES	CORNUS FLORIDA 'CHEROKEE CHIEF'		✓	✓	✓	✓	✓	✓		✓	✓	✓	✓		✓							✓		✓		✓	✓	
TREES	CORNUS X STELLAR HYBRIDS		✓	✓	✓	✓	✓	✓		✓	✓	✓	✓		✓							✓		✓		✓		
TREES	CRATAEGUS PHAENOPYRUM		✓	✓	✓	✓				✓		✓			✓								✓	✓	✓	✓	✓	
TREES	ILEX OPACA 'OLD HEAVY BERRY'			✓	✓	✓	✓			✓	✓	✓	✓		✓								✓	✓	✓		✓	
TREES	MAGNOLIA X 'GALAXY'			✓	✓	✓	✓	✓		✓	✓	✓	✓		✓								✓	✓		✓		
TREES	MAGNOLIA GRANDIFLORA			✓	✓	✓	✓			✓	✓	✓	✓										✓	✓	✓	✓		
TREES	MALUS 'DONALD WYMAN'		✓	✓	✓	✓	✓			✓	✓	✓			✓							✓		✓		✓		
TREES	OXYDENDRUM ARBOREUM			✓	✓	✓	✓	✓		✓	✓	✓	✓										✓	✓	✓	✓		
TREES	PRUNUS CERASIFERA 'NEWPORT'		✓	✓	✓	✓				✓		✓			✓								✓	✓	✓	✓		
TREES	PRUNUS SUBHIRTELLA VAR. PENDULA		✓	✓	✓	✓				✓		✓			✓								✓	✓		✓		
VINES	EUONYMUS FORTUNEI 'VEGETUS'		✓	✓	✓	✓				✓		✓			✓				✓					✓			✓	
VINES	JASMINUM OFFICINALE				✓	✓	✓	✓		✓		✓				✓	✓							✓		✓		
VINES	VITIS COIGNETIAE			✓	✓	✓	✓			✓		✓											✓	✓	✓			✓
VINES	WISTERIA FLORIBUNDA			✓	✓	✓	✓	✓		✓	✓	✓			✓								✓	✓	✓	✓	✓	

A Zone Map of the United States

A plant's winter hardiness is critical in deciding whether it is suitable for your garden. The map below divides the United States into 11 climatic zones based on average minimum temperatures, as compiled by the United States Department of Agriculture. Find your zone and check the zone information in the plant selection guides *(pages 100-105)* or the Encyclopedia *(pages 108-153)* to help you choose the plants most likely to flourish in your climate.

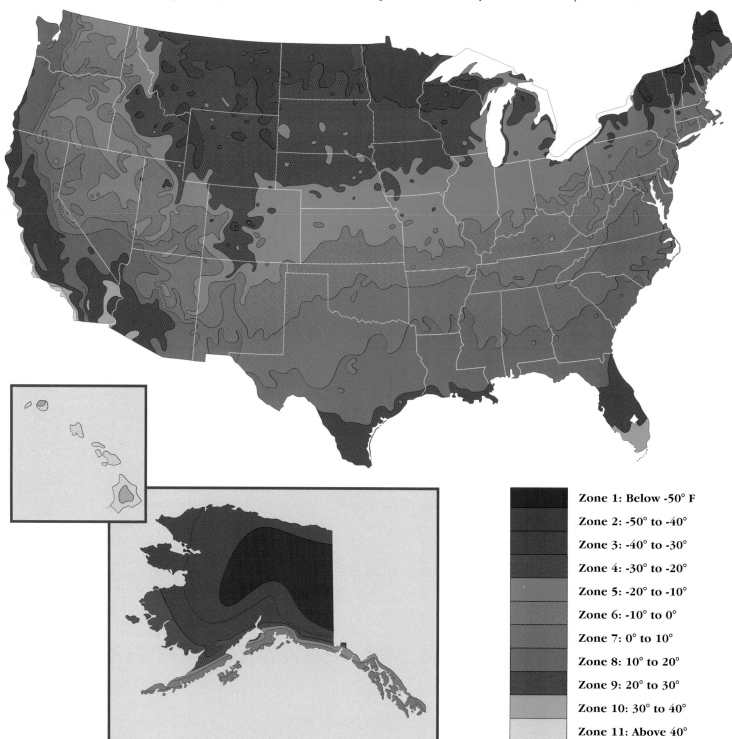

Zone 1: Below -50° F

Zone 2: -50° to -40°

Zone 3: -40° to -30°

Zone 4: -30° to -20°

Zone 5: -20° to -10°

Zone 6: -10° to 0°

Zone 7: 0° to 10°

Zone 8: 10° to 20°

Zone 9: 20° to 30°

Zone 10: 30° to 40°

Zone 11: Above 40°

Cross-Reference Guide to Plant Names

Adam's-needle—
Yucca filamentosa
African lily—*Agapanthus*
Alumroot—*Heuchera*
American aloe—
Agave americana
Andromeda—*Pieris japonica*
Arborvitae—*Thuja*
Azalea—*Rhododendron*
Baby's-breath—*Gypsophila*
Balloon flower—*Platycodon*
Balsam—
Impatiens balsamina
Bear's-breech—*Acanthus*
Beautyberry—*Callicarpa*
Beggar-ticks—*Bidens*
Bellflower—*Campanula*
Bethlehem sage—
Pulmonaria
Birch—*Betula*
Blackberry lily—
Belamcanda chinensis
Black-eyed Susan—
Rudbeckia hirta
Bleeding heart—*Dicentra*
Blue flag—*Iris versicolor*
Boneset—*Eupatorium*
Bugbane—*Cimicifuga*
Burning bush—
Euonymus alata
Butterfly bush—*Buddleia*
Cardoon—
Cynara cardunculus
Castor bean—*Ricinus*
Catmint—*Nepeta*
Cedar—*Juniperus*
Century plant—*Agave*
Cherry—*Prunus*
Chinese silver grass—
Miscanthus
Chokeberry—*Aronia*
Cinquefoil—*Potentilla*
Colewort—
Crambe cordifolia
Columbine—*Aquilegia*
Coneflower—*Rudbeckia*
Coral bells—
Heuchera sanguinea
Corn cockle—*Agrostemma*
Cornelian cherry—*Cornus mas*
Crab apple—*Malus*
Cranesbill—*Geranium*

Crape myrtle—
Lagerstroemia
Cypress vine—
Ipomoea quamoclit
Daffodil—*Narcissus*
Daylily—*Hemerocallis*
Dogwood—*Cornus*
Dusty miller—
Artemisia stellerana
Dusty-miller—
Senecio vira-vira
English laurel—
Prunus laurocerasus
Eulalia—*Miscanthus*
False cypress—
Chamaecyparis
False spirea—*Astilbe*
Feverfew—
Chrysanthemum parthenium
Firethorn—*Pyracantha*
Floss flower—*Ageratum*
Flowering tobacco—
Nicotiana
Forget-me-not—*Myosotis*
Fountain grass—
Pennisetum
Foxglove—*Digitalis*
Gay-feather—*Liatris*
Globe thistle—*Echinops*
Golden rain tree—
Koelreuteria
Grape—*Vitis*
Hardy ageratum—
Eupatorium coelestinum
Hawthorn—*Crataegus*
Heavenly bamboo—
Nandina
Hellebore—*Helleborus*
Holly—*Ilex*
Hyacinth—*Hyacinthus*
Hyacinth bean—
Dolichos lablab
Inca lily—*Alstroemeria*
Inkberry—*Ilex glabra*
Japanese aralia—
Fatsia japonica
Jewelweed—*Impatiens*
Joe-Pye weed—*Eupatorium*
Jonquil—*Narcissus jonquilla*
Juniper—*Juniperus*
Jupiter's-beard—
Centranthus ruber

Lady's-mantle—*Alchemilla*
Lamb's ears—
Stachys byzantina
Lavender—*Lavandula*
Leadwort—*Ceratostigma*
Lilac—*Syringa*
Lily—*Lilium*
Lily-of-the-Nile—*Agapanthus*
Lilyturf—*Liriope*
Lungwort—*Pulmonaria*
Lupine—*Lupinus*
Maple—*Acer*
Marigold—*Tagetes*
Mist flower—
Eupatorium coelestinum
Monkshood—*Aconitum*
Moonflower—*Ipomoea alba*
Moor grass—*Molinia*
Morning glory—*Ipomoea*
Mugwort—*Artemisia*
Mullein pink—
Lychnis coronaria
New Zealand flax—
Phormium tenax
Nippon daisy—
Chrysanthemum nipponicum
Northern sea oats—
Chasmanthium
Oregon grape—
Mahonia aquifolium
Painted daisy—
Chrysanthemum coccineum
Panic grass—*Panicum*
Pear—*Pyrus*
Peony—*Paeonia*
Peruvian lily—*Alstroemeria*
Pine—*Pinus*
Pink—*Dianthus*
Pink golden-drops—
Onosma alboroseum
Plantain lily—*Hosta*
Plumbago—*Ceratostigma*
Plume poppy—
Macleaya cordata
Poppy—*Papaver*
Pot marigold—
Calendula officinalis
Purple coneflower—
Echinacea
Quaking aspen—
Populus tremuloides
Ragwort—*Ligularia dentata*

Redbud—*Cercis*
Reed grass—*Calamagrostis*
Rose campion—
Lychnis coronaria
Rose mallow—*Hibiscus*
Rue—*Ruta*
Russian sage—
Perovskia atriplicifolia
Sage—*Salvia*
Sea holly—*Eryngium*
Sea kale—*Crambe maritima*
Shasta daisy—
Chrysanthemum x *superbum*
Siberian bugloss—
Brunnera macrophylla
Smoke tree (smokebush)—
Cotinus
Sneezeweed—*Helenium*
Soapweed—*Yucca glauca*
Sorrel tree—*Oxydendrum*
Sourwood—*Oxydendrum*
Speedwell—*Veronica*
Spider flower—*Cleome*
St.-John's-wort—*Hypericum*
Stonecrop—*Sedum*
Strawberry—*Fragaria*
Sunflower—*Helianthus*
Sweet pea—
Lathyrus odoratus
Sweet William—
Dianthus barbatus
Switch grass—
Panicum virgatum
Thistle—*Onopordum*
Thorn apple—*Datura*
Thrift—*Armeria*
Tickseed—*Coreopsis*
Tree mallow—*Lavatera*
Vine lilac—
Hardenbergia violacea
White sage—
Artemisia ludoviciana
Wild rye—*Elymus*
Willow—*Salix*
Windflower—*Anemone*
Winterberry—*Ilex glabra*
Witch hazel—*Hamamelis*
Wolfsbane—*Aconitum*
Wormwood—*Artemisia*
Yarrow—*Achillea*
Yaupon—*Ilex vomitoria*
Yew—*Taxus*

Encyclopedia of Plants

Presented here is a selection of plants mentioned in this book as components of good garden combinations. The plants are listed alphabetically by their Latin botanical names; common names appear in bold type below the Latin. If you know a plant only by its common name, see the cross-reference chart on page 107 or the index.

A botanical name consists of the genus and a species, both usually printed in italics. Many species contain one or more cultivars, whose names appear between single quotation marks. An "x" preceding the name indicates a hybrid. "Hardiness" is explained on the USDA Plant Hardiness Map (page 106). For annuals, hardiness refers to their ability to withstand frost. Hardy annuals, as small seedlings, can survive all but extreme cold; half-hardy annuals can tolerate a light frost; tender annuals should not be planted outdoors until all danger of frost has passed.

Acanthus
(a-KAN-thus)
BEAR'S-BREECH

Acanthus mollis

Hardiness: *Zones 7-10*

Plant type: *perennial*

Height: *3 to 4 feet*

Interest: *flowers, foliage*

Soil: *well-drained to dry acid loam*

Light: *full sun to partial shade*

Acanthus's spreading clumps of evergreen, stiffly arching, deeply lobed 2-foot-long leaves make for bold specimen plantings or sculpturesque border backdrops. Spikes of tubular flowers bloom along tall stalks.

Selected species and varieties: *A. mollis*—rose or white summer-blooming flowers above shiny dark green leaves on plants hardy only to Zone 8. *A. spinosus* (spiny bear's-breech)—spiny, leathery, deep green leaves and profuse mauve, sometimes white, summer flowers.

Growing conditions and maintenance: Plant bear's-breech in light shade where summers are hot. Allow ample space for the plant's arching leaves to develop. Propagate from seed or by division in the spring.

Acer
(AY-ser)
MAPLE

Acer griseum

Hardiness: *Zones 2-8*

Plant type: *large shrub or small tree*

Height: *6 to 30 feet*

Interest: *foliage, bark, twigs*

Soil: *well-drained*

Light: *full sun to light shade*

From shrubs to shade trees, the smaller maple species offer varied textures and colors in summer, vibrant foliage in fall.

Selected species and varieties: *A. buergeranum* (trident maple)—spreading shrub or tree to 25 feet tall and as wide, with scaly orange-brown bark. *A. ginnala* (Amur maple)—generally grows 15 to 18 feet, with inconspicuous but fragrant spring flowers. *A. griseum* (paperbark maple)—oval growth to 30 feet tall, with cinnamon brown exfoliating bark. *A. nikoense* (Nikko maple)—vase shaped, to 30 feet. *A. palmatum* (Japanese maple)—6 to 25 feet, with finely textured foliage; 'Bloodgood' has reddish purple leaves; 'Dissectum Atropurpureum' grows as a mounding shrub, with deep red foliage; 'Sangokaku' produces bright coral twigs.

Growing conditions and maintenance: *A. buergeranum* prefers acid soil and is moderately drought tolerant; *A. ginnala* is not particular about soil, is highly drought tolerant, and can be container grown; *A. griseum* adapts well to different soils; *A. nikoense* prefers moist, acid soil; *A. palmatum* prefers humidity and must be protected from hot, dry winds.

Achillea
(ak-il-EE-a)
YARROW

Achillea x Galaxy Hybrids 'Paprika'

Hardiness: *Zones 3-8*

Plant type: *perennial*

Height: *1 to 3 feet*

Interest: *flowers, foliage*

Soil: *dry, poor to average, well-drained*

Light: *full sun*

Broad, flat clusters of tiny flowers rise on sturdy stems above yarrow's graceful, ferny, aromatic gray-green foliage. The soft-textured clumps are especially effective in masses.

Selected species and varieties: *A.* 'Coronation Gold'—bright yellow summer-to-fall flowers on 36-inch stems. *A.* x 'Moonshine'—pale yellow summer-to-fall flower clusters above very finely cut 18-inch foliage. *A. millefolium* 'Red Beauty' (common yarrow)—deep red summer-to-fall flowers on 24-inch stems. Galaxy Hybrids—summer-to-fall blooms on 12- to 36-inch stems; 'Appleblossom' has light pink flowers; 'Hoffnung', pale yellow blooms; 'Paprika', cherry red flowers fading to pink then yellow.

Growing conditions and maintenance: Space yarrows 1½ to 2 feet apart in average soil; stake tall varieties, especially *A. millefolium* cultivars and plants grown in fertile soil. Propagate cultivars from stem cuttings in summer or by division in spring or fall.

Aconitum
(ak-o-NY-tum)
MONKSHOOD

Aconitum carmichaelii

Hardiness: *Zones 3-8*

Plant type: *perennial*

Height: *2 to 5 feet*

Interest: *flowers, foliage*

Soil: *moist, well-drained, fertile*

Light: *partial shade to full sun*

Flowers resembling tiny helmets bloom along the tips of stiffly erect stems. Monkshood's coarsely textured clumps of deeply lobed leaves blend well at the edges of woodlands or in the back of a border among ferns and hostas. The roots are poisonous.

Selected species and varieties: *A.* x hybrids—'Bicolor' has white summer-to-fall-blooming flowers edged in blue on 4-foot stems; 'Bressingham Spire', long-lasting, summer-blooming violet blossoms on compact 3-foot stems; 'Sparks Variety' (also *A. henryi),* deep blue summer flowers on 5-foot stalks. *A. carmichaelii* (azure monkshood)—clear blue summer blooms in rigid clumps to 4 feet tall. *A. napellus* (helmet flower)—vigorous 3- to 4-foot-tall stems with deep blue summer flowers; 'Snow White' has pure white blossoms.

Growing conditions and maintenance: Plant monkshood in early fall, 18 inches apart, with the crowns just below the surface in soil enriched with organic matter. Leave undisturbed. Propagate from fresh seed.

Agapanthus
(ag-a-PAN-thus)
AFRICAN LILY

Agapanthus africanus

Hardiness: *Zones 8-10*

Plant type: *perennial*

Height: *1½ to 4 feet*

Interest: *flowers, foliage*

Soil: *moist, well-drained*

Light: *full sun*

Massive clusters of trumpet-shaped flowers bloom above clumps of arching, sometimes evergreen, straplike leaves.

Selected species and varieties: *A. africanus* (blue African lily)—profuse blue flowers above narrow, curving leaves on stems to 2 feet tall. *A. campanulatus* (bell agapanthus)—pale blue summer-blooming flowers on stems to 4 feet. *A.* 'Headborne Hybrids'—pale to dark to gray-blue summer flowers up to 8 inches across on 2½-foot stalks. *A.* 'Peter Pan'—a dwarf variety with 1½-foot-tall summer flower stalks above 12-inch clumps of evergreen leaves. *A. praecox* ssp. *orientalis* [also listed as *A. umbellatus*] (oriental agapanthus)—rich blue summer flowers on 4-foot-tall stalks above evergreen leaves.

Growing conditions and maintenance: Plant African lilies in containers or 2 feet apart in gardens in soil enriched with organic matter. Water well during the growing season; allow to dry out during dormancy. Flower stalks tend to lean toward the sun. Propagate by dividing the fleshy roots.

Agave
(a-GAH-vay)
CENTURY PLANT

Agave parryi

Hardiness: *Zones 9-10*

Plant type: *succulent perennial*

Height: *18 inches to 40 feet*

Interest: *foliage*

Soil: *well-drained to dry, sandy*

Light: *full sun*

Century plant's rosettes of coarse, wickedly spiny evergreen leaves are accentuated—generally at the end of the plant's long life—by erect, often extremely tall stalks bearing heavy spikes of fragrant flower bells. Grown for the strapping, pointed leaves, century plants are impressive accents to mix with finer-textured plants.

Selected species and varieties: *A. americana* (American aloe)—arching, blue-green leaves in mounds 6 feet wide. *A. attenuata* (foxtail agave)—rosettes of waxy, pale green leaves up to 5 feet across. *A. parryi*—rosettes of powdery gray-green leaves up to 3 feet across.

Growing conditions and maintenance: Protect young plants from frost and winter moisture. *A. americana* can be very hazardous to handle, even after it dies; be certain about the choice of plant and location before starting one. Propagate by transplanting offsets.

Ageratum
(aj-er-AY-tum)
FLOSS FLOWER

Ageratum houstonianum

Hardiness: *tender*

Plant type: *annual*

Height: *6 to 18 inches*

Interest: *flowers, foliage*

Soil: *moist, well-drained*

Light: *full sun*

A profusion of fluffy flowers with thread-like petals crowns ageratum's clumps of heart-shaped leaves. With soft colors and a compact mounding habit, dwarf varieties create excellent garden edgings.

Selected species and varieties: *A. houstonianum*—bears tiny blue to bluish purple, sometimes white or pink flower puffs from summer through fall; 'Adriatic' has early-blooming bright blue violet flowers; 'Blue Danube', a dwarf 6 to 7 inches tall, purple-blue flowers; 'Hawaii White', white blossoms on compact 6-inch-tall plants.

Growing conditions and maintenance: Plant ageratums in soil enriched with organic matter. Pinch early growth to encourage compactness. Removing spent flowers ensures late-season reflowering. Propagate from seed sown indoors in early spring. Ageratums will self-sow under ideal conditions.

Alchemilla
(al-kem-ILL-a)
LADY'S-MANTLE

Alchemilla mollis

Hardiness: *Zones 3-8*

Plant type: *perennial or ground cover*

Height: *4 to 18 inches*

Interest: *foliage*

Soil: *moist, well-drained*

Light: *partial shade to full sun*

Lady's-mantle forms sprawling mats of round, deeply veined, cupped leaves with softly downy undersides that are attractive at the front of the border or as a coarse-textured seasonal ground cover. Frothy clusters of tiny flowers rise on stiff stalks in summer.

Selected species and varieties: *A. alpina*—dwarf species forms mats of silver-edged foliage only about 6 inches tall with inconspicuous spring-to-summer-blooming chartreuse flowers. *A. conjuncta*—has pale green ⅛-inch flowers and star-shaped green leaves edged with silver. *A. mollis*—mats of broad gray-green leaves grow up to 10 inches high with clusters of yellow flowers from spring to summer on stems to 18 inches tall.

Growing conditions and maintenance: Plant lady's-mantle 1½ feet apart and provide partial shade in hot climates. Propagate from seed, by division, or by transplanting self-sown seedlings.

Aloe
(AL-oh)
ALOE

Aloe striata

Hardiness: *Zones 9-10*

Plant type: *succulent perennial*

Height: *1½ to 3 feet*

Interest: *foliage, form*

Soil: *well-drained to dry*

Light: *full sun*

Aloe's rosettes of sword-shaped, fleshy evergreen leaves make striking specimens among finer-textured plantings. Branched clusters of long-lasting flowers rise from their centers on stiff stalks.

Selected species and varieties: *A. saponaria* (soap aloe)—stubby, green-and-white-variegated leaves 8 inches long and coral pink to orange spring-to-fall-blooming flowers on stalks up to 3 feet tall. *A. striata* (coral aloe)—pink-edged green leaves up to 20 inches long and coral pink to orange winter-to-spring flowers on 3-foot-tall stalks.

Growing conditions and maintenance: Aloes tolerate seaside conditions, poor soil, and drought; excess water promotes root rot. They prefer a frost-free location and suffer serious injury at temperatures below 25° F. Once aloes are established, the only care they require is occasional deep watering. Propagate by transplanting suckered offsets.

Anemone
(a-NEM-o-nee)
WINDFLOWER

Anemone hupehensis 'September Charm'

Hardiness: *Zones 4-9*

Plant type: *perennial*

Height: *3 inches to 4 feet*

Interest: *flowers, foliage*

Soil: *moist, well-drained, fertile*

Light: *full sun to partial shade*

Showy, open-faced flowers rise on wiry stems above windflower's clumps of finely cut leaves. The plant is useful for border edgings or backgrounds.

Selected species and varieties: *A. blanda* (Grecian windflower)—2-inch-wide blue spring-blooming flowers on 3- to 8-inch-tall stems; 'Bridesmaid' has white flowers; 'Charmer', pale pink flowers. *A. coronaria* (poppy anemone)—red, blue, or white 3-inch-wide spring flowers on 8- to 12-inch stems; the 'de Caen' series has single petals; the 'St. Brigid' series, semidouble petals. *A. x hybrida* 'Queen Charlotte'—3- to 4-inch semidouble pink blossoms in summer or fall on stems to 4 feet tall. *A. hupehensis* (Japanese anemone)—summer-to-fall flowers on stems to 18 inches tall; 'September Charm' grows silvery rose pink flowers.

Growing conditions and maintenance: Protect anemones from wind and hot sun. Propagate by division.

Aquilegia
(ak-wil-EE-jee-a)
COLUMBINE

Aquilegia canadensis

Hardiness: *Zones 3-9*

Plant type: *perennial*

Height: *6 inches to 3 feet*

Interest: *flowers*

Soil: *moist, well-drained, acid*

Light: *full sun to partial shade*

Columbines produce intricate, dainty, erect or nodding blossoms with long, curving spurs above fine, lacy foliage.

Selected species and varieties: *A. caerulea* (Rocky Mountain columbine)—3-inch erect blue-and-white spring-blooming flowers on 1- to 2-foot-tall stems. *A. canadensis* (American columbine)—red-and-yellow nodding spring blossoms on 2- to 3-foot stems. *A. flabellata* 'Nana' (dwarf fan columbine)—blue-and-yellow spring flowers on plants to 12 inches tall. *A. x hybrida* (hybrid columbine)—spring flowers on plants 1 to 3 feet tall; 'Biedermeier' has white-tipped petals on 12-inch plants; 'Crimson Star', red-and-white flowers; 'McKana Hybrids', long-spurred flowers in many shades; 'Snow Queen', white blossoms.

Growing conditions and maintenance: Columbines will not tolerate dry soil. Plants die out after 4 to 5 years but sometimes self-sow; propagate from seed or by transplanting self-sown plants. Propagation by division is possible but requires great care in order not to damage plants.

Aronia
(a-RO-nee-a)
CHOKEBERRY

Aronia arbutifolia 'Brilliantissima'

Hardiness: *Zones 4-9*

Plant type: *deciduous shrub*

Height: *6 to 10 feet*

Interest: *berries, foliage, flowers*

Soil: *well-drained*

Light: *full sun to partial shade*

Chokeberry bears a profusion of tiny flowers that produce glossy red berries in hanging clusters that persist into winter. The glossy, dark green, oval leaves turn bright scarlet in fall. The upright colonies of suckers look best when massed for display.

Selected species and varieties: *A. arbutifolia* 'Brilliantissima'—⅓-inch white spring-blooming flowers touched with red, followed by clusters of ¼-inch red berries on shrubs to 10 feet tall.

Growing conditions and maintenance: Plant chokeberries in almost any garden soil. Flowering, foliage color, and fruiting all occur best in full sun. Propagate from seed, from cuttings, or by transplanting rooted suckers.

Artemisia
(ar-tem-IS-ee-a)
WORMWOOD

Artemisia x 'Powis Castle'

Hardiness: *Zones 3-9*

Plant type: *perennial*

Height: *4 inches to 6 feet*

Interest: *foliage*

Soil: *poor, well-drained to dry*

Light: *full sun*

Wormwood's finely textured gray-green leaves—a few varieties are evergreen—complement the more dramatic hues in a border. Its form ranges from low and mounding to tall and erect, in most cases with inconspicuous flowers.

Selected species and varieties: *A. absinthium*—aromatic foliage to 4 feet tall; 'Lambrook Silver' has silvery gray evergreen leaves. *A. lactiflora* (white mugwort)—sprays of creamy summer flowers above dark green foliage on stems to 6 feet. *A. ludoviciana* (white sage)—silvery willowlike leaves on 2- to 4-foot plants; 'Silver Queen' has divided leaves. *A.* x 'Powis Castle'—2- to 3-foot-high mounds of lacy, silvery green leaves. *A. schmidtiana* (silvermound artemisia)—compact 2-foot-high mounds of filigreed silvery leaves; 'Nana' grows to only a few inches. *A. stellerana* (dusty miller)—deeply lobed silver-gray leaves on 1- to 2-foot plants.

Growing conditions and maintenance: Space smaller plants 1 foot apart, taller ones 2 feet apart. Most artemisias rot in hot and humid conditions. Propagate from seed or by division.

Aster
(AS-ter)
ASTER

Aster x frikartii 'Mönch'

Hardiness: *Zones 4-8*

Plant type: *perennial*

Height: *1 to 5 feet*

Interest: *flowers*

Soil: *moist, well-drained*

Light: *full sun*

Versatile asters offer forms ranging from compact mounds to open branching clumps, all crowned with flowers composed of feathery fringes of petals surrounding colorful centers.

Selected species and varieties: *A. amellus* (Italian aster)—1½-inch purple summer-to-fall-blooming flowers with yellow centers on bushy plants 1 to 3 feet tall. *A.* x *frikartii* 'Mönch'—long-lasting 3-inch lavender-blue summer-to-fall flowers on 3-foot plants. *A. lateriflorus*—clusters of ½-inch white-to-pale-purple summer-to-fall flowers on horizontally branching plants to 4 feet long. *A. novae-angliae* (New England aster)—clumps 3 to 5 feet tall with 1- to 2-inch, summer-to-fall flowers; 'Hella Lacy' has deep purple blooms; 'Harrington's Pink', pink flowers; 'Treasure', violet-blue flowers.

Growing conditions and maintenance: Space plants 2 to 3 feet apart to ensure good air circulation and prevent mildew. Stake tall species. Propagate by division or from stem cuttings.

Astilbe
(a-STIL-bee)
FALSE SPIREA

![Astilbe chinensis 'Pumila']

Astilbe chinensis 'Pumila'

Hardiness: *Zones 4-8*

Plant type: *perennial*

Height: *8 inches to 4 feet*

Interest: *flowers, foliage*

Soil: *moist, well-drained, fertile*

Light: *partial shade to full sun*

Astilbe's spreading mounds of serrated leaflets crowned by feathery flower plumes serve nicely as fillers or backdrops in shade gardens.

Selected species and varieties: *A.* x *arendsii*—summer-blooming flowers in a range of colors; 'Bridal Veil' grows arching white sprays 18 to 30 inches tall; 'Cattleya', rose pink spikes; 'Erica', bright pink blooms; 'Fanal', garnet flowers and bronzy leaves; 'Fire', coral red spires; 'Peach Blossom', salmon pink flowers; 'Professor van der Wielan', arching 3-foot white sprays; 'White Gloria', dense white plumes. *A. chinensis* 'Pumila'—deep magenta summer flowers on 12-inch plants. *A. taquetii* (fall astilbe)—late blooming; 'Purplelanze' has reddish purple flowers; 'Superba', magenta blooms.

Growing conditions and maintenance: Plant astilbes 1½ to 2 feet apart in a cool location. Water well and mulch if in full sun. Propagate by division every 3 or 4 years in early spring or midsummer.

Aucuba
(aw-KEW-ba)
AUCUBA

Aucuba japonica 'Picturata'

Hardiness: *Zones 7-10*

Plant type: *shrub*

Height: *6 to 10 feet*

Interest: *leaves, berries*

Soil: *moist, well-drained*

Light: *partial shade to shade*

Aucuba's glossy, evergreen, pointed leaves line tidy clumps of stems. The plant softens the landscape beneath tall trees, provides a transition between heavily wooded areas and garden borders, and can be massed as a screen.

Selected species and varieties: *A. japonica* (spotted laurel)—erect or arching 6- to 10-foot-tall stems with open clusters of purple spring-blooming flowers on male plants, followed by ½-inch red fruits on female plants in fall through winter; 'Variegata' (gold dust plant) has yellow-speckled leaves; 'Nana' grows 3 to 5 feet tall with abundant, prominent berries; 'Picturata' has yellow markings on each leaf surrounded by flecks of yellow.

Growing conditions and maintenance: Aucuba grows best in locations with year-round shade and soil enriched with organic matter. Young leaves blacken if exposed to strong sun. The shrubs tolerate urban pollution well. Pollination from a male bush nearby is essential for female shrubs to set berries.

Bergenia
(ber-JEN-ee-a)
BERGENIA

Bergenia cordifolia

Hardiness: *Zones 3-8*

Plant type: *perennial or ground cover*

Height: *8 to 18 inches*

Interest: *foliage, flowers*

Soil: *moist, well-drained*

Light: *partial shade to full sun*

Bergenia's leaf rosettes create a dense, bold-textured ground cover of broad, fleshy, crinkly foliage topped by masses of tiny, waxy spring flowers on red stalks. Leaves are evergreen in milder climates, burnish bronze or maroon where winters are colder.

Selected species and varieties: *B. cordifolia* (heartleaf bergenia)—leathery, heart-shaped, 1-foot-wide leaves and deep pink flowers. *B. crassifolia* (leather bergenia)—spoon-shaped leaves coloring maroon in winter and rose purple flowers. *B. hybrids*—'Abendglut' ('Evening Glow') has deep purple flowers; 'Morgenröte' ('Morning Red'), purplish red blooms; 'Silberlicht' ('Silver Light'), white blossoms aging to pink.

Growing conditions and maintenance: Plant bergenias 1 foot apart in organically rich soil. Provide adequate moisture in sunny locations. Propagate by division after flowering in spring.

Brunnera
(BRUN-er-a)
BRUNNERA

Brunnera macrophylla 'Variegata'

Hardiness: *Zones 4-9*

Plant type: *perennial or ground cover*

Height: *1 to 2 feet*

Interest: *foliage, flowers*

Soil: *moist, well-drained*

Light: *light shade to full sun*

Brunnera forms compact mounds of broad, heart-shaped leaves topped by frothy clusters of tiny flowers. The deeply textured foliage spreads into an informal ground cover beneath trees, among newly planted shrubs, or paired with spring bulbs.

Selected species and varieties: *B. macrophylla* (Siberian bugloss)—¼-inch deep blue spring-blooming flowers with prominent yellow eyes above deep green leaves; 'Langtrees' has silver-speckled foliage; 'Variegata', leaves edged in yellow or cream.

Growing conditions and maintenance: Plant brunnera in soils enriched with organic matter. Plants need constant moisture in full sun. Propagate from seed, by division in spring or fall, or by transplanting self-sown seedlings.

Buddleia
(BUD-lee-a)
BUTTERFLY BUSH

Buddleia davidii 'Empire Blue'

Hardiness: *Zones 5-9*

Plant type: *shrub*

Height: *6 to 20 feet*

Interest: *flowers, texture*

Soil: *well-drained, fertile*

Light: *full sun*

Its arching stems lined with narrow, gray-green leaves, the butterfly bush is effective massed at the edge of a border or lawn. Elongated clusters of fragrant flowers with contrasting centers bloom in spring and summer.

Selected species and varieties: *B. alternifolia* 'Argentea'—4-inch leaves with silky hairs and soft purple flowers on plants to 20 feet tall. *B. davidii* (summer lilac)—leaves to 10 inches long on shrubs to 10 feet; 'Black Knight' has deep purple blooms; 'Dubonnet', long sprays of dark purple flowers; 'Empire Blue', violet flowers; 'Royal Red', 20-inch-long red-purple flower clusters.

Growing conditions and maintenance: Remove spent flowers to prolong bloom. In northern zones, grow *B. davidii* as a perennial, cutting to the ground in fall for flowers on new shoots in spring. *B. alternifolia* 'Argentea' flowers on the previous year's growth.

Caladium
(ka-LAY-dee-um)
ELEPHANT'S-EAR

Caladium x hortulanum 'Aaron'

Hardiness: *Zones 8-10*

Plant type: *bulb*

Height: *1 to 2 feet*

Interest: *foliage*

Soil: *moist, well-drained, fertile*

Light: *full sun to partial shade*

Caladium's heart-shaped green, pink, red, or white leaves are veined and edged in contrasting colors. The foliage clumps make a fine edging or accent.

Selected species and varieties: *C. x hortulanum* (fancy-leaved caladium)—6- to 18-inch-long leaves on 1- to 2-foot-tall stems; 'Aaron' has green-edged white leaves; 'Candidum', white leaves veined and edged in green; 'Frieda Hempel', green-edged red leaves; 'Pink Beauty', pink leaves with deeper pink veins and green edges; 'White Christmas', white leaves with symmetrical green veining; 'White Queen', greenish white leaves.

Growing conditions and maintenance: Plant caladiums in organic soil and water well during their growing season. They do poorly in dry air. In areas with frost, dig tubers in fall and store dry for the winter. Propagate by separating tubers into sections having at least two buds each before planting in spring after all danger of frost has passed.

Callicarpa
(kal-i-CAR-pa)
BEAUTYBERRY

Callicarpa americana

Hardiness: *Zones 5-10*

Plant type: *shrub*

Height: *3 to 8 feet*

Interest: *fruit*

Soil: *well-drained*

Light: *full sun to light shade*

Clusters of colorful ⅛-inch berries dangle from the tips of beautyberry's arching stems for several weeks after the leaves have fallen in autumn. The oval, pointed leaves, arranged like ladders on either side of the stems, turn yellowish, sometimes pinkish, before dropping.

Selected species and varieties: *C. americana* (American beautyberry)—inconspicuous lavender summer flowers followed by magenta fruit clusters encircling stem tips; var. *lactea* produces white berries, Zones 7-10. *C. japonica*—violet to metallic purple berries; 'Leucocarpa' grows white berries after inconspicuous pink or white summer flowers, Zones 5-8.

Growing conditions and maintenance: Prune to within 4 to 6 inches of the ground in early spring to create new shoots; only these produce flowers and fruit. Callicarpas are easy to grow from softwood cuttings or seed and are easily transplanted.

Camellia
(kah-MEEL-ee-a)
CAMELLIA

Camellia japonica

Hardiness: *Zones 6-10*

Plant type: *shrub or small tree*

Height: *6 to 25 feet*

Interest: *flowers, foliage*

Soil: *moist, well-drained, acid*

Light: *light shade*

Camellias' graceful, loose pyramids of evergreen foliage become outstanding garden accents from fall through spring, when the plants become covered with flowers whose fluffy yellow centers are rimmed by single or double rows of ruffled petals.

Selected species and varieties: *C. japonica* (Japanese camellia)—lustrous dark green leaves on shrubs or trees 10 to 25 feet tall with 5-inch blossoms. *C. sasanqua* (sasanqua camellia)—glossy dark green leaves on 6- to 10-foot-tall shrubs with 2- to 3-inch flowers. *C. reticulata* (temple flower)—dull green leaves on lanky shrubs to 20 feet with 7-inch blooms. *C.* hybrids—'Polar Ice', with white flowers; 'Winter's Charm', with double lavender-pink blooms; 'Winter's Star', with reddish pink flowers; hardy to Zone 6.

Growing conditions and maintenance: Plant camellias in organically rich soil. Choose light conditions carefully; excessive sun or shade will cause reduced flowering. Protect from winter winds and mulch heavily. Prune after flowering.

Campanula
(kam-PAN-yew-la)
BELLFLOWER

Campanula carpatica 'Blue Chips'

Hardiness: *Zones 3-8*

Plant type: *perennial*

Height: *4 inches to 5 feet*

Interest: *flowers, foliage*

Soil: *moist, well-drained*

Light: *full sun to partial shade*

Bellflower species range from dwarf cushions to tall upright clumps. Tubular or flaring summer flowers bloom in clusters or spikes.

Selected species and varieties: *C. carpatica* (Carpathian bellflower)—compact plants under 1 foot tall; 'Blue Chips' has blue flowers; 'White Chips', white ; 'China doll', lavender; 'Wedgewood Blue', blue-violet. *C. glomerata* (clustered bellflower)—clusters of summer-blooming blue flowers; 'Joan Elliott', purple flowers on 1½-foot plants; 'Superba', violet-blue blossoms on stems to 2½ feet. *C. latifolia* 'Macrantha'—blue-purple flowers on 4- to 5-foot stems lined with coarse, toothed leaves. *C. persicifolia* (peachleaf bellflower)—solitary deep blue to white blooms; 'Alba' has white flowers on 3-foot plants; 'Telham Beauty', light blue blooms. *C. portenschlagiana* (Dalmatian bellflower)—purple-blue flowers above 4- to 8-inch mounds of coarse leaves.

Growing conditions and maintenance: Plant small bellflowers 12 to 18 inches apart, larger ones 2 feet apart. Dig up and divide every 3 to 4 years to maintain vigor. Propagate from seed or by division.

Canna
(CAN-ah)
INDIAN SHOT

Canna x generalis 'Brandywine'

Hardiness:	*Zones 9-10*
Plant type:	*perennial*
Height:	*18 inches to 8 feet*
Interest:	*flowers*
Soil:	*moist, well-drained, fertile*
Light:	*full sun*

Canna's exotic flowers in lush colors grow in bold spikes at the tips of fleshy stems lined with broad, deeply veined leaves. Cannas provide a flashy summer-to-fall accent in the border or make a bold statement in masses.

Selected species and varieties: *C.* x *generalis* (canna lily)—dwarf to giant cultivars with 4-inch flowers in a range of colors; 'Brandywine' is a dwarf with scarlet flowers; 'Conestoga', a dwarf with light yellow flowers; 'Le Roi Humbert' has red flowers on 6- to 8-foot stems; 'Mohawk', orange flowers and bronze leaves; Pfitzer strain includes 'Pretoria' and 'Striata' dwarfs with leaves striped green and cream.

Growing conditions and maintenance: Plant cannas in soil enriched with organic matter. In Zones 7 and 8, lift rhizomes in fall after the first killing frost and store in moist peat moss. Propagate by dividing rhizomes in spring before planting.

Ceratostigma
(ser-at-o-STIG-ma)
PLUMBAGO, LEADWORT

Ceratostigma plumbaginoides

Hardiness:	*Zones 5-10*
Plant type:	*perennial or ground cover*
Height:	*8 inches to 4 feet*
Interest:	*foliage, flowers*
Soil:	*well-drained*
Light:	*full sun to partial shade*

Plumbago is useful as a ground cover or a shrubby perennial at the back of a border. The plant will be covered with masses of flat 1-inch flowers over a long season of bloom. The foliage colors attractively in fall to contrast with the blossoms.

Selected species and varieties: *C. plumbaginoides* (common leadwort, dwarf plumbago)—blue flowers bloom from late summer through frost above 8- to 12-inch-tall tufts of glossy, nearly evergreen 3-inch leaves that color reddish bronze in fall in cooler climates. *C. willmottianum* (Chinese plumbago)—shrubby mounds of foliage up to 4 feet tall covered with deep blue, 1-inch-wide flowers from late summer through frost.

Growing conditions and maintenance: Plant plumbago 18 inches apart. It does not tolerate soggy soil or competition from tree roots. Mulch over winter in Zones 5 and 6. Shear before new spring growth begins to promote flowering. Propagate by division in spring every 2 to 4 years.

Cercis
(SER-sis)
REDBUD

Cercis occidentalis

Hardiness:	*Zones 4-10*
Plant type:	*tree or shrub*
Height:	*6 to 30 feet*
Interest:	*flowers*
Soil:	*moist, well-drained*
Light:	*full sun to light shade*

Clusters of tiny spring flowers cling to redbud's erect branches like colorful foam for weeks before leaves appear. Young foliage emerges purplish red, turns green, then colors yellow in fall as flat pods develop. Redbud is an outstanding specimen plant.

Selected species and varieties: *C. canadensis* (eastern redbud)—a tree growing to 30 feet tall, with rosy red flowers; var. *alba* has white flowers; 'Forest Pansy', purple leaves. *C. chinensis* (Chinese redbud)—a shrub to 12 feet tall, with profuse, early-blooming rosy purple flowers; 'Avondale' has intense rose-purple blossoms. *C. occidentalis* (western redbud) —magenta flowers on a small tree or shrub to 15 feet tall, with leathery blue-green leaves. *C. reniformis* 'Oklahoma' —wine red flowers and waxy blue-green leaves on a shrub or tree to 18 feet tall.

Growing conditions and maintenance: Although they prefer moist, well-drained soil, redbuds, particularly *C. canadensis,* are highly adaptable to most soil conditions except sogginess. Water during drought. Propagate from seed.

Chamaecyparis
(kam-ee-SIP-a-ris)
FALSE CYPRESS

Chamaecyparis obtusa 'Crippsii'

Hardiness: *Zones 4-8*

Plant type: *tree or shrub*

Height: *6 to 90 feet*

Interest: *foliage*

Soil: *moist, well-drained, fertile*

Light: *full sun*

False cypresses mature into pyramidal or columnar specimen trees with drooping branch tips. The flat sprays of evergreen foliage resemble tiny fans made of overlapping scales with a tracery of white on their undersides.

Selected species and varieties: *C. lawsoniana* (Port Orford cedar)—narrow pyramid of ascending branches with drooping tips on mature trees to 60 feet or more, with deeply furrowed bark. *C. nootkatensis* 'Pendula' (weeping Alaska cedar)—conical tree to 45 feet with gracefully pendulous branches. *C. obtusa* (Hinoki false cypress)—tree to 75 feet with a 10- to 20-foot spread; 'Crippsii' has yellowish branch tips; 'Nana' is slow growing to 3 feet tall and as wide; 'Nana Gracilis', to 6 feet tall. *C. pisifera* 'Filifera Aurea' (goldthread false cypress)—dense pyramid of stringy branches with yellow branchlets to 10 feet.

Growing conditions and maintenance: Although they prefer full sun, false cypresses will tolerate light shade. They do best in cool, humid climates and should be protected from hot, drying winds.

Chasmanthium
(kaz-MAN-thee-um)
NORTHERN SEA OATS

Chasmanthium latifolium

Hardiness: *Zones 4-8*

Plant type: *ornamental grass*

Height: *3 feet*

Interest: *flowers*

Soil: *well-drained*

Light: *full sun to light shade*

Northern sea oats send up erect stems lined with slender, rough-edged leaves. The stems are tipped with drooping clusters of summer-blooming flowers that color attractively in fall and persist through the winter. Attractive as specimens or backdrop foliage, clumps of sea oats provide welcome interest in a winter garden.

Selected species and varieties: *C. latifolium* [also classified as *Uniola latifolia*] (spangle grass)—gracefully drooping 5- to 10-inch clusters of pale green flowers on 3-foot leafy stems coloring bronze in fall then fading to brown in winter.

Growing conditions and maintenance: Chasmanthium grows taller in shady situations. Cut back in spring before new growth begins. Propagate by dividing clumps in spring.

Chrysanthemum
(kri-SAN-the-mum)
CHRYSANTHEMUM

Chrysanthemum coccineum

Hardiness: *Zones 3-9*

Plant type: *perennial*

Height: *6 inches to 3 feet*

Interest: *flowers, foliage texture*

Soil: *well-drained, fertile*

Light: *full sun*

Chrysanthemum flower forms vary widely, from daisylike blossoms in single or double rows of petals to spider or football mums to tiny button mums. The sprawling or upright mounds of attractively lobed or ferny foliage blend well with other border plantings or can be massed for effect.

Selected species and varieties: *C. coccineum* [also classified as *Tanacetum coccineum*] (painted daisy, pyrethrum) —wiry stalks lined with fine-textured, ferny leaves support 2- to 3-inch flowers with yellow centers; 'Robinson Hybrids' produce exceptionally large flowers ranging from white through crimson and blooming on 2-foot-long stems in spring and early summer. *C. indicum* 'Mei Kyo' [also called *Dendranthema* x 'Mei Kyo']—double-petaled lavender fall blooms on 3-foot plants. *C.* x *koreanum* [also called *Dendranthema koreana*] 'Venus'—semidouble coral pink fall flowers on 2- to 3-foot plants. *C.* x *morifolium* [also called *Dendranthema* x *morifolium*] (hardy chrysanthemum)— clusters of 1- to 6-inch summer-to-fall flowers in white, yellow, orange, red, bronze, and lavender on 1- to 3-foot plants with aromatic foliage. *C. nipponicum* [also called *Nipponanthemum nipponicum*] (Nippon daisy)—fall flowers with a single row of white petals surrounding a green-tinged eye on shrubby plants to 2½ feet tall. *C.* x *rubellum* [also called *C. zawadskii*, *Dendranthema* x *rubellum*, and *D. zawadskii* hybrids] 'Clara Curtis'—medium pink petals fringing yellow centers persisting from summer through frost on neat clumps of 2-foot stems. *C.* x *superbum* [also called *C. maxima* and *Leucanthemum* x *superbum*] (Shasta daisy)—5- to 6-inch double- or single-petaled white summer-to-fall flowers on stems to 2½ feet; 'Aglaia' has a tangled fringe of double petals; 'Majestic', extremely large 6-inch single-petaled flowers; 'Marconi', double or semidouble petals on 2-foot plants. *C. weyrichii* [also called *Dendranthema weyrichii*] (Japanese daisy)—dwarf, creeping plants to 12 inches tall with

Chrysanthemum nipponicum

flowers blooming late summer through fall above deeply cut foliage; 'White Bomb' has late-blooming white blossoms; 'Pink Bomb', large pink flowers.

Growing conditions and maintenance: Plant chrysanthemums in fall in soil enriched with organic matter. Although all other species are sun loving, *C. coccineum* requires afternoon shade in warm zones. Pinch fall-blooming plants twice before midsummer for profuse blooms. Cut painted daisies back after they bloom in spring to encourage a second bloom. Cut stems back after flowering. Propagate by division in fall.

Cimicifuga
(si-mi-SIFF-yew-ga)
BUGBANE

Cimicifuga ramosa 'Brunette'

Hardiness:	*Zones 3-8*
Plant type:	*perennial*
Height:	*3 to 7 feet*
Interest:	*foliage, flowers, fruit*
Soil:	*moist, well-drained, fertile*
Light:	*full sun to partial shade*

Bugbane's lacy leaflets create airy columns of foliage topped by long wands of tiny, frilled flowers. Use it as an accent specimen, naturalized in a woodland garden, or massed at the edge of a stream or pond.

Selected species and varieties: *C. americana* (American bugbane)—dense spikes of creamy blossoms on branched 2- to 6-foot-tall flower stalks in late summer to fall. *C. ramosa* (branched bugbane)—3-foot wands of fragrant white flowers on reddish stalks in fall; 'Atropurpurea' grows to 7 feet with bronzy purple leaves; 'Brunette' has purplish black foliage and pink-tinged flowers on 3- to 4-foot stalks. *C. simplex* 'White Pearl'—2-foot wands of white flowers on branching, arched 3- to 4-foot flower stalks followed by round, lime green fruits.

Growing conditions and maintenance: Plant bugbane in cooler areas of the garden in soil enriched with organic matter. Propagate by division in spring.

Clematis
(KLEM-a-tis)
VIRGIN'S BOWER

Clematis x jackmanii

Hardiness:	*Zones 3-9*
Plant type:	*vine*
Height:	*4 to 30 feet*
Interest:	*flowers*
Soil:	*moist, well-drained, fertile*
Light:	*full sun to light shade*

Clinging to supports, climbing through shrubs, or trailing along walls or fences, twining clematis offers attractive, sometimes evergreen foliage and billows of showy, flat-faced spring-, summer-, or fall-blooming flowers. Fluffy seeds develop for added fall interest.

Selected species and varieties: *C. armandii* (Armand clematis)—glossy evergreen, drooping leaflets and fragrant, shimmering white, 2-inch spring flowers on vines to 16 feet; 'Apple Blossom' produces cup-shaped flowers that emerge pink, fade to white; 'Farquhariana', pink flowers; 'Snowdrift', very fragrant waxy white flowers on drooping stems. *C. heracleifolia* var. *davidiana*—semiherbaceous subshrub 2 to 4 feet tall with dense clusters of fragrant, 1-inch-long tubular blue summer flowers. *C.* x *jackmanii* (Jackman hybrids)—summer-to-fall flowers up to 7 inches across with petals like pointed stars in single or double rows in white, soft pink, carmine, orchid, deep lavender, pale violet, mauve, purple, and rich shades of blue on 12- to 18-foot vines. *C. lanuginosa* (Lanuginosa hybrids)—6-inch spring-to-summer flowers on 6-foot vines; 'Crimson King' grows abundant single and double crimson flowers; 'Fairy Queen', large pink blooms; 'Lady Northcliffe', large, deep lavender flowers; 'Nelly Moser', abundant, large pale mauve-pink flowers with a carmine bar down the sepals. *C. montana* var. *rubens*—2-inch rosy red spring flowers amid bronzy leaves on vigorous 25-foot vines. *C. paniculata* (sweet autumn clematis)—fragrant white 1¼-inch flowers in frothy profusion from summer through fall on rampant vines to 30 feet. *C. recta* 'Purpurea' (ground clematis)—fragrant 1-inch-wide white flower stars amid deep purple leaves from spring through summer on short 2- to 5-foot vines. *C. viticella*—2-inch midsummer flowers on 15-foot vines; 'Alba Luxurians' has white blooms with a mauve tint and purple anthers; 'Caerulea', violet flowers; 'Plena', double violet flowers; 'Rubra Grandiflora', large carmine flowers.

Growing conditions and maintenance: Plant clematis in a constantly moist soil. Mulch plants heavily in full sun to keep roots cool. Spring-blooming varieties bloom on the previous year's wood; summer- or fall-blooming kinds bloom

Clematis viticella

on spring growth. Prune a month after flowering to shape plants and increase flowers the following year. Prune new plants severely for the first several years. Propagate from seed or cuttings.

Cleome
(klee-O-me)
SPIDER FLOWER

Cleome hasslerana 'Rose Queen'

Hardiness: *tender*

Plant type: *annual*

Height: *3 to 4 feet*

Interest: *flowers*

Soil: *moist, well-drained*

Light: *full sun to light shade*

Enormous clusters of 1-inch cleome flowers with trailing 2- to 3-inch stamens bloom from summer through frost at the tips of erect stems lined with palm-shaped leaflets. The tall, showy blossoms are a dramatic accent in masses or a good background planting in a border.

Selected species and varieties: *C. hasslerana* [also called *C. spinosa*]—clumps of 6-foot-tall stems hold clusters of fragrant flowers with spidery stamens followed by slim seed pods; 'Cherry Queen' has rosy red flowers; 'Helen Campbell', white blossoms; 'Rose Queen', rosy pink flowers; 'Violet Queen', blue-violet blossoms.

Growing conditions and maintenance: Start cleome seed indoors 4 to 6 weeks before the last frost or plant directly in the garden once soil has warmed. Keep soil moist. Cleome reseeds itself from year to year.

Coreopsis
(ko-ree-OP-sis)
TICKSEED

Coreopsis grandiflora 'Sunray'

Hardiness: *Zones 4-9*

Plant type: *perennial*

Height: *6 inches to 3 feet*

Interest: *flowers, foliage*

Soil: *well-drained to dry*

Light: *full sun*

Coreopsis's daisylike flowers grow atop mats or cushions of foliage. The plant is excellent for edgings or naturalizing.

Selected species and varieties: *C. auriculata* 'Nana' (eared tickseed)—6- to 9-inch mat with 1-inch yellow spring-blooming flowers. *C. grandiflora*—yellow or orange 1- to 1½-inch single, semidouble, or double summer flowers on 2-foot stems; 'Sunray' has 4-inch double flowers. *C. lanceolata* (lance coreopsis)—late-spring-to-summer 1½- to 2½-inch yellow flowers on stems to 3 feet; 'Goldfink' is a 10-inch-tall cultivar. *C. rosea* (pink coreopsis)—inch-wide pink summer-to-fall flowers with yellow centers on plants to 2 feet. *C. verticillata* (threadleaf coreopsis)—cushions of lacy leaves; 'Golden Showers' has yellow flowers on plants to 3 feet; 'Moonbeam', creamy yellow flowers on 18- to 24-inch plants; 'Zagreb', yellow flowers on 8- to 18-inch plants.

Growing conditions and maintenance: Plant coreopsis 12 to 18 inches apart. Remove spent flowers to prolong bloom. Transplant the self-sown seedlings of *C. verticillata*. Propagate from seed or by division in spring.

Cornus
(KOR-nus)
DOGWOOD

Cornus florida 'Cherokee Chief'

Hardiness: *Zones 2-9*

Plant type: *tree or shrub*

Height: *7 to 30 feet*

Interest: *flowers, foliage, berries, bark*

Soil: *moist, well-drained, acid*

Light: *full sun to light shade*

Naturalized at the edges of woodland gardens, in a shrub border, or as an overstory for a border of spring bulbs, dogwoods offer three seasons of interest. Flowers with petal-like bracts surrounding prominent centers bloom in spring. Attractive berries appear as the leaves color red in fall. And several species offer brightly colored bark to enliven a winter landscape.

Selected species and varieties: *C. alba* (Tartarian dogwood)—8- to 10-foot-tall shrub spreading to 10 feet with reddish green stems that color blood red in winter; 'Sibirica' (Siberian dogwood) has creamy 2-inch flowers followed by clusters of blue-tinted white berries on clumps of stems that turn bright coral red with the cold; 'Argenteo-marginata' has creamy leaf margins. *C. florida* (flowering dogwood)—branches in loose, flat tiers on trees to 30 feet tall bear large buds that open into 3- to 5-inch spring blooms with creamy white, pink, or red notched bracts surrounding prominent centers, followed by clusters of bright red fall-to-winter berries; 'Cherokee Chief' has deep ruby bracts; 'Cloud Nine' is a more heat-tolerant cultivar with profuse

blooms. *C. kousa* var. *augustata*—horizontal to upright branches develop into round trees, evergreen in milder climates, to 20 feet tall with pointed flower bracts and fall berries resembling puffy raspberries; 'Autumn Rose' has creamy green young leaves, white flowers, and pink to red fall foliage; 'Dubloon', white flowers with overlapping bracts on slender trees; 'Radiant Rose', reddish leaves and large pink flowers. *C.* x Stellar Hybrids—vigorous, borer-resistant trees blooming midseason; *C.* 'Aurora' (cv. Rutban) has velvety white overlapping petals; *C.* 'Celestial' (cv. Rutdan), young bracts like greenish cups opening to flat white flowers; *C.* 'Stellar Pink' (cv. Rutgan), pastel pink overlapping bracts. *C. mas* (cornelian cherry)—shrub or tree to 25 feet with tiny yellow flower puffs lining naked twigs in very early spring, followed by red fruits in late summer or fall. *C. sericea* 'Flaviramea' (red-osier dogwood)—2½-inch white flowers on clumps of yellow stems to 10 feet.

Cornus alba 'Argenteo-marginata'

Growing conditions and maintenance: Plant dogwoods in soil enriched with organic matter. Prune Siberian dogwood or red-osier dogwood heavily in spring to encourage new shoots, which develop the most intense winter color. Propagate from seed or cuttings.

Cosmos
(KOS-mos)
COSMOS

Cosmos bipinnatus 'Sonata'

Hardiness: *tender*

Plant type: *annual*

Height: *10 inches to 4 feet*

Interest: *flowers*

Soil: *well-drained to dry*

Light: *full sun to light shade*

Daisylike flowers crown cosmos's loose clumps of wiry stems from summer through frost. Smaller varieties are useful as edgings or fillers, taller ones as backdrops.

Selected species and varieties: *C. atrosanguineus* (black cosmos)—chocolate-scented 1½-inch flowers with maroon rays and deep purple centers on clumps to 3½ feet tall. *C. bipinnatus* (common cosmos)—clumps to 4 feet or more with white, pink, violet, or red single- or double-petaled flowers; 'Sensation' has lacy foliage; 'Sonata', white flowers; 'Seashells', two-toned pink, rolled ray flowers. *C. sulphureus* (yellow cosmos)—radiant yellow, gold, orange, or red early flowers; 'Bright Lights' grows to 3 feet; 'Ladybird', to 10 inches.

Growing conditions and maintenance: Heavy fertilization diminishes flower production. Clumps may need staking. Propagate from seed by sowing directly into the garden after danger of frost has passed.

Cotoneaster
(ko-toe-nee-AS-ter)
COTONEASTER

Cotoneaster apiculatus

Hardiness: *Zones 4-7*

Plant type: *shrub*

Height: *18 inches to 6 feet*

Interest: *foliage, berries*

Soil: *well-drained*

Light: *full sun*

Tiny deep green, sometimes evergreen leaves line stiff, spreading branches that grow in dense mounds as wide as or wider than their height. White or pink spring flowers are followed in fall by red berries persisting through winter. Cotoneasters make excellent ground covers or bank plants.

Selected species and varieties: *C. adpressus* (creeping cotoneaster)—prostrate plants 18 inches tall and 6 feet wide. *C. apiculatus* (cranberry cotoneaster)—tangle of branches 3 feet tall and 6 feet wide. *C. dammeri* 'Skogholmen' (bearberry cotoneaster)—1-foot-high branches trailing 3 feet with evergreen leaves. *C. divaricatus* (spreading cotoneaster)—mounds of arching branches 6 feet tall and as wide. *C. horizontalis* (rockspray cotoneaster)—scalelike leaves along twiggy ladders on shrubs to 3 feet tall and twice as wide or wider.

Growing conditions and maintenance: Although they prefer well-drained, fertile soil, cotoneasters will do well in virtually any soil. Propagate from softwood cuttings or by detaching rooted stem tips and carefully transplanting them.

Crambe
(KRAM-bee)
CRAMBE

Crambe forms broad mounds of wrinkly, gray-green, heart-shaped leaves with deep lobes attractive as edgings or fillers. In late spring or early summer, stout stems carry an enormous branching cloud of tiny, strongly scented white flowers above the fleshy leaves to create an unusual accent in a border.

Selected species and varieties: *C. cordifolia* (colewort)—leafy mounds 4 feet across crowned by an equally wide froth of flowers on stalks to 6 feet tall. *C. maritima* (sea kale)—2-foot-wide mounds of blue-green leaves with a powdery coating topped by a billow of tiny white flowers on a stalk up to 3 feet tall.

Growing conditions and maintenance: Plant colewort and sea kale at least 4 feet apart. Sea kale tolerates the sandy, salty conditions in seaside gardens. Propagate from fresh seed sown immediately after ripening or from 4- to 6-inch root cuttings.

Crambe cordifolia

Hardiness: *Zones 5-9*

Plant type: *perennial*

Height: *2 to 6 feet*

Interest: *foliage, flowers*

Soil: *well-drained, slightly alkaline*

Light: *full sun*

Crataegus
(kra-TEE-gus)
HAWTHORN

Crataegus viridis 'Winter King'

Hardiness: *Zones 4-7*

Plant type: *tree or shrub*

Height: *20 to 35 feet*

Interest: *flowers, berries*

Soil: *well-drained*

Light: *full sun*

Hawthorns develop neat, round crowns of lobed, triangular leaves with finely toothed edges that give them a delicate texture as a specimen tree or in a shrub border. The foliage has a reddish cast when young, turns green through the summer, then colors attractively in fall. Clusters of small white spring flowers produce bright red berries that persist through winter. Long thorns along its woody branches are a drawback.

Selected species and varieties: *C. phaenopyrum* (Washington hawthorn)—multiple-stemmed shrub or tree to 30 feet with foliage that turns scarlet in fall. *C. viridis* 'Winter King' (green hawthorn)—round to vase-shaped tree to 35 feet tall with lustrous green foliage coloring purple or red in fall.

Growing conditions and maintenance: Plant hawthorns in loose, slightly alkaline soil. Thorns make pruning or shearing difficult, so allow room for the tree or shrub's mature spread. Propagate from seed.

Cynara
(SIN-ah-ra)
CYNARA

Cynara cardunculus

Hardiness: *Zones 8-9*

Plant type: *perennial*

Height: *6 to 8 feet*

Interest: *foliage, flowers*

Soil: *well-drained*

Light: *full sun*

Related to the edible globe artichoke, cynara forms clumps of thick stems lined with spiny, lacy, silver-gray leaves with woolly undersides that provide a bold accent in a border. Fuzzy, thistlelike flower globes tip each stem from summer through fall. Both leaves and flowers are prized by floral artists for fresh and dried arrangements.

Selected species and varieties: *C. cardunculus* (cardoon)—deep blue-violet flower heads at the tips of 6-foot stems lined with spiny leaves up to 3 feet long.

Growing conditions and maintenance: Plant cardoon in moist soil enriched with organic matter. Propagate from seed or by transplanting suckers that grow from the base of established clumps.

Daphne
(DAF-nee)
DAPHNE

Daphne x burkwoodii

Hardiness: *Zones 4-9*

Plant type: *shrub*

Height: *6 inches to 4 feet*

Interest: *foliage, flowers*

Soil: *moist, well-drained, alkaline*

Light: *light shade*

Evergreen shrubs with narrow, oval, 1- to 3-inch leaves, daphnes are prized for their clusters of fragrant spring flowers. Use their dense mounds of foliage in a shrub border or at the edges of woodland gardens.

Selected species and varieties: *D.* x *burkwoodii*—creamy white to pink spring blooms sometimes followed by a second flowering in fall on shrubs 3 to 4 feet tall and as wide or wider. *D. cneorum* 'Ruby Glow' (garland flower)—clusters of deep pink, ½-inch flowers on plants 6 to 12 inches tall and spreading 2 feet or more. *D. odora* (winter daphne) 'Variegata'—very fragrant pale pink flowers on plants 3 to 4 feet tall and equally wide with leaves edged in yellow.

Growing conditions and maintenance: Plant daphnes in loose soil or distribute peat moss around the roots to encourage stems to root, increasing the plant's spread. Prune if necessary immediately after it flowers. Propagate from seed or from cuttings.

Datura
(da-TOOR-a)
THORN APPLE

Datura inoxia ssp. quinquecuspida

Hardiness: *tender or Zones 9-10*

Plant type: *annual or perennial*

Height: *2 to 5 feet*

Interest: *flowers*

Soil: *moist, well-drained*

Light: *full sun to light shade*

Thorn apple's large flower trumpets bloom above coarse, oval leaves on shrubby plants useful as fillers or as backdrops in a border. Each summer-blooming flower opens at sunset and lasts only a day. Though the flowers are sometimes fragrant, the leaves are unpleasantly scented, and most parts of daturas are extremely poisonous. Plant them only in places where they are out of the reach of children and pets.

Selected species and varieties: *D. inoxia* ssp. *quinquecuspida* (downy thorn apple)—7-inch white-to-pink trumpets with ripply edges on spreading perennial plants to 3 feet tall. *D. metel* (Hindu datura)—2- to 5-foot annual with 8-inch leaves and 7-inch white flowers tinged yellow or purple.

Growing conditions and maintenance: Shelter daturas from wind. Cut *D. inoxia* ssp. *quinquecuspida* back in early spring. Propagate from seed started indoors 6 to 8 weeks before moving outdoors to warmed soil.

Delphinium
(del-FIN-ee-um)
DELPHINIUM

Delphinium 'Blue Fountains'

Hardiness: *Zones 3-7*

Plant type: *perennial*

Height: *2 to 8 feet*

Interest: *flowers*

Soil: *moist, well-drained, fertile*

Light: *full sun*

Enormous showy spikes of 2-inch flowers on stiff stalks bloom atop delphinium's clumps of finely cut, lobed leaves. The spurred flowers often have deeply contrasting centers. Delphiniums make impressive specimens in a border.

Selected species and varieties: *D.* x *belladonna* (belladonna delphinium)—blue or white flowers on branching 3- to 4-foot-tall stems. *D.* 'Blue Fountains'—dwarf delphinium 2½ to 3 feet tall with flowers in shades of blue. *D. elatum* Pacific Hybrids—blue, violet, lavender, pink, or white mostly double flowers on stalks usually 4 to 6 feet tall.

Growing conditions and maintenance: Plant delphiniums in slightly alkaline soil enriched with organic matter. Remove dead flowers after bloom and cut foliage back as it yellows to encourage a second blooming. Stake tall varieties. Propagate from seed.

Dianthus
(dy-AN-thus)
PINK

Dianthus barbatus 'Newport Pink'

Hardiness: *Zones 3-9*

Plant type: *perennial or biennial*

Height: *3 to 20 inches*

Interest: *flowers, foliage*

Soil: *moist, well-drained, slightly alkaline*

Light: *full sun to partial shade*

Pinks form mats of grassy, sometimes evergreen foliage with flowers that are often fragrant. Sweet William's taller, leafy clumps carry flat clusters of unscented flowers.

Selected species and varieties: *D.* x *allwoodii* (Allwood pink)—4- to 20-inch-tall mounds of blue-gray foliage; 'Helen' grows double salmon flowers; 'Robin', coral red double blooms. *D. barbatus* (sweet William)—biennial that self-sows freely; 'Indian Carpet' is a dwarf with flowers in mixed hues; 'Newport Pink' has coral pink blooms. *D. deltoides* (maiden pink)—mats of grass green leaves and flower stems to 1 foot; 'Flashing Light' has deep carmine flowers; 'Zing Rose', rose red blooms. *D. gratianopolitanus* (cheddar pink)—compact, part woody, with strongly fragrant flowers; 'Spotty' bears red-and-white bicolored blooms; 'Tiny Rubies', deep pink double flowers.

Growing conditions and maintenance: Space plants 12 to 18 inches apart. Divide every 2 to 3 years to maintain vigor. Propagate by division or by transplanting self-sown seedlings.

Dicentra
(dy-SEN-tra)
BLEEDING HEART

Dicentra spectabilis 'Alba'

Hardiness: *Zones 2-9*

Plant type: *perennial*

Height: *1 to 3 feet*

Interest: *flowers, foliage*

Soil: *moist, well-drained*

Light: *partial shade*

One-inch-long flowers resembling hearts or pantaloons dangle in profusion above bleeding heart's soft, lacy foliage. The plant serves well as a specimen or a filler in a shade or woodland garden.

Selected species and varieties: *D. eximia* 'Alba' (fringed bleeding heart)—loose clusters of white summer-blooming flowers above pale green foliage that remains attractive all season. *D.* hybrids—similar to *D. eximia* in habit and culture; 'Adrian Bloom' has crimson summer flowers and blue-green foliage; 'Luxuriant', red flowers from summer through frost; 'Zestful', pink summer flowers. *D. spectabilis* 'Alba' (common bleeding heart)—1½-inch white spring-to-summer flowers above feathery foliage that dies back by late summer.

Growing conditions and maintenance: Plant fringed bleeding heart 1 to 2 feet apart, common bleeding heart 2 to 3 feet. Cut fringed bleeding heart back after summer flowering to encourage fall flowers. Propagate by division.

Digitalis
(di-ji-TAL-us)
FOXGLOVE

Digitalis purpurea 'Foxy'

Hardiness: *Zones 3-9*

Plant type: *perennial or self-sowing biennial*

Height: *2 to 5 feet*

Interest: *flowers, foliage*

Soil: *moist, well-drained, acid*

Light: *partial shade*

Foxglove's striking summer-blooming flower trumpets line the tips of stiff stalks above clumps of coarse, hairy leaves.

Selected species and varieties: *D. grandiflora* (yellow foxglove)—yellow flowers with spotted throats on stalks to 3 feet tall. *D.* x *mertonensis* (strawberry foxglove)—coppery pink flowers on plants to 4 feet. *D. purpurea* (common foxglove)—purple, sometimes pink, white, or brownish red flowers with spotted throats on plants to 5 feet; foliage may be poisonous to pets; 'Alba' grows white flowers; 'Apricot', peach blooms; 'Excelsior Hybrids', pink, mauve, yellow, or white blooms that encircle the stalks; 'Foxy' produces blooms in mixed colors from seed the first year; 'Shirley Hybrids', profuse flowers on stalks to 5 feet.

Growing conditions and maintenance: Plant foxgloves 12 to 18 inches apart in organically rich soil. Propagate from seed, by transplanting self-sown seedlings, or by division in fall.

Echinacea
(ek-i-NAY-see-a)
PURPLE CONEFLOWER

Echinacea purpurea 'Magnus'

Hardiness: *Zones 3-9*

Plant type: *perennial*

Height: *2 to 4 feet*

Interest: *flowers*

Soil: *well-drained*

Light: *full sun to light shade*

Purple coneflowers form bold, stiff clumps of coarsely textured, hairy leaves. The daisylike flowers have softly drooping petals surrounding prominent conical centers. Purple coneflower's rigid form can be used as an accent or planted among softer-textured border specimens to balance its strong presence.

Selected species and varieties: *E. purpurea*—summer blooms 2 to 3 inches across on stiff stems lined with broad, pointed, tooth-edged leaves; 'Bright Star' has rosy red petals surrounding dark maroon centers; 'Magnus', a fringe of broad, rosy purple straight petals; 'White Swan', pure white blossoms.

Growing conditions and maintenance: Plant purple coneflowers 2 feet apart in any well-drained soil. Light shade enhances colors in hot climates. Plants may need staking in extremely fertile soils. Propagate by division.

Echinops
(EK-in-ops)
GLOBE THISTLE

Echinops ritro 'Taplow Blue'

Hardiness: *Zones 3-8*

Plant type: *perennial*

Height: *3 to 5 feet*

Interest: *flowers*

Soil: *well-drained*

Light: *full sun*

Globe thistle provides a striking blue accent over a long season of bloom. Tiny bristling spheres bloom on stiff stalks lined with crisp, hairy, deeply lobed leaves with spiny tips. Plant globe thistles among softer foliage that will hide the sparse foliage at the base of their rigid forms.

Selected species and varieties: *E. ritro* (small globe thistle)—blue-violet or deep blue flower spheres in summer for 6 to 8 weeks; 'Taplow Blue' has silvery blue 3-inch flower spheres on 4- to 5-foot plants; 'Veitch's Blue', ½- to 2-inch dark steel blue flower heads on 3- to 3½-foot stalks.

Growing conditions and maintenance: Plant globe thistles 2 feet apart. Plants tolerate heat well, but flowers will be a more intense blue in areas with cool nights. Propagate by clump division or root cuttings in spring.

Eryngium
(e-RIN-jee-um)
SEA HOLLY

Eryngium bourgatii

Hardiness: *Zones 4-9*

Plant type: *perennial*

Height: *1 to 6 feet*

Interest: *foliage, flowers*

Soil: *dry, sandy*

Light: *full sun*

Ruffs of spiny bracts cradle sea holly's conical flower heads with tiny, tightly packed florets. The long-lasting summer-blooming flowers rise on stiff stalks above crisp, leathery, often wavy leaves with deeply cut, spiny margins.

Selected species and varieties: *E. alpinum* (bluetop sea holly)—frilled bracts on 1- to 2-foot-tall plants. *E. bourgatii* (Mediterranean sea holly)—narrow, pointed bracts and wavy, gray-green leaves with prominent white veins on plants to 2 feet. *E. giganteum* (stout sea holly)—wide bracts like silvery holly leaves on plants 4 to 6 feet tall. *E. planum* (flat-leaved eryngium)—light blue flower heads with blue-green bracts on plants to 3 feet. *E. yuccifolium* (rattlesnake master)—narrow, drooping gray-green leaves with spiny edges on 4-foot stalks.

Growing conditions and maintenance: Plant sea hollies 12 to 18 inches apart. Plants may need staking in fertile soils. Propagate by separating and transplanting plantlets that appear at the base of mature plants.

Euonymus
(yew-ON-i-mus)
SPINDLE TREE

Euonymus fortunei 'Emerald Charm'

Hardiness: *Zones 3-8*

Plant type: *ground cover or shrub*

Height: *4 inches to 30 feet*

Interest: *foliage*

Soil: *well-drained*

Light: *full sun to shade*

The genus includes deciduous shrubs with brilliant fall color and evergreen shrubs and ground covers with an almost endless variety of white, cream, or yellow markings.

Selected species and varieties: *E. alata* (winged spindle tree)—winged branches and flaming red fall color on shrubs to 20 feet tall; 'Compacta' grows to 10 feet. *E. europaea* (common spindle tree)—upright shrubs to 30 feet with leaves turning yellow or purple in fall; 'Red Cascade' has rosy red seeds. *E. fortunei* (winter creeper euonymus)—evergreen ground cover or low hedge; 'Emerald Charm' is an erect 3-foot shrub; 'Longwood' produces low mats of ¼-inch leaves; var. *radicans* is a climber or trailer with 2-inch leaves; 'Gold Prince' grows in mounds 2 feet high with gold-tipped leaves that later turn all green; 'Vegetus' is a freely fruiting shrub or trailing vine to 5 feet. *E. kiautschovica* (spreading euonymus)—semi-evergreen shrub to 10 feet with conspicuous spring flowers.

Growing conditions and maintenance: Euonymus will grow in any soil, but likes neither sogginess nor drought.

Eupatorium
(yew-pa-TOR-ee-um)
BONESET

Eupatorium coelestinum

Hardiness: *Zones 5-10*

Plant type: *perennial*

Height: *1 to 6 feet*

Interest: *flowers*

Soil: *moist*

Light: *full sun to partial shade*

Boneset produces flat, dense clusters of fluffy, frizzy ½-inch flowers on erect stems lined with hairy, triangular leaves. The sturdy clumps will naturalize in marshy areas at the edges of meadows or in wild gardens. The flowers provide a fall foil for yellow or white flowers such as chrysanthemums and are excellent for cutting.

Selected species and varieties: *E. coelestinum* (mist flower, hardy ageratum, blue boneset)—bluish purple to violet ½-inch flowers crowded in clusters at the tips of 1- to 2-foot-tall stalks in late summer to fall. *E. fistulosum* (hollow Joe-Pye weed)—flat clusters of mauve flowers on hollow purple stems to 6 feet in late summer through fall.

Growing conditions and maintenance: Plant boneset in soil enriched with organic matter. Cut foliage back several times through the summer for bushier plants. Propagate by division in spring.

Fatsia
(FAT-see-a)
JAPANESE ARALIA

Fatsia japonica

Hardiness: *Zones 8-10*

Plant type: *shrub*

Height: *6 to 10 feet*

Interest: *foliage, flowers*

Soil: *well-drained*

Light: *shade*

Fatsia develops into round mounds of leathery, evergreen, palm-shaped leaves that create bold, somewhat exotic accents in a border.

Selected species and varieties: *F. japonica* (Japanese fatsia, glossy-leaved paper plant)—shrub 6- to 10-feet tall with 15-inch leaves on 1-foot-long stalks and 1½-inch clusters of white flowers in fall through winter, followed by small black berries.

Growing conditions and maintenance: Plant fatsia in moist but well-drained sites protected from strong winds or the reflected heat of light-colored walls or fences. Propagate from cuttings.

Fothergilla
(faw-ther-GIL-a)
FOTHERGILLA

Fothergilla major

Hardiness: *Zones 4-8*

Plant type: *shrub*

Height: *2 to 10 feet*

Interest: *foliage, flowers*

Soil: *well-drained, acid*

Light: *full sun to light shade*

A small shrub notable for the excellent coloring of its foliage in both summer and fall, fothergilla produces upright spikes of fluffy, honey-scented spring flowers before the leaves appear.

Selected species and varieties: *F. gardenii* 'Blue Mist' (witch alder)—oval blue-green leaves with a powdery coating on loose mounds 2 to 3 feet tall and as wide or wider turning yellow-green in fall. *F. major* (featherbush)—dense shrub 6 to 10 feet tall and as wide with 2-inch flower spikes and deep green summer leaves turning yellow, orange, and red in fall.

Growing conditions and maintenance: Acid soil is essential for fothergilla's survival. Propagate from softwood cuttings.

Geranium
(jer-AY-nee-um)
CRANESBILL

Geranium 'Johnson's Blue'

Hardiness: *Zones 3-8*

Plant type: *perennial*

Height: *6 inches to 2 feet*

Interest: *flowers, foliage*

Soil: *moist, well-drained*

Light: *full sun to partial shade*

Cranesbill's spreading mounds of fine-textured foliage and dainty spring-to-summer-blooming flowers are effective naturalized in a woodland garden.

Selected species and varieties: *G. endressii* 'Wargrave Pink' (Pyrenean cranesbill)—salmon pink flowers on 18-inch-tall plants. *G. macrorrhizum* (bigroot geranium)—pink flowers above 1-foot-high mounds of aromatic foliage; 'Ingwersen's Variety' has glossy foliage; 'Spessärt', soft maroon flowers. *G. maculatum* 'Album' (wild geranium)—clusters of 1-inch white flowers above deeply fingered leaves. *G. sanguineum* (bloody cranesbill)—1-inch-wide magenta flowers above 6- to 12-inch clumps of fine leaves; 'Album' has white flowers; var. *striatum* [also called *G.* 'Lancastriense'], red-veined pink blossoms. *G.* 'Johnson's Blue'—clear blue flowers with deep blue veins.

Growing conditions and maintenance: Plant cranesbill 1½ to 2 feet apart in cool areas. Propagate from seed, from summer cuttings, or by division.

Hakonechloa
(hah-kon-eh-KLO-a)
HAKONECHLOA

Hakonechloa macra 'Aureola'

Hardiness: *Zones 6-9*

Plant type: *ornamental grass*

Height: *12 to 18 inches*

Interest: *leaves*

Soil: *well-drained*

Light: *light shade*

Golden variegated hakonechloa forms shaggy mounds of colorfully striped, narrow leaves that are effective as specimens that add a colorful punctuation mark in a planting or in dramatic masses.

Selected species and varieties: *H. macra* 'Aureola' (golden variegated hakonechloa)—broad, vigorous clumps 12 to 18 inches tall of 8- to 12-inch narrow leaves striped yellow and green.

Growing conditions and maintenance: Hakonechloa will grow in full sun but provides best color in partial shade. Propagate by dividing clumps.

Hamamelis
(ha-ma-MEL-is)
WITCH HAZEL

Hamamelis x intermedia 'Jelena'

Hardiness: *Zones 5-8*

Plant type: *shrub or small tree*

Height: *15 to 20 feet*

Interest: *flowers, foliage*

Soil: *moist, well-drained, acid*

Light: *full sun to partial shade*

Witch hazel's flowers bloom along bare branches in late winter and early spring, before leaves emerge. The oval foliage colors yellow to red in fall. Witch hazel extends the season of bloom in a shrub border, stands alone as a specimen accent, or provides a backdrop for a spring bulb or wildflower garden.

Selected species and varieties: *H.* x *intermedia*—loosely branched, upright shrub or tree to 20 feet tall, producing flowers with four narrow petals like dangling wrinkled ribbons; 'Arnold Promise' has 1-inch-long, fragrant yellow-petaled flowers with reddish centers; 'Diana', red flowers; 'Jelena', 1-inch-long petals that are red at their base lightening through orange to yellow at their tips; 'Primavera', profuse yellow flowers.

Growing conditions and maintenance: Plant witch hazel in soil enriched with organic matter. Sunny conditions produce denser growth than shade. Propagate from seed or from cuttings.

Helenium
(hel-EE-nee-um)
SNEEZEWEED

Helenium autumnale 'Bruno'

Hardiness: *Zones 3-8*

Plant type: *perennial*

Height: *2½ to 6 feet*

Interest: *foliage, flowers*

Soil: *moist, well-drained*

Light: *full sun*

Sneezeweed's clumps of erect stems lined with willowy leaves form a backdrop for shorter border plantings or provide a fall-blooming filler among plants that bloom earlier in the season. Daisylike flowers with fan-shaped petals and prominent centers bloom at the ends of sneezeweed's branching tips.

Selected species and varieties: *H. autumnale* (common sneezeweed)—flowers up to 2 inches wide bloom in summer and persist through frost on 5- to 6-foot-tall stems; 'Brilliant' has profuse bronze blossoms; 'Bruno', mahogany flowers on 4-foot plants; 'Butterpat', clear yellow petals surrounding bronze centers on 4- to 5-foot plants; 'Moerheim Beauty', reddish bronze blossoms on 4-foot stems.

Growing conditions and maintenance: Plant sneezeweed 18 to 24 inches apart. Plants may need staking. Divide every 3 to 4 years to prevent crowding and to propagate.

Helianthus
(hee-lee-AN-thus)
SUNFLOWER

Helianthus annuus 'Russian Giant'

Hardiness: *hardy or Zones 3-9*

Plant type: *annual or perennial*

Height: *2 to 10 feet*

Interest: *flowers*

Soil: *moist, well-drained*

Light: *full sun*

Sunflowers produce daisylike flower heads of widely varying size filled with seeds in late summer through frost. Some form clumps of ornamental foliage for backdrops or naturalizing.

Selected species and varieties: *H. annuus* (common sunflower)—annual with 3- to 14-inch-wide flowers with a fringe of yellow to orange ray flowers encircling broad centers; 'Russian Giant' grows 10 feet tall; 'Italian White', to 4 feet with cream-colored flowers; 'Sunburst', to 4 feet with deep crimson, lemon, bronze, or gold 4-inch blooms. *H. salicifolius* (willow-leaved sunflower)—2-inch yellow flowers above narrow, willowy leaves on 4- to 6-foot plants.

Growing conditions and maintenance: Plant sunflowers 2 feet apart. Stake tall stalks. Propagate either species from seed and *H. salicifolius* by division.

Hemerocallis
(hem-er-o-KAL-is)
DAYLILY

Hemerocallis 'Stella de Oro'

Hardiness: *Zones 3-9*

Plant type: *perennial*

Height: *1 to 3 feet*

Interest: *flowers, foliage*

Soil: *moist, well-drained*

Light: *full sun to partial shade*

Daylilies form dense clumps of arching, grasslike leaves. Branching stalks bear a succession of flower trumpets 2 to 6 inches across, often with frilled, spotted, or double petals. Each blossom lasts only a single day.

Selected species and varieties: Hybrid daylilies provide flowers in yellow, orange, peach, melon, pink, red, lavender, maroon, and bronze. Cultivars bloom in spring, summer, or fall. Spring-blooming daylilies include 36-inch-tall, fragrant yellow 'Hyperion'; 28-inch fragrant golden apricot 'Ruffled Apricot'. Summer bloomers include 30-inch, pale orchid 'Catherine Woodbury'; 14-inch light yellow 'Eenie Weenie'; canary yellow, orange-throated, low-growing 'Stella de Oro'. Fall bloomers include 28-inch, lemon yellow 'Bountiful Valley'; 34-inch, carmine 'Oriental Ruby'.

Growing conditions and maintenance: Plant daylilies in soil that has been enriched with organic matter, spacing small varieties 18 to 24 inches apart, taller ones 2 to 3 feet apart. Propagate by division every 3 to 6 years.

Heuchera
(HEW-ker-a)
ALUMROOT

Heuchera micrantha 'Palace Purple'

Hardiness: *Zones 3-9*

Plant type: *perennial*

Height: *1 to 2 feet*

Interest: *foliage, flowers*

Soil: *moist, well-drained, fertile*

Light: *full sun to partial shade*

Alumroot's round, evergreen leaves with scalloped edges, often veined or tinted, form neat mounds that are attractive as edgings or fillers or massed as a ground cover. Wiry, branched flower stalks carry loose clusters of dainty flowers high above the foliage.

Selected species and varieties: *H. micrantha* 'Palace Purple'—pink flowers held on 18-inch stems above purplish green foliage. *H.* cultivars—long-lasting blossoms from spring to summer; 'Firebird' has deep scarlet blossoms on 18-inch stalks; 'June Bride', white flowers on 18-inch stems; 'Pluie de Feu', cherry red blossoms on 18-inch stems; 'Pewter Veil', purple-tinged silvery leaves; 'Scintillation', red flowers on 30-inch stems; 'Snowflake', white flowers.

Growing conditions and maintenance: Plant heuchera 12 to 18 inches apart in soil enriched with organic matter. Propagate from seed or by division every 3 years.

Hosta
(HOS-ta)
PLANTAIN LILY

Hosta fortunei 'Gold Standard'

Hardiness: *Zones 3-9*

Plant type: *perennial*

Height: *8 inches to 3 feet*

Interest: *foliage*

Soil: *moist, well-drained, fertile*

Light: *partial to full shade*

Hosta's neat, wide-spreading mounds of broad, pointed leaves in a bounty of sizes, shapes, textures, and colors are excellent as accent specimens, ground covers, fillers, or edgings for shady gardens. Foliage is often wavy, quilted, or deeply veined and banded with contrasting hues of green, yellow, cream, or white. Tubular flowers dangle along erect stems rising among the leaves.

Selected species and varieties: *H. fortunei* (giant plantain lily)—funnel-shaped, lavender-tinged white flowers above dark green to blue-green foliage; 'Albopicta' produces lilac summer blossoms on 1½-foot-tall stems above creamy yellow young foliage banded in dark green maturing to solid green; 'Gold Standard', chartreuse leaves edged in dark green that color gold in full sun. *H. plantaginea* (fragrant plantain lily)—white, trumpet-shaped flowers on stems 1½ to 2½ feet above yellow-green, glossy, 10-inch-long leaves; 'Aphrodite' grows fragrant double-petaled white summer flowers on 2-foot stems above light green leaves; 'Royal Standard', white flowers above deeply veined, deep green leaves. *H.* x 'Honeybells'—pale lilac summer flowers above wavy, yellow-green leaves. *H. sieboldiana* (seersucker plantain lily)—gray-green leaves to 10 inches wide forming clumps 4 feet wide, with insignificant flowers; 'Elegans' has white summer flowers on 2- to 3-foot stalks above steel blue leaves; 'Frances Williams', white summer flowers and crinkled blue-green leaves edged in gold. *H.* cultivars—'Blue Cadet' is a dwarf hosta with small blue leaves and lavender summer blossoms; 'Blue Umbrellas' has deeply veined blue-green leaves covered with a powdery bloom; 'Ginko Craig', light green leaves touched with white at

Hosta 'Blue Cadet'

the edges and 12-inch violet summer blooms; 'Piedmont Standard', white summer flowers above heart-shaped golden leaves; 'Sum and Substance', glossy, heart-shaped golden green leaves and lavender summer flowers.

Growing conditions and maintenance: Plant hostas in soil enriched with organic matter. Some cultivars tolerate full sun but foliage color may fade. Propagate by division in spring.

Hyacinthus
(by-a-SIN-thus)
HYACINTH

Hyacinthus orientalis 'Blue Jacket'

Hardiness: *Zones 3-7*

Plant type: *bulb*

Height: *8 to 12 inches*

Interest: *flowers*

Soil: *moist, well-drained*

Light: *full sun*

Hyacinth's flower spikes, crowded with 1-inch-long flowers whose petals curve backward, add color and sweet fragrance to the spring border. The spikes rise from a small bundle of canoe-shaped leaves. Hyacinths are impressive in mass plantings and add a touch of texture and height when interplanted among other spring bulbs.

Selected species and varieties: *H. orientalis* (common hyacinth)—flowers in white, yellow, blue, purple, red, and pink; 'Anna Marie' has light pink flowers; 'Blue Jacket', navy blue flowers on black stems; 'Carnegie', cream flowers; 'City of Harlem', pale yellow blooms; 'Delft Blue', deep medium blue flowers; 'Lady Derby', pink blossoms.

Growing conditions and maintenance: Plant hyacinths 6 to 8 inches deep in organically rich soil. Bulbs produce the largest flower their first year, small blooms thereafter. Replace bulbs every 2 to 3 years.

Hydrangea
(hy-DRANE-jee-a)
HYDRANGEA

Hydrangea anomala ssp. petiolaris

Hardiness: *Zones 3-9*

Plant type: *vine, shrub, or tree*

Height: *3 to 80 feet*

Interest: *flowers, foliage, bark*

Soil: *moist, well-drained*

Light: *full sun to light shade*

Hydrangeas punctuate the garden with huge flower clusters above coarse, lustrous leaves that color attractively in fall. Older stems often have peeling bark, adding winter interest.

Selected species and varieties: *H. anomala* ssp. *petiolaris* (climbing hydrangea) —vine to 80 feet long with white spring-to-summer-blooming flower clusters as much as 10 inches across. *H. arborescens* 'Grandiflora' (hills-of-snow hydrangea)—white summer-to-fall flower clusters 6 to 8 inches across on shrubs to 5 feet. *H. macrophylla* (bigleaf hydrangea)—pink or blue summer flowers on shrubs 3 to 10 feet tall. *H. paniculata* 'Grandiflora' (peegee hydrangea)—tree or shrub to 25 feet with 12- to 18-inch white summer flower clusters. *H. quercifolia* 'Snowflake' (oakleaf hydrangea)— shrub to 6 feet with leaves resembling those of oaks and double-petaled summer flowers in 1½-inch clusters.

Growing conditions and maintenance: Plant hydrangeas in soil richly amended with organic matter. *H. arborescens* does better in partial shade. Propagate from cuttings.

Ilex
(EYE-lex)
HOLLY

Ilex aquifolium

Hardiness: *Zones 3-10*

Plant type: *tree or shrub*

Height: *3 to 50 feet*

Interest: *foliage, flowers, berries*

Soil: *moist, well-drained, acid*

Light: *full sun to light shade*

Hollies are prized as specimens and in groupings for their tidy shapes and the textures of their glossy, mostly evergreen, often spiny leaves. The clusters of tiny, sometimes fragrant flowers that bloom in spring are followed in fall by berries that provide winter interest. Dense branching and foliage make several species ideal for formal hedges.

Selected species and varieties: *I. aquifolium* (English holly)—dense branching on trees 30 to 50 feet tall with evergreen leaves of varying sizes on the same plant and red berries. *I.* x *attenuata* 'Foster #2' (topal holly)—small, oval evergreen leaves with spiny edges on compact, pyramidal, red-berried shrubs. *I. cornuta* 'Burfordii' (Chinese holly)—rounded oval, evergreen leaves with short spines on dense shrubs 10 to 20 feet high and as wide with red berries. *I. crenata* (Japanese holly)—dense, fine-textured shrubs with oval, spineless, evergreen leaves and black berries; 'Convexa' grows 4 to 9 feet tall and wide and is good for hedges; 'Helleri' is a dwarf growing to 5 feet; 'Hetzii', a 6- to 8-foot shrub good for hedges. *I. glabra* (inkberry)—narrow,

spineless evergreen foliage on shrubs to 8 feet tall and slightly wider with black berries; 'Compacta' is a dwarf with dense branching. *I. opaca* (American holly)— scalloped evergreen leaves to 3 inches long with spiny edges on trees 15 to 30 feet tall and as wide with red berries; 'Cardinal' is a compact shrub with smaller leaves and abundant berries; 'Goldie' has yellow berries; 'Old Heavy Berry' is an extremely prolific berry producer. *I. pedunculosa* (longstalk holly)—pointed oval, wavy, evergreen leaves without spines on trees 15 to 20 feet tall with red berries on long stalks. *I.* 'Sparkleberry'— dense column of oval, deciduous foliage

Ilex 'Sparkleberry'

and profuse red berries that last through winter on shrubs to 12 feet. *I. vomitoria* (yaupon)—15- to 30-foot upright tree or shrub with purplish new leaves turning glossy deep green and with profuse red berries that last through winter.

Growing conditions and maintenance: Grow hollies in soil enriched with organic matter. They tolerate light shade but are better berry producers in full sun. Berry production requires the proximity of both male and female plants. Propagate from cuttings.

Impatiens
(im-PAY-shens)
BALSAM, JEWELWEED

Impatiens wallerana 'Shady Lady' series

Hardiness: *tender*

Plant type: *annual*

Height: *6 inches to 3 feet*

Interest: *flowers, foliage*

Soil: *moist, well-drained*

Light: *shade to full sun*

Massed as edgings or ground covers, impatiens brighten a shady garden with tiny flowers in jeweled hues from summer through frost.

Selected species and varieties: *I. balsamina* (garden balsam)—1- to 2-inch flowers with double petals in mixed colors on plants to 3 feet tall. *I.* x New Guinea—'Spectra Hybrids' produce flowers up to 3 inches on 2-foot plants with showy leaves often veined or variegated in yellow, pink, or red; 'Tango' has orange flowers among bronze leaves. *I. wallerana* (garden impatiens)—flat-faced, 1-inch-wide blossoms in mixed colors; 'Shady Lady' series make excellent shade plants 12 to 15 inches tall; 'Super Elfin' produces spreading plants 6 to 12 inches tall.

Growing conditions and maintenance: Plant impatiens in soil enriched with organic matter. Keep well watered. Start seeds indoors 3 to 4 months before the last frost or purchase bedding plants.

Imperata
(im-per-AY-ta)
JAPANESE BLOOD GRASS

Imperata cylindrica 'Red Baron'

Hardiness: *Zones 6-9*

Plant type: *ornamental grass*

Height: *12 to 18 inches*

Interest: *foliage*

Soil: *well-drained*

Light: *full sun to partial shade*

Spring shoots of Japanese blood grass emerge green, then turn red as clumps mature in summer and remain ornamental through fall. The erect clumps of straplike leaves are particularly striking massed in a border.

Selected species and varieties: *I. cylindrica* 'Red Baron'—nonflowering clumps of ¼- to ½-inch-wide leaf blades turning bright red in early summer and remaining colorful until late fall.

Growing conditions and maintenance: Japanese blood grass will grow in partial shade but color will be less intense than in full sun. Remove any parts of the plant that revert to the green of the parent species immediately. Propagate by division in spring.

Ipomoea
(eye-po-MEE-a)
MORNING GLORY

Ipomoea nil 'Scarlett O'Hara'

Hardiness: *tender*

Plant type: *annual vine*

Height: *10 to 30 feet*

Interest: *flowers*

Soil: *well-drained*

Light: *full sun*

Twining on trellises and fences or cascading over walls and banks, morning glories produce a profusion of trumpet-shaped blossoms that persist from summer until frost, opening in the morning or evening or on cloudy days.

Selected species and varieties: *I. alba* (moonflower)—fragrant, white 6-inch flower trumpets banded in green among lustrous heart-shaped leaves on vines to 30 feet long. *I. nil* 'Scarlett O'Hara' (imperial Japanese morning glory)—6-inch red flowers among heart-shaped leaves on vines to 10 feet. *I. tricolor* 'Heavenly Blue'—early-blooming, deep sky blue flower trumpets 5 inches across with contrasting throats on vines to 10 feet. *I. quamoclit* (cypress vine)—1½-inch tubular red flowers with flaring lips on vines to 20 feet with threadlike, paired leaflets.

Growing conditions and maintenance: Fertile soil and high moisture will produce abundant leaves but few flowers. Start seed indoors before the last frost.

Iris
(EYE-ris)
IRIS

Iris reticulata 'Harmony'

Hardiness: *Zones 3-10*

Plant type: *perennial*

Height: *2 inches to 4 feet*

Interest: *flowers, foliage*

Soil: *moist, well-drained*

Light: *full sun to light shade*

An array of forms make irises a bold punctuation mark in a border, a dainty ground cover, or a showy display in masses. Fans of stiff, sword-shaped leaves spread into dense clumps, with flowers unfurling on stiff stalks. The complex flowers, presenting in an enormous range of hues, tints, and shades, have erect, arched or flared inner petals and longer, broader outer petals that droop attractively.

Selected species and varieties: *I. cristata* (crested iris)—grassy 6-inch-tall leaves and blue-violet spring-blooming flowers banded in white and yellow; 'Alba' has pure white petals; 'Shenandoah Sky', pale blue flowers; 'Summer Storm', deep blue blossoms. *I. danfordiae* (Danford iris)—grassy leaves up to 12 inches long and 1-inch green-spotted yellow-orange flowers in spring. *I. ensata* [also called *I. kaempferi*] (Japanese water iris)—graceful, stiff leaves to 2 feet with summer flowers on 4-foot stalks; 'Eleanor Perry' has deep lilac flowers; 'Great White Heron', semidouble-petaled white blossoms. *I. laevigata* 'Variegata'—green leaves edged with cream-and-lavender-blue summer flowers on 18-inch plants. *I. pallida* 'Aureo-Variegata' (Dalmation iris)—crinkled pale blue summer flowers and 3-foot gray-green leaves striped with yellow. *I. reticulata* (netted iris)—fragrant early spring flowers on 3- to 4-inch stems followed by 9-inch leaves; 'Harmony' has blue flowers with yellow and white blotches. *I. sibirica* (Siberian iris)—2- to 4-foot clumps of leaves with late spring flowers on stalks to 4 feet; 'Caesar's Brother' has blue-black flowers; 'Dreaming Spires', deep-lavender-and-blue blossoms; 'White Swirl', ruffled white petals and a yellow-splashed throat. *I. tectorum* 'Alba' (roof iris)—white flowers touched with yellow in spring on 1-foot plants. *I.* hybrids—orchidlike summer bearded iris blossoms on stalks from 6 inches to 4 feet; 'Bride's Halo' has mixed white and yellow petals; 'Cup Race', shimmering white petals; 'Debby Rairdon', white-and-cream blossoms; 'Loop the Loop', violet-edged white petals; 'Navy Strut', ruffled purple

Iris tectorum 'Alba'

petals; 'Stepping Out', purple-and-white blossoms; 'Victoria Falls', large numbers of ruffled, pale blue flowers.

Growing conditions and maintenance: Plant irises in soil enriched with organic matter. To propagate, dig bulbs or rhizomes in fall after foliage dies back, divide, and replant for bloom the following spring or summer.

Jasminum
(JAZ-min-um)
JASMINE

Jasminum nudiflorum

Hardiness: *Zones 6-10*

Plant type: *vine or shrub*

Height: *5 to 30 feet*

Interest: *flowers, foliage*

Soil: *well-drained*

Light: *full sun to light shade*

Jasmine perfumes the garden with sweetly fragrant flowers on evergreen or deciduous vines or shrubs. The plant clambers up supports or sprawls along the ground as a mounding ground cover.

Selected species and varieties: *J. grandiflorum* [also called *J. officinale* forma *grandiflorum*] (Spanish jasmine)—semi-evergreen vine to 15 feet tall with 1½-inch white summer-blooming flowers. *J. nudiflorum* (winter jasmine)—spreading, deciduous nonclimber to 15 feet with unscented yellow spring flowers 1 inch across. *J. officinale* (common white jasmine)—semi-evergreen vine to 30 feet with clusters of 1-inch white summer-to-fall flowers. *J. polyanthum* (pink jasmine)—clusters of white flowers tinged pink on evergreen to semi-evergreen climbing shrubs to 20 feet. *J. sambac* (Arabian jasmine)—intensely fragrant 1-inch white flowers on shrubby evergreen climbers to 5 feet.

Growing conditions and maintenance: Grows well in poor soil. May become invasive. Pinch to shape plants or train into shrubs. Propagate from seed or cuttings.

Juniperus
(joo-NIP-er-us)
JUNIPER

Juniperus conferta 'Emerald Sea'

Hardiness: *Zones 3-9*

Plant type: *tree, shrub, or ground cover*

Height: *4 inches to 30 feet*

Interest: *form, foliage, berries*

Soil: *well-drained to dry*

Light: *full sun*

Junipers are extremely hardy plants producing fine-needled foliage in shades of green to blue-green, silvery blue, or gold in forms that suit a multitude of landscaping uses. Branches may trail over walls or among rocks, spread horizontally into dense ground covers, layer in tidy columns or pyramids, arch upward into fountainlike sprays, or droop gracefully into weeping forms. Fleshy blue-black berries develop on female plants. The species here offer choices for ground covers, screens, hedges, or specimen plantings that anchor plantings of other shrubs, perennials, or bulbs by offering consistent year-round color, texture, and form.

Selected species and varieties: *J. chinensis* 'Gold Coast' (Chinese juniper)—compact ground cover mounding to 3 feet tall and spreading up to 5 feet with golden yellow foliage; 'Mint Julep' produces a loose fountain of bright green foliage 4 to 6 feet tall and slightly wider; var. *sargentii* (Sargent's juniper) has blue-green foliage on plants 18 to 24 inches tall and up to 10 feet wide. *J. conferta* 'Blue Pacific' (shore juniper)—9- to 12-inch

plants with blue-green foliage on branches trailing up to 8 feet; 'Emerald Sea' grows slightly greener, salt-tolerant foliage. *J. horizontalis* (creeping juniper)—scalelike needles coloring purplish in winter along feathery twigs; 'Bar Harbor' produces salt-tolerant blue-green foliage in tight mats 1 foot high and up to 8 feet wide; 'Blue Chip' has silvery blue foliage; 'Wiltonii' (blue rug juniper), trailing mats of intense silvery blue foliage only 4 to 6 inches high. *J. procumbens* 'Nana' (dwarf Japanese garden juniper)—spreading mounds of blue-green foliage up to 2 feet tall and 10 feet wide. *J. sabina* 'Broadmoor' (Savin juniper)—dark green foliage on plants

Juniperus procumbens 'Nana'

spreading up to 10 feet wide from a central cushion of branches up to 3 feet tall. *J. scopulorum* 'Skyrocket' (Rocky Mountain juniper, Colorado red cedar)—deep blue-green foliage on extremely narrow columns of branches only 2 feet wide but 15 to 30 feet tall; 'Tolleson's Weeping' has silver-blue or green foliage lining stringy, weeping twigs; 'Wichita Blue' is an upright pyramid of blue foliage to 18 feet or taller.

Growing conditions and maintenance: Plant junipers in acid soil, allowing room for each shrub's mature spread. If necessary, prune to shape plants in spring.

Lagerstroemia
(la-gur-STREE-mee-a)
CRAPE MYRTLE

Lagerstroemia indica 'Natchez'

Hardiness: *Zones 7-9*

Plant type: *shrub or tree*

Height: *15 to 25 feet*

Interest: *flowers, foliage, bark*

Soil: *moist, well-drained*

Light: *full sun*

One-inch-wide crape myrtle flowers with papery, wrinkled petals bloom from summer to fall in clusters up to 1 foot long at the tips of new stems. Crape myrtles are attractive as specimens or add fall color and winter texture to a shrub border.

Selected species and varieties: *L. indica* (common crape myrtle)—small shrub to tree in habit, with lustrous, deep green oval leaves coloring red to orange in fall before dropping to reveal smooth gray bark shredding to shades of brown; 'Natchez' has white flower clusters on shrubs up to 20 feet tall and equally wide; 'Potomac', pink flower clusters on upright shrubs to 10 feet; 'Tuscarora', coral blooms on shrubs or small trees to 15 feet.

Growing conditions and maintenance: Plant crape myrtles in hot, sunny locations. Cutting plants to the ground in spring controls size and produces larger flowers the following year. Prune to train multiple-stemmed shrubs into small trees. Propagate from seed or cuttings.

Lathyrus
(LATH-er-us)
VETCHLING, WILD PEA

Lathyrus latifolius

Hardiness: *Zones 4-9 or half-hardy*

Plant type: *perennial, annual vine, or bush*

Height: *6 inches to 9 feet*

Interest: *flowers*

Soil: *well-drained*

Light: *full sun to partial shade*

Lathyrus bears flowers with puffy or furled petals on branching flower stalks. Use it as a trailing ground cover, a climbing vine for a screen or backdrop, or as a bushy accent among spring bulbs.

Selected species and varieties: *L. latifolius* (perennial pea)—twining vine to 9 feet tall with 1-inch-wide summer flowers. *L. odoratus* (sweet pea)—fragrant spring or summer flowers up to 2 inches wide on compact, 6-inch to 2½-foot-tall annual bushes or twining vines to 5 feet long or more. *L. vernus* (spring vetchling)—bushy, sprawling perennial 10 to 15 inches high with ferny foliage and profuse rose-violet spring flowers fading to greenish blue.

Growing conditions and maintenance: Plant lathyrus in well-drained garden loam. Propagate all species from seed, perennial pea and spring vetchling also by division. Remove spent flowers to prolong blooming season.

Lavandula
(lav-AN-dew-la)
LAVENDER

Lavandula stoechas

Hardiness: *Zones 5-9*

Plant type: *perennial or small shrub*

Height: *1 to 3 feet*

Interest: *foliage, flowers*

Soil: *well-drained*

Light: *full sun*

Lavender forms neat cushions of erect stems lined with fragrant, willowy, gray or gray-green leaves tipped with spikes of tiny flowers. Lavender's attractive evergreen foliage blends into rock gardens or at the edges of borders and can be clipped into a low hedge.

Selected species and varieties: *L. angustifolia* (true lavender, English lavender)—whorls of lavender-to-purple ¼-inch flowers in summer on compact, round plants 1 to 2 feet tall; 'Hidcote' produces deep violet-blue flowers and silvery gray foliage. *L. latifolia* (spike lavender)—branched stalks of lavender-to-purple summer flowers above broader leaves than true lavender on plants to 2 feet tall. *L. stoechas* (French lavender)—dense whorls of tufted purple flowers in summer on plants to 3 feet tall.

Growing conditions and maintenance: Plant lavender 12 to 18 inches apart in soil that is not overly rich. Cut stems back to 8 inches in early spring to encourage compact growth and to remove old woody stems that produce few flowers. Propagate from seed or by division.

Ligularia
(lig-yew-LAY-ree-a)
GOLDEN-RAY

Ligularia przewalskii 'The Rocket'

Hardiness: *Zones 4-9*

Plant type: *perennial*

Height: *2 to 6 feet*

Interest: *foliage, flowers*

Soil: *moist*

Light: *full sun*

Ligularia's summer-to-fall flowers bloom on erect stalks above clumps of coarse-textured, 12- to 24-inch-wide leaves. Use it as a bold border accent or massed for effect in marshy areas.

Selected species and varieties: *L. dentata* (ragwort)—yellow-orange flowers held above 3- to 4-foot-high mounds of foliage; 'Desdemona' grows deep purple lower leaves and leaf stems; 'Othello', compact mounds of purplish foliage. *L. macrophylla*—small yellow flowers tipping 4- to 6-foot stalks above 2-foot leaves. *L. przewalskii* 'The Rocket'—wands of yellow flowers atop 5- to 6-foot stalks. *L. tussilaginea*—low clumps of leathery green leaves and yellow flowers on 2-foot stalks; 'Argentea' has creamy leaf edges; 'Aureo-maculata', leaves freckled yellow gold; 'Cristata', ruffled leaf edges.

Growing conditions and maintenance: Plant ligularia 2 to 3 feet apart in soils that are constantly moist. Propagate species and cultivars by division in the spring or fall; species can also be propagated from seed.

Lilium
(LIL-ee-um)
LILY

Lilium candidum

Hardiness:	*Zones 3-9*
Plant type:	*bulb*
Height:	*2 to 6 feet*
Interest:	*flowers*
Soil:	*moist, well-drained*
Light:	*full sun to light shade*

Showy, curvaceous flower trumpets ornamented with prominent stamens and sometimes spotted or contrasting throats make lilies outstanding border specimens. Massed for effect, lilies can provide a succession of blossoms from spring through fall growing singly or in clusters at the tips of erect stems lined with narrow, grassy leaves. Lilies are also effective naturalized in front of a shrub border or at the sunny edge of a woodland garden, which will act as a backdrop for their ornate blossoms.

Selected species and varieties: *L. auratum* (gold-banded lily)—up to 35 fragrant, ruffled, white summer- or fall-blooming trumpets 6 to 12 inches across, spotted red and banded with gold, at the tips of stems to 6 feet tall. *L. canadense* (meadow lily, Canada lily)—clusters of 3-inch, nodding, red, yellow, or orange flower bells on stems to 5 feet in summer. *L. candidum* (Madonna lily)—a dozen or more intensely fragrant, snow white spring or summer flowers on stems to 5 feet. *L. martagon* (Turk's-cap lily)—clusters of purple-to-pink 1½-inch flowers with petals curved tightly back

into miniature turbans on stems to 6 feet, blooming from spring to summer. *L. regale* (royal lily)—fragrant white trumpets 5 inches wide with yellow throats on 6-foot stems. *L. speciosum* (showy Japanese lily)—waxy pink, red, or white fragrant summer flowers with raised spots on stems to 6 feet. *L. tigrinum* (tiger lily)—drooping, 4-inch, red-orange blossoms dotted black on 4-foot stalks from summer to fall. Asiatic Hybrids—spring-to-summer upturned flowers 6 inches across in every color but blue, sometimes bi- or tricolored, on 3- to 4-foot stems; 'Avignon' produces mellow orange blooms on 2- to 3-foot stems. Oriental Hybrids—late-summer-to-fall bowl-shaped or flat-faced blossoms up to 10 inches across in white to pink or red

Lilium 'Avignon'

on 2- to 3-foot stems. Trumpet Hybrids [also called Aurelian Hybrids]—summer-blooming bowl-shaped or sunburst-shaped flowers up to 12 inches across in white, gold, or pink on stems to 6 feet.

Growing conditions and maintenance: Plant lilies in porous, slightly acid soil with constant moisture, setting bulbs at a depth three times their height; plant Madonna lilies only an inch deep. If cultivating tiger lilies, use only virus-free stock or plant far from other lily species. Lilies do best in full sun when their roots are heavily mulched or receive light shade to keep them cool. Stake tall lilies. Propagate by division or by removing and planting tiny bulbils, which grow in leaf axils.

Liriope
(li-RYE-o-pee)
LILYTURF

Liriope muscari 'Christmas Tree'

Hardiness:	*Zones 4-10*
Plant type:	*perennial*
Height:	*18 inches*
Interest:	*foliage, flowers*
Soil:	*moist to dry, well-drained, fertile*
Light:	*full sun to full shade*

Tidy tufts of evergreen, grassy lilyturf leaves create dense ground covers or border edgings. Spikes of ¼-inch flowers in whorls lining erect flower stalks held above the leaves are followed by attractive blue-black berries.

Selected species and varieties: *L. muscari* (big blue lilyturf)—grasslike leaves ½-inch wide and up to 18 inches long with deep blue summer flowers; 'Christmas Tree' has conical spikes of lilac flowers; 'Majestic', large violet-blue blossoms in heavy clusters; 'Monroe's White', white flowers; 'Variegata', yellow-edged new foliage.

Growing conditions and maintenance: Plant lilyturf in any light conditions; a sunny spot will produce more flowers. Foliage may suffer winter burn in colder areas; shear to the ground as new growth begins in the spring. Propagate by division in spring.

Lupinus (loo-PY-nus) **LUPINE**	*Macleaya* (mak-LAY-a) **PLUME POPPY**	*Magnolia* (mag-NO-lee-a) **MAGNOLIA**

Lupinus 'Russell Hybrids'

Macleaya cordata

Magnolia x soulangiana 'Rustica Rubra'

Hardiness: *Zones 4-6*

Plant type: *perennial*

Height: *3 to 4 feet*

Interest: *flowers*

Soil: *moist, well-drained, acid*

Light: *full sun to light shade*

Hardiness: *Zones 3-8*

Plant type: *perennial*

Height: *6 to 10 feet*

Interest: *foliage, flowers*

Soil: *moist, well-drained*

Light: *full sun*

Hardiness: *Zones 3-9*

Plant type: *shrub or tree*

Height: *10 to 80 feet*

Interest: *flowers, foliage, bark, seeds*

Soil: *moist, well-drained, acid*

Light: *full sun to light shade*

Lupine's elongated spikes of small, but-terfly-shaped flowers at the tips of stiff stalks lined with whorls of narrow leaves dramatically embellish the flower bor-der. The stalks grow in clumps that can be used as accents or massed effectively.

Selected species and varieties: *L.* 'Russell Hybrids'—plants to 4 feet tall with showy 18- to 24-inch-long summer-blooming flower spires that open from the bottom up in a multitude of colors and combina-tions; dwarf strains 1½ feet tall include 'Little Lulu' and 'Minarette'.

Growing conditions and maintenance: Plant lupines in acidic soil enriched with organic matter. Lupines will not tolerate hot summers. Plants may require stak-ing. Propagate from seed or from root cuttings taken with a small piece of crown in early spring.

Plume poppy's massive clumps of fo-liage, growing almost as wide as high, develop into imposing, shrubby speci-mens at the back of a border, as tempo-rary screens, or as an anchor in the cen-ter of an island bed. Feathery clusters of tiny flowers bloom at the tips of erect stems lined with broad, deeply lobed leaves that cover the plants, producing a frothy effect.

Selected species and varieties: *M. cor-data* (tree celandine)—creamy ½-inch flowers above gray-green leaves up to 1 foot across with wavy edges and silvery undersides.

Growing conditions and maintenance: Plant plume poppies 3 to 4 feet apart. Shady conditions and fertile soils will ac-centuate their invasive tendencies. Prop-agate from seed, by division in spring, or by transplanting plantlets that develop along the roots.

Evergreen in warmer climates, semi-evergreen or deciduous in colder areas, magnolias produce broad, cup-shaped or star-shaped spring- or summer-blooming flowers amid coarse, often leathery and glossy leaves. In fall, knob-by, conical seed pods split open to re-veal glossy red or orange seeds. The smooth gray bark is a cool winter accent. Whether as loose, rounded shrubs or pyramidal trees, magnolias are outstand-ing as specimens and are also effective as part of a shrub border.

Selected species and varieties: *M.* x 'Galaxy'—pyramidal tree to 30 feet tall and 10 feet wide with profuse reddish-purple-to-pink, 6-inch, early-spring flow-ers. *M. grandiflora* (southern magno-lia, bull bay)—low-branching pyramidal evergreen tree to 80 feet tall and half as wide with glossy, leathery oval leaves up to 8 inches long that are woolly brown on their undersides and fragrant, cream-colored, spring blossoms up to 12 inches across; 'Edith Bogue' is a hardy cultivar to 35 feet tall; 'Little Gem', 15 to 20 feet tall and half as wide. *M.* Kosar de Vos Hy-brids—erect, deciduous shrubs to 12 feet tall with star-shaped, late-spring blossoms; 'Randy' has flowers that are white inside, purple-tinged outside; 'Ricky', deep red-purple flowers tinted white to purple inside. *M.* x *loebneri*—shrub or small tree 30 feet tall and as wide or wider; 'Merrill' produces profuse, fragrant white flowers 3 inches across in spring; 'Leonard Messel', pink flowers. *M.* x 'Nimbus'—hardy tree to 30 feet with fragrant, 6-inch ivory flowers. *M.* x *soulangiana* (saucer magnolia)—deciduous shrub or small tree to 30 feet with dark green leaves, maturing to pyramidal or rounded form; 'Brozzonii' has 10-inch, white late-spring flowers tinged purple; 'Rustica Rubra', 5½-inch cup-shaped flowers that are white inside,

Magnolia Kosar de Vos Hybrids 'Ricky'

rosy red on the outside; 'Verbanica', late-spring, rose-tinted flowers with straplike petals. *M. stellata* 'Centennial' (star magnolia)—fragrant, pink-tinged white flowers 4 inches across with straplike petals on deciduous shrub or small tree to 20 feet tall and half as wide. *M. virginiana* (sweet bay magnolia)—deciduous shrub to 20 feet tall and as wide in the North, pyramidal tree to 60 feet in the South, with lemon-scented, 3-inch white flowers from spring through summer.

Growing conditions and maintenance: Plant magnolias in soil enriched with organic matter. Allow room for the spread of mature shrubs or trees and avoid compacting soil in root zone. If necessary, prune to shape plants after flowers fade. Propagate from seed or cuttings.

Mahonia
(ma-HO-nee-a)
HOLLY GRAPE

Mahonia bealei

Hardiness:	*Zones 5-8*
Plant type:	*shrub or ground cover*
Height:	*10 inches to 12 feet*
Interest:	*foliage, flowers*
Soil:	*moist, well-drained, acid*
Light:	*light shade*

Mahonia's glossy, scalloped, spiny leaflets resemble those of some hollies. The crisp evergreen foliage gives plants a coarse texture. Showy clusters of 1- to 3-inch flowers bloom in very early spring, followed in fall by fleshy, deep blue fruits.

Selected species and varieties: *M. aquifolium* (mountain grape, holly barberry)—lustrous 1- to 2½-inch leaflets that color bronze in fall on shrubs to 6 feet tall and almost as wide with grapelike berries. *M. bealei* (leatherleaf mahonia)—5-inch leaflets, bluish green above and gray-green underneath, on shrubs to 12 feet tall. *M. repens* (creeping mahonia)—blue-green leaflets turning purple in fall on spreading plants 10 inches high.

Growing conditions and maintenance: Plant mahonia in soil that has been enriched with organic matter. Propagate by digging and replanting suckers growing from the roots.

Malus
(MAY-lus)
FLOWERING CRAB APPLE

Malus 'Callaway'

Hardiness:	*Zones 4-9*
Plant type:	*tree or shrub*
Height:	*6 to 25 feet*
Interest:	*flowers, foliage, fruit*
Soil:	*moist, well-drained, acid*
Light:	*full sun*

Buds open into a froth of spring blossoms that cover the branches of flowering crab apples even before leaves appear. Small fruits less than 2 inches across follow in fall. Flowering crab apples are excellent specimen trees.

Selected species and varieties: *M.* 'Callaway'—1½-inch white flowers and maroon fruit on round trees to 25 feet tall. *M.* 'Donald Wyman'—1¾-inch white flowers and red fruit on trees 20 feet tall and as wide or wider. *M.* 'Katherine'—2-inch pink double-petaled flowers fading to white and yellow fruit on round trees to 20 feet. *M.* 'Prince Georges'—fragrant double-petaled 2-inch pink flowers on nonfruiting, round trees to 20 feet. *M. sargentii* (Sargent crab apple)—spreading shrub to 15 feet tall and twice as wide with 1-inch white flowers and red fruit.

Growing conditions and maintenance: Flowering crab apples tolerate a wide range of soil conditions. Prune plants lightly while young to establish desired shape and remove suckers. Pruning should be done immediately after they flower. Propagate from cuttings.

Miscanthus
(mis-KAN-thus)
EULALIA

Miscanthus sinensis 'Zebrinus'

Hardiness: *Zones 5-9*

Plant type: *ornamental grass or perennial*

Height: *3 to 10 feet*

Interest: *leaves, flowers*

Soil: *well-drained*

Light: *full sun*

Miscanthus forms graceful clumps of narrow, arching leaves surmounted by tall flower stalks. Fans of minute flowers along drooping stems remain effective as specimens or backdrops throughout fall and winter.

Selected species and varieties: *M. sinensis* (Chinese silver grass)—clumps of tapering ⅜-inch-wide leaves to 4 feet tall and flower stalks to 10 feet; 'Malepartus' has pinkish summer plumes silvering as they age and bronze fall foliage; 'Morning Light', white-striped leaves and reddish bronze fall flowers on stalks to 6 feet; 'Purpurascens' turns red-orange in fall; 'Variegatus' has wide white-striped leaves; 'Yaku Jima' is an 18-inch dwarf; 'Zebrinus' has leaves banded horizontally with yellow.

Growing conditions and maintenance: Plant Chinese silver grass clumps 3 feet apart in any well-drained soil. Cut old foliage back to 6 inches in early spring, before new growth emerges. Propagate by division in spring.

Myosotis
(my-oh-SO-tis)
FORGET-ME-NOT

Myosotis sylvatica 'Blue Bird'

Hardiness: *hardy or Zones 3-8*

Plant type: *annual, biennial, or perennial*

Height: *8 to 12 inches*

Interest: *flowers, foliage*

Soil: *moist, well-drained*

Light: *partial shade to full sun*

Airy clusters of dainty flowers with prominent eyes open above forget-me-not's low mounds of delicate foliage. Forget-me-nots provide a soft filler or a delicate border edging.

Selected species and varieties: *M. sylvatica* (woodland or garden forget-me-not)—8- to 10-inch-tall stems in clumps almost as wide lined with soft, elongated leaves and tipped with ¼-inch blue flowers with large yellow centers from spring through summer; 'Blue Bird' has bright blue flowers on 1-foot plants; 'Royal Blue', very early deep indigo blossoms on 1-foot plants; 'Victoria Mixed', white, blue, rose, and pink flowers on compact 8-inch plants.

Growing conditions and maintenance: Plant forget-me-nots in soil enriched with organic matter. Though an annual, *M. sylvatica* self-sows prolifically to perform like a perennial. Sow seed from late summer through fall to bloom the following spring.

Nandina
(nan-DEE-na)
HEAVENLY BAMBOO

Nandina domestica 'Moyers Red'

Hardiness: *Zones 6-9*

Plant type: *shrub*

Height: *1 to 8 feet*

Interest: *foliage, berries*

Soil: *moist, well-drained*

Light: *full sun to light shade*

Heavenly bamboo's tall clumps of erect canes are lined with evergreen leaflets often colored attractively in fall and winter. Large clusters of spring-blooming flowers are followed by heavy clusters of bright red berries that decorate the clumps throughout winter. Use heavenly bamboo as a winter accent among other evergreens and under deciduous shade trees.

Selected species and varieties: *N. domestica* (sacred bamboo)—clumps of canes 2 feet wide and up to 8 feet tall with leaflets up to 20 inches long and 1-foot-long clusters of white spring flowers; 'Harbour Dwarf' grows in graceful clumps 3 feet tall and as wide or wider; 'Moyers Red' has glossy leaves turning reddish purple through winter.

Growing conditions and maintenance: Plant heavenly bamboo in sites sheltered from drying winds. Cut older canes back to produce thicker shrubs. Propagate by transplanting tiny plants from around self-seeding parent.

Narcissus
(nar-SIS-us)
DAFFODIL

Narcissus 'Dutch Master'

Hardiness: *Zones 3-8*

Plant type: *bulb*

Height: *6 inches to 2 feet*

Interest: *flowers*

Soil: *well-drained*

Light: *full sun to light shade*

A symbol of spring, daffodils rise singly or in clusters on thick stems from arching clumps of narrow leaves. Each flower's cup or corona is surrounded by a ruff of petal-like segments or perianth. They make bright accents in a border, where other plants will fill in as their foliage fades. Narcissus are also ideal for naturalizing.

Selected species and varieties: Trumpet daffodils—single flowers with cups as long as or longer than the perianth; 'Beersheba' has pure white flowers on 14-inch stems; 'Dutch Master', large yellow cups cradled in a perianth sweeping slightly forward on 15-inch stems; 'Lunar Sea', white cups surrounded by a yellow perianth on 18-inch stems; 'Mount Hood', creamy white flowers tinged slightly yellow. Large-cupped daffodils—single flowers with shorter cups; 'Carlton' produces pure golden yellow flowers with large cups; 'Flower Record', red-rimmed orange cups and white perianths; 'Ice Follies', lemon yellow cups fading to white and white perianths. Double daffodils—one or more flowers per stem with doubled, ruffled, and frilled cups or perianths; 'Cheerfulness' produces white flowers; 'Yellow Cheerfulness', fragrant yellow flowers touched with orange at their centers; 'White Lion', heavily doubled white fragrant flowers resembling small gardenias, with a few yellow petals at the center. *N. bulbocodium* var. *conspicuus* (hoop-petticoat daffodil)—large funnel-shaped yellow cups. *N. cyclamineus*—large cups surrounded by a backswept perianth; 'February Gold' produces pure yellow blooms. *N. jonquilla* (jonquil)—clusters of very fragrant flowers; 'Trevithian' grows 2 to 4 fragrant flowers with shallow golden cups and lemon yellow perianths on 18-inch stems. *N. poeticus* 'Actaea' (pheasant's-

Narcissus 'Ice Follies'

eye narcissus)—tiny golden cups rimmed with red and a white perianth. *N. tazetta* 'Geranium' (polyanthus narcissus, bunch-flowered narcissus)—clusters of fragrant flowers with very small, ruffled orange cups and white perianths. *N.* 'Tête-à-Tête'—1 to 3 golden yellow blossoms on each 6-inch stem.

Growing conditions and maintenance: Plant narcissus in porous soil enriched with organic matter, setting bulbs out in fall at a depth one and a half times their height. After flowering, allow leaves to fade before trimming back. Narcissus can be left undisturbed for years. Propagate by digging and dividing bulb clumps.

Nepeta
(NEP-e-ta)
CATMINT

Nepeta mussinii 'Blue Wonder'

Hardiness: *Zones 3-9*

Plant type: *perennial*

Height: *1 to 3 feet*

Interest: *foliage, flowers*

Soil: *well-drained*

Light: *full sun*

Catmint forms loose cushions of fragrant stems lined with soft, oval, pointed leaves and tipped with spikes of tiny white, mauve, or blue flower whorls that form a haze of color above the foliage. The plant is effective massed as a dense ground cover.

Selected species and varieties: *N.* x *faassenii* (blue catmint)—18- to 36-inch-high mounds of silvery gray foliage with lavender-blue spring-to-summer-blooming flowers; 'Six Hills Giant' grows taller and is more robust than the species. *N. mussinii* (Persian catmint)—sprawling 1-foot-high mounds with lavender summer flowers; 'Blue Wonder' has deep blue blossoms on compact plants to 15 inches.

Growing conditions and maintenance: Plant catmint 1 to 1½ feet apart in any well-drained soil. It can be invasive. Shearing plants after flowering may produce a second season of bloom. Propagate blue catmint from cuttings, Persian catmint from seed, either species by division.

Nicotiana
(ni-ko-she-AN-a)
FLOWERING TOBACCO

Nicotiana alata 'Lime Green'

Hardiness: *tender*

Plant type: *annual*

Height: *1 to 6 feet*

Interest: *flowers, foliage*

Soil: *moist, well-drained*

Light: *full sun to partial shade*

Flowering tobacco produces coarse clumps of large, sticky leaves useful as a border filler or specimen. Loose clusters of fragrant, flat-faced flowers with extremely elongated tubular throats grow at the tips of soft stems. Flowers of some varieties close in sunlight but open on cloudy days or in the evening. Leaf juices are poisonous.

Selected species and varieties: *N. alata* (jasmine tobacco)—1- to 2-foot-tall clumps with flowers that bloom from spring to fall above 4- to 10-inch leaves; 'Domino' series has compact cushions of foliage to 15 inches and early-spring flowers in mixed colors; 'Lime Green' has whitish green summer-to-fall flowers on 18-inch plants. *N. langsdorfii*—nodding green flowers with turquoise anthers at the tips of stems to 5 feet. *N. sylvestris* (woodland tobacco)—drooping white flowers tinged pink or purple on branching plants 3 to 6 feet tall with 1-foot leaves.

Growing conditions and maintenance: Plant nicotiana in ordinary soil. Remove dead flower stalks in midsummer for further bloom. Propagate from seed.

Onopordum
(o-no-POR-dum)
SCOTCH THISTLE

Onopordum acanthium

Hardiness: *hardy*

Plant type: *annual or biennial*

Height: *6 to 8 feet*

Interest: *flowers, foliage*

Soil: *well-drained to dry*

Light: *full sun*

Scotch thistle produces fuzzy, globular flower heads on tall, stiffly erect branching stems lined with spiny, gray-green leaves. The unusual flowers and foliage add both color and texture as vertical accents in a border.

Selected species and varieties: *O. acanthium* (cotton thistle, silver thistle)—stiff, downy leaves to 2 feet long, deeply lobed and scalloped into spiny segments on branching stems 6 to 9 feet tall tipped in late spring to summer with round, prickly, purple-to-white flowers that have flat, fuzzy tops up to 2 inches in diameter.

Growing conditions and maintenance: Scotch thistle thrives in hot, dry locations. Propagate from seed; plants also self-sow for a display the following year.

Oxydendrum
(ok-si-DEN-drum)
SOURWOOD

Oxydendrum arboreum

Hardiness: *Zones 5-9*

Plant type: *tree*

Height: *15 to 30 feet*

Interest: *foliage, flowers, bark, seeds*

Soil: *moist, well-drained, acid*

Light: *full sun to light shade*

Sourwood provides four seasons of interest as a specimen tree. Its young spring leaves are tinted bronze, turn glossy green in summer, then brilliant red in fall. Clusters of summer flowers cover the tree like a haze; these are followed by feathery fans of narrow, pointed seed capsules that persist through the winter, when leaves fall to reveal deeply furrowed gray-brown-to-black blocky bark.

Selected species and varieties: *O. arboreum* (lily-of-the-valley tree, titi)—pyramidal tree to 30 feet tall and about half as wide, with lustrous, oval, pointed leaves 5 to 8 inches long and drooping 10-inch clusters of small, creamy white flower bells in summer.

Growing conditions and maintenance: Plant sourwood in soil that is rich in organic matter. Trees will flourish in light shade but flowering may be diminished. Mulch to protect shallow roots. Propagate from seed.

Paeonia
(pee-O-nee-a)
PEONY

Paeonia 'Gay Paree'

Hardiness: *Zones 3-8*

Plant type: *perennial*

Height: *3 feet*

Interest: *flowers, foliage*

Soil: *moist, well-drained, fertile*

Light: *full sun to light shade*

Sweetly fragrant peonies decorate a border in spring or early summer with enormous, showy blossoms up to 10 inches across. Peonies have been extensively hybridized into several forms: single peonies with a single row of petals encircling centers with fluffy golden stamens; Japanese peonies with single or double rows of petals surrounding centers filled with modified stamens that look like finely cut petals; semidouble and double peonies with large outer petals framing a fluffy pompom of frilled and ruffled inner petals. The flowers tip the ends of branching 3-foot-tall stems lined with broad, lobed leaves that remain attractive into fall.

Selected species and varieties: Single peonies—'Bowl of Beauty' has creamy centers surrounded by pink petals; 'Illini Warrior', rugged red flowers; 'Krinkled White', crepey white petals; 'President Lincoln', dark red blooms; 'Sea Shell', clear, bright pink blossoms. Japanese peonies—'Bu-te' produces pure white flowers; 'Isani-Gidui', white flowers with buff centers; 'Gay Paree', pink petals surrounding a white center; 'Mrs. Wilder

Bancroft', deep red petals; 'Sword Dance', dark red flowers with fluffy yellow centers. Double peonies—'Elsa Sass' has pure white petals; 'Festiva Maxima', white-streaked red blooms; 'Raspberry Sundae', light pink flowers with deep pink centers; 'Nick Shaylor', very pale pink flowers touched with red; 'Dinner Plate', shell pink blooms; 'Mrs. Franklin D. Roosevelt', rosy pink flowers fading to white; 'Vivid Rose', bright rose pink petals; 'Kansas', bright red flowers; 'Bonanza', rich reddish pink blooms.

Growing conditions and maintenance: Plant peonies in full sun in soil enriched with organic matter. Light shade pre-

Paeonia 'Bowl of Beauty'

vents delicate pastels from fading, but deep shade inhibits flowering. Propagate by dividing the thick, tuberous roots, setting the buds or eyes along the roots 1 inch deep in the soil.

Panicum
(PAN-i-kum)
PANIC GRASS

Panicum virgatum 'Heavy Metal'

Hardiness: *Zones 5-9*

Plant type: *ornamental grass*

Height: *3 to 6 feet*

Interest: *foliage, flowers*

Soil: *moist, well-drained*

Light: *full sun*

Branching stalks up to 6 feet tall bearing feathery clusters of tiny buff flowers rise from panicum's 3-foot-high clumps of arching, attractively colored leaves in fall. The seed heads that follow remain attractive through winter. Use panicum as a specimen or filler or at the edge of a woodland garden.

Selected species and varieties: *P. virgatum* (switch grass)—loose, open flower clusters above green leaves coloring yellow and red in fall before fading to winter brown; 'Haense Herms' has red summer foliage lasting until frost and grayish dried seed heads on 3- to 3½-foot stalks; 'Heavy Metal', 3- to 4-foot flower stalks above stiff, deep blue leaves that color yellow in fall; 'Strictum' has blue-green, more-erect foliage.

Growing conditions and maintenance: Switch grass thrives in moist soil but will tolerate much drier conditions, even drought, though it will spread more slowly. It will also tolerate salt spray and seaside conditions. Cut it back nearly to ground level in early spring, before new growth begins. Propagate by division.

Papaver
(pa-PAY-ver)
POPPY

Papaver nudicaule 'Oregon Rainbows'

Hardiness: *Zones 3-7*

Plant type: *perennial*

Height: *15 inches to 4 feet*

Interest: *flowers*

Soil: *well-drained*

Light: *full sun to light shade*

Poppy's showy spring flowers surround prominent centers above clumps of coarse, hairy, deeply lobed leaves.

Selected species and varieties: *P. nudicaule* (Iceland poppy, Arctic poppy)—short-lived perennial with a single row of white, yellow, orange, salmon, or pink petals; 'Oregon Rainbows' produces often bi- or tricolored flowers on 20-inch-tall stems; 'Sparkling Bubbles' grows in colors from pastels through rose or scarlet on 15-inch stems. *P. orientale* (Oriental poppy)—double rows of ruffled petals around black stamens on stems to 4 feet; 'Helen Elizabeth' produces salmon pink flowers; 'Doubloon', orange flowers; 'Glowing Rose', watermelon red blooms; 'Harvest Moon', 10-inch yellow-orange flowers; 'Pinnacle', ruffled red-and-white blooms; 'Warlord', red flowers.

Growing conditions and maintenance: Grow poppies 1½ feet apart in soil that is free from excess winter moisture. Since foliage dies back after flowering, plant poppies among leafy perennials that will fill the resulting void. Propagate *P. orientale* from seed or root cuttings. *P. nudicaule* will flower from seed the first year.

Parrotia
(pa-ROTE-ee-a)
IRONWOOD

Parrotia persica

Hardiness: *Zones 4-8*

Plant type: *shrub or tree*

Height: *20 to 40 feet*

Interest: *foliage, bark*

Soil: *well-drained*

Light: *full sun*

Parrotia's trunk and horizontal branches are covered with flaky bark that peels away to give the plant an attractive, mottled green-gray-and-brown texture. Tiny, inconspicuous flowers with red stamens bloom along young branches before the leaves emerge in spring. The oval foliage colors attractively in fall. Use parrotia as a specimen tree or part of a shrub border.

Selected species and varieties: *P. persica* (Persian parrotia)—grows to 30 feet tall with a spread as wide or wider and with 3- to 4-inch-long lustrous green leaves in brilliant shades of yellow and orange turning rosy pink and scarlet in fall.

Growing conditions and maintenance: Plant Persian parrotia in slightly acidic soil, leaving space for its mature spread. Allow young plants to develop as multi-stemmed shrubs or prune to a single trunk. Propagate from seed or cuttings.

Pennisetum
(pen-i-SEE-tum)
FOUNTAIN GRASS

Pennisetum setaceum 'Rubrum'

Hardiness: *Zones 5-9 or tender*

Plant type: *perennial or annual*

Height: *2 to 4 feet*

Interest: *foliage, flowers*

Soil: *moist, well-drained*

Light: *full sun*

Perennial and annual fountain grasses produce narrow spikes of tiny, bristly summer flowers above dense mounds of arching leaves. The flowers last through fall, and the leaf clumps of perennial fountain grass remain effective through winter. Use fountain grass as a border specimen or massed as a backdrop.

Selected species and varieties: *P. alopecuroides* (perennial or Chinese fountain grass)—rosy silver flowers in 5- to 7-inch spikes above leaf mounds 3 to 4 feet tall and as wide; 'Hameln' is a fine-textured 2-foot dwarf. *P. setaceum* (annual fountain grass)—nodding foot-long flower spikes in shades of pink to purple above leaf mounds 2 to 4 feet tall and as wide until frost; 'Rubrum' has burgundy leaves and deep purple flowers.

Growing conditions and maintenance: Plant fountain grass 2 to 3 feet apart. Cut back to 6 inches before growth begins in spring. Propagate either species from seed, cultivars by division of clumps in the spring.

Perovskia
(per-OV-skee-a)
RUSSIAN SAGE

Perovskia atriplicifolia

Petunia
(pe-TOO-nee-a)
PETUNIA

Petunia x hybrida

Phlox
(flox)
PHLOX

Phlox divaricata 'Fuller's White'

Hardiness: *Zones 5-9*

Plant type: *perennial*

Height: *3 to 4 feet*

Interest: *foliage, flowers*

Soil: *well-drained*

Light: *full sun*

Russian sage's mounds of fine-textured, aromatic gray foliage are an effective filler in the border and remain attractive through winter. In summer, spires of tiny flowers tip each stem.

Selected species and varieties: *P. atriplicifolia* (azure sage)—tiny lavender flowers spaced along 12-inch flower spikes above downy gray, finely divided leaves on clumps of woody stems to 4 feet tall and as wide.

Growing conditions and maintenance: Plant Russian sage in soil that is not overly rich. Cut woody stems back in spring before new growth begins. Propagate from seed or cuttings.

Hardiness: *half-hardy*

Plant type: *annual*

Height: *8 to 18 inches*

Interest: *flowers*

Soil: *well-drained*

Light: *full sun*

Open flower trumpets bloom in profusion from summer to frost along petunias' trailing or upright stems amid small, hairy, pointed leaves. Petunias are effective cascading over walls or banks or when massed as bedding plants.

Selected species and varieties: *P. x hybrida* (common garden petunia)—blossoms from white through yellow to pink, red, purple, blue-purple, and lavender, often speckled, splotched, veined, or striped in a contrasting color on compact, bushy or trailing plants; grandifloras have flowers up to 6 inches across, sometimes ruffled, fringed, or deeply veined, on bushy plants or trailing stems to 18 inches; multifloras have copious 2- to 3-inch blossoms with smooth-edged petals on compact plants.

Growing conditions and maintenance: Grow petunias from seed, starting indoors 10 to 12 weeks before the last frost date. Pinch to develop bushy plants; remove dead blooms to encourage further flowering.

Hardiness: *Zones 3-9*

Plant type: *perennial*

Height: *6 inches to 4 feet*

Interest: *flowers, foliage*

Soil: *moist, well-drained*

Light: *full sun to full shade*

Clusters of dainty flowers cover phlox's mounds or mats of soft foliage in spring, summer, or fall. Taller species are suitable for fillers or massing; shorter species spread into ground-covering mats.

Selected species and varieties: *P. divaricata* (wild blue phlox)—plants to 15 inches tall with spring-to-summer-blooming flowers; 'Fuller's White' has prolific creamy white blooms. *P. maculata* (wild sweet William)—3-foot plants with fragrant, conical, summer-to-fall clusters; 'Alpha' has rosy pink flowers with darker centers. *P. paniculata* (summer phlox)—4-foot stems tipped with flower clusters to 8 inches wide in summer and fall; 'Fairest One' has salmon petals and white centers. *P. stolonifera* (creeping phlox)—ground-covering mats with 6- to 12-inch flower stems in spring and summer.

Growing conditions and maintenance: Space low-growing phlox varieties 12 to 18 inches apart, taller ones up to 2 feet apart. *P. divaricata* grows well in moist, shady spots. *P. maculata* and *P. paniculata* prefer full sun, with ample moisture. *P. stolonifera* grows in any light. Propagate by division or from cuttings.

Phormium
(FOR-mee-um)
FLAX LILY

Phormium tenax

Hardiness: *Zones 9-10*

Plant type: *perennial*

Height: *7 to 15 feet*

Interest: *foliage, flowers*

Soil: *moist, well-drained*

Light: *full sun*

Dramatic fans of stiff, evergreen leaves, sometimes split at their ends or edged with red, make phormium a bold specimen or an effective screen. Tall flower stalks lined with dull red 2-inch flowers rise above the foliage.

Selected species and varieties: *P. tenax* (New Zealand flax)—leathery leaves 6 to 10 feet tall with flower stalks to 15 feet; 'Atropurpureum' produces rich purple leaves; 'Bronze', deep red-brown leaves; 'Maori Sunrise', bronze leaves striped pink and cream; 'Tiny Tim' is a semi-dwarf cultivar with yellow-striped bronze leaves; 'Variegatum' has creamy white striping on green leaves.

Growing conditions and maintenance: Plant New Zealand flax in soil enriched with organic matter. Plants tolerate seaside conditions and pollution. Propagate from seed or by division.

Pieris
(PYE-er-is)
PIERIS

Pieris japonica 'Valley Valentine'

Hardiness: *Zones 5-8*

Plant type: *shrub*

Height: *2 to 12 feet*

Interest: *flowers, foliage*

Soil: *moist, well-drained, acid*

Light: *full sun to light shade*

An evergreen shrub with glossy, oval, pointed leaves and clusters of tiny urn-shaped early spring flowers, pieris extends the season of bloom in a shrub border or provides a year-round backdrop for a perennial garden.

Selected species and varieties: *P. floribunda* (fetterbush, mountain pieris)—rounded shrubs 2 to 6 feet tall and as wide or wider with 4-inch, upright flower clusters. *P. japonica* (lily-of-the-valley bush, Japanese pieris)—upright shrubs to 12 feet with drooping flower clusters to 6 inches; 'Dorothy Wyckoff' has red buds opening into pink flowers; 'Flamingo', deep rose flowers; 'Valley Rose', pastel pink blossoms; 'Valley Valentine', maroon buds opening into rose pink clusters; 'White Cascade', long-lasting white flowers.

Growing conditions and maintenance: Plant pieris in soil enriched with organic matter. Protect from heavy winds. Propagate from seed or cuttings.

Platycodon
(plat-i-KO-don)
BALLOON FLOWER

Platycodon grandiflorus var. mariesii

Hardiness: *Zones 3-8*

Plant type: *perennial*

Height: *10 inches to 3 feet*

Interest: *flowers*

Soil: *well-drained*

Light: *full sun to light shade*

Balloon flower gets it name from the round flower buds that open into shallow saucer-shaped flowers 2 to 3 inches across with translucent, pointed petals. The blue, white, or pink summer-blooming blossoms tip erect stems growing in narrow clumps. Use balloon flowers as accents among lower-growing border plants or massed for a showy display.

Selected species and varieties: *P. grandiflorus* (Japanese bellflower)—2- to 3-foot stems lined with oval, toothed leaves up to 3 inches long in erect clumps; 'Apoyama' is a dwarf only 10 inches tall with blue-violet flowers; *P. g.* var. *mariesii* [sometimes designated a cultivar, 'Mariesii'] has bright blue flowers on compact 18-inch plants; 'Shell Pink', pastel pink flowers.

Growing conditions and maintenance: Plant balloon flowers 18 inches apart in nonboggy, slightly acid soil. Propagate from seed or by division.

Prunus
(PROO-nus)
CHERRY

Prunus subhirtella var. pendula

Hardiness: *Zones 3-9*

Plant type: *shrub or tree*

Height: *10 to 50 feet*

Interest: *flowers, fruit*

Soil: *well-drained*

Light: *full sun to moderate shade*

A froth of small blossoms decorates prunus in spring, followed by brightly colored summer-to-fall fruits. The foliage colors attractively in fall. Use prunus as a specimen tree or as a shady overstory for a section of the border.

Selected species and varieties: *P. cerasifera* 'Newport' (cherry plum, myrobalan plum)—palest pink flowers followed by inch-wide purple fruits on shrubby trees to 30 feet tall with purple leaves. *P. x* 'Hally Jolivette'—rounded trees to 15 feet with pink buds opening to double white flowers. *P. laurocerasus* (common cherry laurel, English laurel)—spreading evergreen shrub to 10 feet with fragrant white flowers. *P. maackii* (Manchurian cherry, Amur chokecherry)—rounded tree to 45 feet with yellow-brown bark peeling to cinnamon and elongated clusters of white flowers followed by red fruits maturing to black. *P. x* 'Okame'—handsome reddish pink flowers on hardy trees to 30 feet. *P. sargentii* (Sargent cherry)—clusters of clear pink flowers followed by tiny purple-black fruits on trees to 50 feet with lustrous green leaves coloring bronze in fall.

P. serrulata (Japanese flowering cherry)—round or vase-shaped trees to 25 feet with single or double flowers in clusters and glossy leaves coloring bronze in fall; 'Amanogawa' has fragrant pink flowers on trees only 4 to 5 feet wide; 'Kwanzan', a profusion of double pink flowers; 'Shirofugen', heavily double pink flowers maturing to white and leaves bronzy when young. *P. subhirtella* var. *pendula* (weeping Higan cherry)—gracefully drooping branches on trees to 40 feet with pink flowers; var. *autumnalis* has semidouble pink flowers, occasional blossoms opening in fall. *P. x yedoensis* (yoshino cherry)—flat-topped trees to 40 feet with pinkish white flowers.

Growing conditions and maintenance: *P. laurocerasus* prefers soil rich in organic matter but should not be overfertilized. It is less cold tolerant than other

Prunus x yedoensis

species but will stand up to wind and salt spray, will grow in light shade, and takes pruning well. *P. sargentii* and *P. x* 'Hally Jolivette' do best in full sun. Propagate from seed or cuttings.

Pulmonaria
(pul-mo-NAY-ree-a)
LUNGWORT

Pulmonaria saccharata 'Sissinghurst White'

Hardiness: *Zones 3-8*

Plant type: *perennial*

Height: *8 to 18 inches*

Interest: *flowers, foliage*

Soil: *well-drained*

Light: *light to full shade*

Pulmonaria's clusters of spring flower trumpets nod at the tops of stems rising from clumps of broadly oval, hairy leaves spreading twice their height. They are effective when massed as a coarse ground cover or used as accent specimens.

Selected species and varieties: *P. angustifolia* (blue lungwort)—½-inch blue flower trumpets on 12-inch-tall stems in spring; ssp. *azurea* has sky blue blossoms. *P. saccharata* (Bethlehem sage)—pink flowers aging to blue on 18-inch stems above leaves mottled green and white; 'Janet Fiske' produces leaves marbled almost to white; 'Margery Fish', very large silvery leaf spots; 'Mrs. Moon', subdued silvery white leaf spots; 'Sissinghurst White', white flowers above speckled leaves.

Growing conditions and maintenance: Plant lungwort 1 to 1½ feet apart. Can be grown in sun but looks poor by midsummer. Propagate by division in fall.

145

Pyracantha
(py-ra-KAN-tha)
FIRETHORN

Pyracantha coccinea 'Mohave'

Hardiness: *Zones 6-9*

Plant type: *shrub*

Height: *2 to 16 feet*

Interest: *foliage, flowers, berries*

Soil: *well-drained*

Light: *full sun*

Firethorn's shiny, dark brown branches are lined with ½-inch thorns and evergreen or semi-evergreen leaves. Clusters of tiny white spring flowers are followed by bright berries. Use massed as informal hedges, or espaliered against walls or trellises.

Selected species and varieties: *P. coccinea* (scarlet firethorn)—1- to 1½-inch oval leaves and red-orange fall berries; 'Apache' grows bright red berries on shrubs to 5 feet tall and as wide or wider; 'Mohave' is a cold-hardy, heavily berried, evergreen shrub to 12 feet tall and as wide; 'Navajo' has red-orange fruit on dense, 6-foot-round mounds of branches; 'Teton' grows narrow columns of branches 16 feet tall and half as wide with yellow-orange berries.

Growing conditions and maintenance: Firethorns can grow in light shade but flower much less. Prune anytime to shape plants. Propagate from seed or cuttings.

Rhododendron
(roh-doh-DEN-dron)
RHODODENDRON

Rhododendron catawbiense 'Nova Zembla'

Hardiness: *Zones 4-8*

Plant type: *shrub*

Height: *3 to 12 feet*

Interest: *foliage, flowers*

Soil: *moist, well-drained, acid*

Light: *light shade to full sun*

Though the division is not hard-and-fast, azaleas are generally small-leaved, deciduous or sometimes evergreen shrubs with funnel-shaped flowers, while rhododendrons have whorls of large, leathery, oval, evergreen leaves with woolly undersides and trusses of bell-shaped flowers. Both have been extensively hybridized so that cultivars are available in a rainbow of colors. Mainstays in shrub borders, useful as an understory beneath tall conifers or hardwoods at the edge of a woodland, and attractive as specimens, both kinds of plants are beloved for their showy spring flowers. Small azaleas and dwarf rhododendrons also make good border fillers and informal edgings. Singly, in clusters, or in domed trusses, flowers with tissue-thin petals cover shrubs in profusion.

Selected species and varieties: *R. carolinianum* (Carolina rhododendron)—hardy, low-growing evergreen to 6 feet; 'Album' has white flowers; 'Luteum', yellow flowers. *R. catawbiense* (mountain rosebay, Catawba rhododendron)—dense evergreen foliage on extremely hardy shrubs 6 to 10 feet tall

and almost as wide with cultivars, including dwarfs and semidwarfs, that flower in almost every color but orange; 'Ironclad Hybrids' are extremely cold hardy; 'Nova Zembla' is also very cold hardy and produces red flowers. *R.* Dexter Hybrids—fine-textured evergreen rhododendrons with very large, often fragrant, ruffled, frilled, and spotted flowers. *R.* Exbury Azaleas and *R.* Knap Hill Azaleas—deciduous shrubs in upright columns to 12 feet with foliage coloring yellow, orange,

Rhododendron Knap Hill 'Peach Sunset'

and red in fall. *R.* Ghent Azaleas—extremely cold-hardy, deciduous upright shrubs. *R.* Glenn Dale Azaleas—cold-hardy evergreens in compact mounding to tall and rangy forms. *R.* Kurume Azaleas—handsome mounding shrubs to 5 feet with fine-textured evergreen foliage. *R.* North Tisbury Azaleas—low-growing, spreading evergreen azaleas excellent for ground covers and sometimes blooming into summer. *R. yakusimanum* (Yakushima rhododendron)—white to pink flower trusses on sun-tolerant mounds to 4 feet, with handsome curving leaves; cold-hardy cultivars are available.

Growing conditions and maintenance: Plant azaleas and rhododendrons in shady sites protected from winter winds in soil enriched with organic matter. Propagate species from seeds, hybrids from cuttings.

Ricinus (RISS-in-us) **CASTOR-OIL PLANT**	*Rodgersia* (ro-JER-zee-a) **RODGERSIA**	*Rosa* (RO-za) **ROSE**

Ricinus communis 'Carmencita'

Rodgersia podophylla

Rosa hybrid tea rose 'Chicago Peace'

Hardiness: *tender*
Plant type: *annual*
Height: *8 to 10 feet*
Interest: *foliage*
Soil: *well-drained*
Light: *full sun*

Hardiness: *Zones 5-7*
Plant type: *perennial*
Height: *3 to 6 feet*
Interest: *flowers, foliage*
Soil: *boggy loam*
Light: *full sun to light shade*

Hardiness: *Zones 2-10*
Plant type: *shrub*
Height: *3 inches to 20 feet*
Interest: *flowers*
Soil: *well-drained*
Light: *full sun*

Ricinus's clumps of large, glossy leaves make an effective, coarse-textured backdrop in sunny borders and, because the plants grow rapidly, they are also used as screens. The insignificant flowers are followed by prickly husks filled with tiny brown seeds. These are extremely poisonous, especially to children, who find them attractive. Thus, care must be taken to locate ricinus plants appropriately.

Selected species and varieties: *R. communis* (castor bean)—broad leaves, emerging red tinged and turning glossy green until frost, up to 3 feet across with narrow, pointed leaflets on plants to 10 feet tall and 3 or 4 feet wide; 'Carmencita' has early-blooming bright red flowers and deep brown leaves.

Growing conditions and maintenance: Plant ricinus in loose, fertile soil. Provide ample water and fertilizer. Propagate from seed, sowing indoors 6 to 8 weeks before the last frost. Plants grow best in hot, humid climates; they may survive as perennials in warm climates.

Rodgersia's large leaves make them dramatic foliage plants and excellent fillers massed in marshy bog or woodland gardens. In summer, huge frothy pyramids of flowers rise on stout stalks followed by reddish seeds in fall.

Selected species and varieties: *R. aesculifolia* (fingerleaf rodgersia)—clumps to 5 feet across of 1-foot-wide leaves formed of leaflets arranged like fingers and creamy 2-foot flower clusters on 5-foot-tall stalks. *R. pinnata* 'Superba'—pink flowers in 10-inch clusters above bronze-tinged foliage on plants to 4 feet tall and as wide. *R. podophylla*—bronze-green, 1-foot-wide leaves shaped like a duck's foot and creamy white flowers on 3-foot stalks. *R. tabularis* (shieldleaf rodgersia)—round leaves up to 3 feet across with scalloped edges and white flower clusters on 4-foot stalks.

Growing conditions and maintenance: Plant rodgersia 3 feet apart in constantly moist soil, as at the edge of a stream or pond. Propagate by division in spring.

Roses offer limitless choices for landscaping, from formal gardens to informal rock garden or border plantings. They can be cultivated as specimens, massed as hedges, pegged as ground covers, or trained against fences and trellises. Velvety petals surround fluffy stamens in flat single rows, in double-petaled cups, or in overlapping rows that create rounded forms, rosettes, and pompoms. The often fragrant flowers bloom singly or in clusters on arching or stiff woody stems lined with small thorns, sometimes appearing in a single flush, sometimes one at a time from summer through fall. Roses are extensively hybridized, and cultivars bloom in almost every color of the rainbow.

Selected species and varieties: Bush roses—large-flowered varieties [also called hybrid tea roses] blooming singly over the season on 2- to 6-foot-tall shrubs; cluster-flowered roses [also called floribunda roses] have small clusters of blossoms blooming over the season on plants to 10 feet. Shrub roses—English roses with large flowers in old-fashioned rosettes on plants to 8 feet; hybrid musk roses have heavily fragrant, almost everblooming clusters on shrubs to 8 feet; hybrid rugosa roses, single- or double-petaled fragrant flowers on arching canes; unclassified modern shrub roses are a variable group with flowers on spreading mounds or upright bushes. Climbing roses—a single flush or repeating blooms along canes to 20 feet; large-flowered climbing roses have single flowers like hybrid tea roses; cluster-flowered climbing roses, smaller blossoms in multiples. Miniature roses—

Rosa climbing rose 'American Pillar'

tiny versions of hybrid tea and floribunda roses only 3 to 18 inches tall. Old garden roses—moss roses with a single flush of flowers on soft, floppy stems; hybrid perpetual roses have fragrant rosettes up to 7 inches across on plants to 8 feet or more; climbing tea roses, large single flowers on stiff, arching canes to 10 feet. Wild roses—arching stems with a flush of single-petaled, often fragrant flowers.

Growing conditions and maintenance: Plant roses in sites with good air circulation and a slightly acidic soil enriched with organic matter. Mulch to suppress weeds and protect roots in winter. Pruning to remove old canes and shape plants is essential to maintain vigor and promote flowering. Propagate species from seed or by dividing rooted suckers, cultivars and species from softwood cuttings.

Rudbeckia
(rood-BEK-ee-a)
CONEFLOWER

Rudbeckia hirta 'Gloriosa Daisy'

Hardiness: *Zones 4-9 or hardy*

Plant type: *perennial or annual*

Height: *10 inches to 7 feet*

Interest: *flowers, foliage*

Soil: *well-drained*

Light: *full sun to light shade*

Coneflowers have prominent dark centers fringed with petal-like ray flowers. The yellow summer flowers bloom on stems lined with large, hairy leaves. Coneflowers are useful as fillers or backdrops in a border or sunny meadow garden.

Selected species and varieties: *R. fulgida* 'Goldsturm' (orange coneflower)—compact 2-foot plants with a profusion of flowers. *R. hirta* (black-eyed Susan)—single or double drooping golden yellow petals around brown-black centers on 2- to 3-foot-tall annual plants; 'Gloriosa Daisy' grows in shades of yellow with mahogany centers, and in bicolors; 'Goldilocks' has semidouble or double petals on compact 10-inch plants; 'Irish Eyes', green centers. *R. maxima* (great coneflower)—1-foot-long attractive gray foliage on 5-foot stems. *R. nitida* 'Herbstsonne'—showy 4-inch flowers with green centers on plants to 7 feet.

Growing conditions and maintenance: Plant coneflowers 1½ to 2 feet apart. They tolerate heat and dry conditions. Propagate from seed or by division; annual coneflowers self-sow.

Salvia
(SAL-vee-a)
SAGE

Salvia coccinea 'Lady in Red'

Hardiness: *Zones 4-10 or tender*

Plant type: *perennial or annual*

Height: *8 inches to 5 feet*

Interest: *flowers, foliage*

Soil: *well-drained*

Light: *full sun to light shade*

Whorled spikes of tiny, hooded, summer-to-fall-blooming flowers line the tips of salvia's erect stems above soft, sometimes downy leaves. Salvias are particularly effective in masses that multiply the impact of their flowers. Tender perennial salvias that cannot withstand frost are grown as annuals in Zone 8 and colder.

Selected species and varieties: *S. argentea* (silver sage)—perennial with branching clusters of white flowers tinged yellow or pink on 3-foot stems above rosettes of woolly, gray-green, 8-inch leaves. *S. azurea* ssp. *pitcheri* var. *grandiflora* (blue sage)—perennial with large, deep blue flowers on stems to 5 feet lined with gray-green leaves. *S. coccinea* (Texas sage)—annual with heart-shaped leaves on 1- to 2-foot branching stems; 'Lady in Red' has slender clusters of bright red flowers. *S. farinacea* 'Blue Bedder' (mealy-cup sage)—annual with whorls of blue-violet flowers on branching stems to 3 feet lined with toothed gray-green leaves; 'Victoria' is a smaller cultivar, to 1½ feet. *S. guaranitica*—annual with deep blue 2-inch flowers on shrubby 3- to 5-foot plants. *S. officinalis* (common sage)—perennial with whorls of tiny white, blue, or purple flowers above hairy, aromatic gray-green leaves used for cooking; 'Purpurascens' has purple-tinged leaves; 'Tricolor', leaf veins turning from cream to pink and red as foliage ages. *S. sclarea* 'Turkestanica' [also called *S. s.* var. *turkestana* or var. *turkestaniana*]—rosy pink flower spikes tipping 3-foot stems above wrinkled, hairy leaves. *S. splendens* (scarlet sage)—annual 8 to 30 inches or taller with soft green leaves; 'Hotline Mix' has very early white to salmon, red, and violet flowers on compact plants to 10 inches. *S.* x *superba* 'East Friesland' (perennial salvia)—violet-purple flowers on 18- to 24-inch plants. *S. uliginosa*—annual with 5-

Salvia officinalis 'Purpurascens'

foot stems tipped with azure blue flowers on branching spikes above broad leaves with toothed edges. *S. viridis* [also called *S. horminum*] (painted sage)—annual with long-lasting purple spikes on 1½-foot plants; 'Claryssa' is more compact than the species with larger flowers.

Growing conditions and maintenance: Plant smaller salvia varieties 18 inches apart, larger ones 2 to 3 feet apart in sites that will be dry in winter. Salvias will tolerate droughty conditions. Removing spent flowers encourages reblooming. Grow annual salvias from seed, all salvias from cuttings or by division.

Sedum
(SEE-dum)
STONECROP

Sedum x 'Autumn Joy'

Hardiness:	*Zones 3-10*
Plant type:	*perennial*
Height:	*4 inches to 2 feet*
Interest:	*foliage, flowers*
Soil:	*well-drained*
Light:	*full sun*

Durable stonecrop bears large clusters of tiny summer-to-fall-blooming flowers on stems lined with fleshy leaves that are often tinged purple or bronze. The plants are attractive in bud as well as while flowering, and dried flower heads of taller species often remain standing through winter. Use trailing and compact stonecrops as ground covers, edgings, or rock garden plants. Mass taller stonecrops as fillers in the border.

Selected species and varieties: *S.* x 'Autumn Joy'—a hybrid with four seasons of interest as gray-green buds emerge in spring, deepen into summer green, then mature to deep pinky red in fall before drying to decorate the winter garden. *S.* x 'Ruby Glow'—compact, 8-inch plants with purple-tinged leaves and rich ruby flower clusters. *S. sieboldii* (October daphne)—trailing 9-inch stems with tiny blue-gray leaves edged in red and dense clusters of deep pink flowers. *S. spectabile* (showy stonecrop)—round clumps of 18- to 24-inch stems lined with fleshy 3-inch leaves, each tipped with a flat cluster of white, pink, or red summer-to-fall flowers; 'Brilliant' has dull red

flowers on 18-inch plants; 'Carmen', rosy pink flowers above gray-green leaves on 18-inch plants; 'Meteor', very large flat clusters of burgundy flowers on 18-inch plants. *S.* x 'Vera Jameson'—purple leaves covered with a whitish bloom on 9-inch plants with dusty pink flower clusters. *S.* x 'Weihenstephaner Gold'—compact 4- to 5-inch plants with scalloped leaves and yellow-orange flowers.

Growing conditions and maintenance: Plant *S. sieboldii* 1 foot apart, other species 1½ to 2 feet apart. Sedum toler-

Sedum x 'Vera Jameson'

ates dry soils and hot locations and can be left undivided for many years. Propagate from stem cuttings in summer or by division in spring.

Stachys
(STAY-kis)
LAMB'S EARS

Stachys byzantina 'Silver Carpet'

Hardiness: *Zones 4-8*

Plant type: *perennial*

Height: *6 to 18 inches*

Interest: *foliage, flowers*

Soil: *well-drained*

Light: *full sun to light shade*

Stachys foliage adds color and texture to the border. Mats of woolly, pointed leaves of low-growing species are ideal for ground covers or informal edgings. The large, corrugated leaves and fine-textured flowers of taller species fill spaces in the border.

Selected species and varieties: *S. byzantina* (lamb's ears, woolly betony)—dense 8-inch-high mats of velvety gray-green oval leaves to 6 inches and woolly, pinkish summer-blooming flower spikes up to 1½ feet tall; 'Silver Carpet' is a non-flowering cultivar. *S. macrantha* (big betony)—stems to 1½ feet, tipped with whorls of purple summer flowers above heart-shaped, rippled green leaves; 'Superba' has lavender pink flowers.

Growing conditions and maintenance: Plant stachys 12 to 18 inches apart in soil that is not overly fertile. Remove old leaves before new growth begins in the spring. Propagate by transplanting self-sown seedlings, from seed, or by division.

Taxus
(TAKS-us)
YEW

Taxus cuspidata 'Capitata'

Hardiness: *Zones 4-7*

Plant type: *shrub or tree*

Height: *4 to 50 feet*

Interest: *foliage*

Soil: *moist, well-drained, fertile*

Light: *full sun to light shade*

Fine-needled evergreen plants, yews are employed as ground covers, shrubbery backdrops, hedges, screens, or specimen plantings.

Selected species and varieties: *T. baccata* (English yew)—dense, wide-spreading branches with dark green needles to 50 feet tall; 'Adpressa', very short needles on bushes to 30 feet; 'Fastigiata', stiff, upright branches in columns to 30 feet tall and 8 feet wide; 'Repandens', a dwarf to 4 feet tall and up to 15 feet wide. *T. cuspidata* (Japanese yew)—medium-textured species cultivated in many forms of shrub or tree; 'Capitata', pyramids of branches to 50 feet; 'Densa', a dwarf spreading to twice its 4-foot height; 'Thayerae', branches angled slightly upward into flat-topped shrubs 8 feet tall and twice as wide. *T. x media* (Anglo-Japanese yew) —medium-size pyramidal shrub or tree; 'Hatfieldii' grows to 12 feet tall; 'Hicksii' forms a narrow column to 20 feet.

Growing conditions and maintenance: Yews must have excellent drainage and should be protected from drying winds. They take well to pruning and shearing. Propagate from cuttings.

Thuja
(THOO-ya)
ARBORVITAE

Thuja occidentalis 'Hetz Midget'

Hardiness: *Zones 2-9*

Plant type: *tree or shrub*

Height: *3 to 30 feet*

Interest: *foliage*

Soil: *moist, well-drained, fertile*

Light: *full sun to light shade*

Arborvitae's fine-textured evergreen foliage develops along dense pyramids of branches in shades of green, yellow-green, and blue-green. Use them as specimens, in shrub borders, or planted into screens or hedges.

Selected species and varieties: *T. occidentalis* (American or eastern arborvitae, white cedar)—shiny green needles that turn brown in winter; 'Hetz Midget' is a dense 3- to 4-foot globe; 'Lutea' forms a golden yellow pyramid to 30 feet; 'Nigra' has dark green foliage on trees 20 feet high and 4 feet wide; 'Rheingold', deep gold foliage on oval shrubs to 5 feet. *T. orientalis* [also called *Platycladus orientalis*] (Oriental arborvitae)—bright green or yellow-green young foliage maturing to dark green and holding its color through winter.

Growing conditions and maintenance: Arborvitaes located in shade will grow loose and open. Plants can be transplanted year round from containers or in balled-and-burlapped form. *T. orientalis* is less cold tolerant than American arborvitae; plant only to Zone 5 or 6. Propagate from cuttings.

Tulipa
(TOO-lip-a)
TULIP

Tulipa 'Plaisir'

Hardiness: *Zones 2-8*

Plant type: *bulb*

Height: *4 inches to 3 feet*

Interest: *flowers*

Soil: *well-drained*

Light: *full sun*

Rising singly or occasionally in clusters from clumps of canoe-shaped leaves, tulips make cheerful spring accents in borders and rock gardens. Tulips come in many forms, including lily-flowered, with pointed petals; Darwin, with curved petals arranged in deep cups; double- or peony-flowered, with multiple rows of overlapping petals; and parrot, with overlapping rippled petals. They grow in almost every color, often splashed with a second hue. The wide selection of hybrid tulips is classified by their parent species, flower form, or time of bloom.

Selected species and varieties: SPECIES TULIPS. *T. clusiana* (lady tulip)—red-and-white flowers above 1-foot-long leaves on stems of equal height; var. *chrysantha* blooms are rosy red outside with yellow inner petals on 6-inch stems; 'Cynthia' has red-striped flowers edged in chartreuse with fringed inner petals on 12-inch stems. *T. dasystemon* [also called *T. tarda*] (Kuen Lun tulip)—clusters of white flowers tinged green with yellow centers on 4-inch stems. *T. praestans* 'Unicum' (leather-bulb tulip)—clusters of red flowers with yellow centers on

8-inch stems. HYBRID TULIPS. Single early tulips—'Bellona' produces fragrant golden yellow flowers; 'Coleur Cardinal', plum-tinged red blooms. Double early tulips—'Electra' is deep cherry red; 'Mr. van der Hoef', double yellow. Triumph and Mendel tulips—'Apricot Beauty' is salmon-rose brushed with apricot; 'Negrita', deep purple; 'Garden Party', white edged with rose. Darwin tulips—'Apeldoorn' is cherry red with a black center; 'Golden Apeldoorn', yellow-gold with a black center; 'Ivory Floradale', creamy ivory flecked with red. Single late tulips—'Blushing Lady' is apricot tinged with rose; 'Temple of Beauty', salmon-tinged orange. Lily-flowered tulips—'West Point' is bright yellow; 'White Triumphator', pure white. Fringed tulips—'Fancy Frills' is ivory with a rosy fringe; 'Fringed Elegance', yellow flecked with pink. Multiflowering tulips—'Georgette' is red-rimmed yellow. Parrot

Tulipa 'Apricot Beauty'

tulips— 'Flaming Parrot' is bright yellow streaked with red; 'Estella Rijnveld', red streaked with white. Double late tulips —'Angelique' is pale pink. Fosteriana tulips—'Madame Lefeber' is brilliant red; 'Orange Emperor', deep orange with a yellow center. Greigii tulips—'Plaisir' is red-streaked creamy yellow; 'Red Riding Hood', deep red with a black center.

Growing conditions and maintenance: Set tulip bulbs out in fall. Plant cultivars generally 5 to 6 inches deep; species bulbs, which may be smaller, 3 times the bulb's diameter. Propagate by dividing bulb clumps.

Verbena
(ver-BEE-na)
VERVAIN

Verbena x hybrida 'Homestead Purple'

Hardiness: *Zones 6-10 or tender*

Plant type: *perennial or annual*

Height: *6 inches to 5 feet*

Interest: *flowers*

Soil: *moist, well-drained*

Light: *full sun*

Vividly colored, small flowers blooming from summer through frost in clusters on wiry stems above mats or clumps of soft green foliage make verbenas useful as ground covers or fillers in the border.

Selected species and varieties: *V. bonariensis* (Brazilian verbena)—3- to 4-foot-tall plants with branching clusters of fragrant, rosy violet flowers above wrinkled leaves. *V. canadensis* (rose verbena)—trailing stems lined with 4-inch leaves and clusters of rose pink flowers on stems to 6 inches. *V. x hybrida* (common garden verbena)—flat flowers in loose, round heads on 6- to 12-inch stems above wrinkled leaves; 'Homestead Purple' has deep purple flowers. *V. tenuisecta* (moss verbena)—spreading stems in 12-inch-tall clumps of finely dissected, ferny leaves and violet or purple flowers in 2-inch clusters.

Growing conditions and maintenance: Plant Brazilian verbena 2 feet apart, smaller varieties 1 foot apart. Rose verbena is hardy to Zone 6, other species to Zone 8. Grow as annuals where frost will kill them. Propagate from seed or from cuttings taken in late summer.

Veronica
(ve-RON-i-ka)
SPEEDWELL

Veronica 'Sunny Border Blue'

Hardiness: *Zones 4-8*

Plant type: *perennial*

Height: *6 inches to 4 feet*

Interest: *flowers, foliage*

Soil: *well-drained*

Light: *full sun to light shade*

Clumps of spreading stems lined with soft-textured, narrow leaves and tipped with long spikes of tiny spring-to-summer flowers make speedwell a good choice for fillers or naturalizing.

Selected species and varieties: V. x hybrids—plants 12 to 24 inches tall; 'Sunny Border Blue' produces blue flowers. *V. incana* (silver speedwell, woolly speedwell)—pale lilac-blue flowers above low clumps of silver-gray foliage; 'Minuet' has pink flowers and gray-green leaves; 'Saraband', 12- to 18-inch plants with violet-blue flowers. *V. longifolia* (longleaf speedwell)—plants to 4 feet; 'Icicle' has white flowers; var. *subsessilis,* lilac blooms. *V. spicata* (spike speedwell)—18-inch plants; 'Blue Fox' has lavender-blue flower spikes; 'Red Fox', rose-to-pink blooms. *V. teucrium* [also called *V. austriaca* ssp. *teucrium*] 'Crater Lake Blue'—compact 12- to 18-inch plants with wide spikes of deep blue flowers.

Growing conditions and maintenance: Plant speedwell 1 to 2 feet apart. Remove spent flowers to extend bloom. Propagate from seed or cuttings or by division in spring or fall.

Viburnum
(vy-BUR-num)
VIBURNUM

Viburnum dilatatum

Hardiness: *Zones 5-8*

Plant type: *shrub*

Height: *6 to 12 feet*

Interest: *foliage, flowers, berries*

Soil: *well-drained*

Light: *full sun to light shade*

Deciduous or evergreen viburnums offer a choice of textures for specimens or backdrop plantings. The showy spring-blooming flowers are followed in fall by colorful fruits.

Selected species and varieties: *V. dilatatum* (linden viburnum)—rounded oval leaves coloring burgundy in fall on shrubs to 10 feet tall with profuse flat clusters of white flowers and scarlet fruits. *V. plicatum* var. *tomentosum* 'Shasta' (double file viburnum)—toothed oval leaves coloring red-purple in fall on horizontally branching shrubs 6 feet tall with profuse white flowers and red fruits. *V. rhytidophyllum* (leatherleaf viburnum)—narrow evergreen leaves on shrubs to 12 feet with 8-inch clusters of yellowy white flowers and red fruit. *V. setigerum* 'Aurantiacum' (tea viburnum)—blue-green leaves coloring red in fall and white flowers followed by handsome orange berries on shrubs to 12 feet.

Growing conditions and maintenance: Viburnums transplant easily and thrive in soil amended with organic matter. When necessary, prune viburnums immediately after they flower.

Vitis
(VY-tis)
GRAPE

Vitis vinifera 'Purpurea'

Hardiness: *Zones 5-8*

Plant type: *vine*

Height: *20 to 50 feet*

Interest: *foliage, bark*

Soil: *well-drained*

Light: *full sun*

With their twining tendrils, grapes quickly scramble over arbors and trellises to create almost instant screens, canopies, or arches. The broad leaves, attractively lobed and incised, color brilliantly in fall. Older stems have shredding, peeling bark.

Selected species and varieties: *V. amurensis* (Amur grape)—5- to 10-inch leaves coloring crimson to purple in fall. *V. coignetiae* (crimson glory vine)—extremely fast-growing vine, up to 50 feet per year, with 4- to 10-inch leaves turning scarlet in fall. *V. vinifera* 'Purpurea' (wine grape, common grape)—4- to 6-inch heart-shaped leaves emerge reddish burgundy, then mature to purple.

Growing conditions and maintenance: Plant grapes in deeply cultivated soil enriched with organic matter. When growing for shade or an arbor, cut canes back in winter to control spread. Propagate from cuttings.

Wisteria
(wis-TEE-ree-a)
WISTERIA

Wisteria sinensis 'Alba'

Hardiness: *Zones 4-9*

Plant type: *vine*

Height: *10 to 50 feet*

Interest: *flowers, form*

Soil: *well-drained*

Light: *full sun*

Robust wisteria climbs by twining young shoots around supports, eventually developing a stout, twisted woody trunk. In spring or summer, vines drip with enormous clusters of flowers. The contorted trunks lend a sculptural accent to a winter garden.

Selected species and varieties: *W. floribunda* (Japanese wisteria)—violet or blue-violet, fragrant spring-blooming flower clusters up to 10 inches long on vines to 50 feet; 'Alba' has white clusters; 'Macrobotrys', red-violet clusters up to 4 feet long. *W. frutescens* (American or southern wisteria)—6-inch pale lilac clusters spotted yellow in summer on vines to 30 feet. *W. sinensis* 'Alba' (Chinese wisteria)—12-inch white clusters in spring.

Growing conditions and maintenance: Plant wisteria in moist soil enriched with organic matter. Prune heavily to restrain its rampant growth or to shape into trees or multistemmed shrubs. Prune away from porches and other structures, as the increasing weight of the vine may eventually pull them down; and from living trees, which may be slowly strangled.

Yucca
(YUK-a)
YUCCA

Yucca filamentosa 'Golden Sword'

Hardiness: *Zones 4-9*

Plant type: *shrub*

Height: *2 to 12 feet*

Interest: *foliage, flowers*

Soil: *well-drained*

Light: *full sun*

Yuccas form stiff rosettes of gray-green, swordlike evergreen leaves with shredding, thready filaments along their edges. Tall flower stalks with dangling blossoms rise high above the leaves in summer.

Selected species and varieties: *Y. filamentosa* (Adam's-needle)—rosettes up to 3 feet wide of gray-green leaves tipped with spines and 2-inch white flowers on branching stalks to 6 feet tall; 'Bright Edge' has creamy leaf edges; 'Golden Sword' is edged in yellow. *Y. glauca* (soapweed)—rosettes to 3 to 4 feet wide of gray-green leaves with pale edges and greenish white flowers on unbranched stalks to 6 feet.

Growing conditions and maintenance: Yuccas tolerate infertile, dry soil, extremes of heat and cold, and strong wind. Remove dead flower stalks and leaves. Propagate by dividing root knobs from the main plant.

Zinnia
(ZIN-ee-a)
ZINNIA

Zinnia elegans 'Border Beauty Rose Shades'

Hardiness: *hardy*

Plant type: *annual*

Height: *8 to 20 inches*

Interest: *flowers*

Soil: *well-drained*

Light: *full sun*

Zinnias brighten the border with pompons of petal-like rays that are sometimes flat and rounded, sometimes rolled into fringes, crowded around centers with yellow or green true flowers. Hues range from riotous yellows, oranges, and reds to subdued pinks, roses, salmons, and creams, even maroon and purple. Flowers cover plants from summer through frost and are best massed for effect as edgings or in the border.

Selected species and varieties: *Z. angustifolia* (narrowleaf zinnia)—compact, 8-inch-tall plants with 1-inch-wide orange blossoms. *Z. elegans* 'Border Beauty Rose Shades' (common zinnia, youth-and-old-age)—3-inch blossoms with flat rays in shades of rose touched with salmon on 20-inch stems. *Z. haageana* 'Persian Carpet' (Mexican zinnia)—bicolored 2-inch flat pointed rays in maroon through chocolate to gold and cream on 15-inch stems.

Growing conditions and maintenance: Zinnias prefer hot, dry weather and good air circulation to prevent mildew. They are among the easiest flowers to grow. Propagate from seed.

Acknowledgments

The editors wish to thank the following for their valuable assistance in the preparation of this volume:
Linda Chisari, Del Mar, Calif.; Howard Cohen, Seattle, Wash.; Brian Coleman, Seattle, Wash.; Sam Daniel, Arlington, Va.; Helen Dawson, La Jolla, Calif.; Mr. and Mrs. James Lynn, Bethesda, Md.; Northwest Perennial Alliance Border, Bellevue Botanical Garden, Bellevue Parks and Community Services Department, Bellevue, Wash.; Daryl Puterbaugh, New York, N.Y.; Chris Rosmini, Los Angeles, Calif.; Nancy Schibanoff, Del Mar, Calif.; Holly and Osamu Shimazu, Glen Echo, Md.; William Smith, Atlanta, Ga.; Judith Stark, Nashotah, Wis.; John Troy, San Antonio, Tex.; Phillip Watson, Fredericksburg, Va.

Picture Credits

Bibliography

Books:

American Horticultural Society: *Encyclopedia of Gardening.* New York: Dorling Kindersley, 1994.

Encyclopedia of Garden Plants. New York: Macmillan, 1989.

Bartels, Andreas. *Gardening with Dwarf Trees and Shrubs.* Translated by Roberta J. Cooper. Portland, Ore.: Timber Press, 1986.

Billington, Jill. *Architectural Foliage.* London: Ward Lock, 1991.

Boisset, Caroline, and Fayal Greene. *The Garden Sourcebook.* New York: Crown, 1993.

Brookes, John. *The Book of Garden Design.* New York: Macmillan, 1991.

Bradley, Fern, and Barbara W. Ellis (Eds.). *Rodale's All-New Encyclopedia of Organic Gardening.* Emmaus, Pa.: Rodale Press, 1992.

Capon, Brian. *Botany for Gardeners: An Introduction and Guide.* Portland, Ore.: Timber Press, 1992.

Challis, Myles. *Large-Leaved Perennials.* London: Ward Lock, 1992.

Chatto, Beth. *The Green Tapestry.* New York: Simon and Schuster, 1989.

Clarke, Graham. *Garden Colour: Autumn and Winter Colour in the Garden.* Topsfield, Mass.: Salem House Publishers, 1986.

Color in Your Garden (Sunset Books). Menlo Park, Calif.: Lane Books, 1973.

Conder, Susan (text), and Andrew Lawson (photography). *Variegated Leaves: The Encyclopedia of Patterned Foliage.* New York: Macmillan, 1993.

Cox, Jeff: *The Perennial Garden.* Emmaus, Pa.: Rodale Press, 1992. *Plant Marriages.* New York: HarperCollins, 1993.

Cresson, Charles O. *Charles Cresson on the American Flower Garden* (Burpee Expert Gardener series). New York: Prentice Hall Gardening, 1993.

Damrosch, Barbara. *Theme Gardens.* New York: Workman Publishing, 1982.

Frederick, William H., Jr. *The Exuberant Garden and the Controlling Hand.* Boston: Little, Brown, 1992.

Garden Color: Annuals and Perennials. Menlo Park, Calif.: Sunset Publishing, 1992.

Glattstein, Judy. *Garden Design with Foliage* (Garden Way Publishing). Pownal, Vt.: Storey Communications, 1991.

Good, Jane (Ed.). *The Gardener's Color Guide.* Buffalo, N.Y.: Camden House, 1993.

Grant, John A., and Carol L. Grant. *Garden Design Illustrated.* Portland, Ore.: Timber Press, 1983.

Harper, Pamela J. *Color Echoes.* New York: Macmillan, 1994.

Hobhouse, Penelope. *Color in Your Garden.* Boston: Little, Brown, 1991.

Hudak, Joseph. *Shrubs in the Landscape.* New York: McGraw-Hill, 1984.

Jefferson-Brown, Michael. *Hardy Ferns.* London: Ward Lock, 1992.

Keen, Mary. *Gardening with Color.* New York: Random House, 1991.

Kelly, John. *Foliage in Your Garden.* New York: Viking, 1988.

Lacey, Stephen. *The Startling Jungle.* New York: Viking, 1986.

Lacy, Allen. *The Garden in Autumn.* New York: Atlantic Monthly Press, 1990.

Lovejoy, Ann. *The American Mixed Border: Gardens for All Seasons.* New York: Macmillan, 1993.

Oehme, Wolfgang, James van Sweden, and Susan Rademacher Frey. *Bold Romantic Gardens.* Reston, Va.: Acropolis Books, 1990.

Ortloff, H. Stuart, and Henry B. Raymore. *Color and Design for Every Garden.* New York: M. Barrows, 1951.

Overy, Angela. *The Foliage Garden.* New York: Harmony Books, 1993.

Quinn, Vernon. *Leaves: Their Place in Life and Legend.* New York: Frederick A. Stokes, 1937.

Reader's Digest Illustrated Guide to Gardening. Pleasantville, N.Y.: Reader's Digest Association, 1978.

Roth, Susan A. *The Four-Season Landscape.* Emmaus, Pa.: Rodale Press, 1994.

Saville, Diana. *Guides to Garden Design: Color.* New York: Canopy Books, 1993.

Squire, David. *The Complete Guide to Using Color in Your Garden.* Emmaus, Pa.: Rodale Press, 1991.

Taylor, Jane. *Drought-Tolerant Plants.* New York: Prentice Hall, 1993.

Taylor, Patricia A. *Easy Care Shade Flowers.* New York: Simon and Schuster, 1993.

Thomas, Graham Stuart. *The Art of Planting.* London: J. M. Dent and Sons, 1984.

Verey, Rosemary. *The Garden in Winter.* London: Windward (W. H. Smith and Son), 1988.

Wilder, Louise Beebe. *Color in My Garden.* New York: Atlantic Monthly Press, 1990 (reprint of 1918 edition).

Wilson, Helen Van Pelt. *Color for Your Winter Yard and Garden.* New York: Charles Scribner's Sons, 1978.

Wyman, Donald. *Dwarf Shrubs.* New York: Macmillan, 1975.

Zucker, Isabel. *Flowering Shrubs and Small Trees.* Revised and expanded by Derek Fell. New York: Grove Weidenfeld, 1990.

Periodicals:

Apps, Darrel. "Perennial Border Design with Foliage." *Fine Gardening,* January/February 1994.

Cowden, Bob. "The White Flower Garden." *Pacific Horticulture,* Fall 1987.

Cox, Jeff. "How to Plan Perennial Color." *Organic Gardening,* March 1985.

Culbertson, William Louis. "Autumn Glory." *Country Living Gardener,* Fall/Winter 1994.

Descloux, Joyce. "Winter Heaths." *Fine Gardening,* July/August 1994.

Harper, Pamela. "Blazing Borders." *Horticulture,* February 1991.

Higgins, Edward. "Chrysanthemums." *Fine Gardening,* January/February 1994.

Hobhouse, Penelope. "Laying Out a Flower Garden." *Country Journal,* June 1984.

Koller, Gary. "Gold-Leaved Plants Keep the Hues of Spring." *Fine Gardening,* September/October 1994.

Lacey, Allen. "A Winning Combination." *Homeground,* Winter 1993.

Lloyd, Christopher. "Splashes of Silver and Gold." *Horticulture,* August/September 1994.

McKinley, Michael. "Inviting Birds into Your Garden." *Fine Gardening,* August 1994.

Schoellkopf, George. "The Frost Fighters." *Town and Country,* September 1994.

Sheldon, Elizabeth. "A Home for Hot Colors." *Fine Gardening,* March/April 1994.

Snyder, Leon C. "Plants for Fall Color." *Arboretum Review No. 27* (University of Minnesota Agricultural Extension Service), 1975.

Wesler, Mickey. "Landscaping for the Birds." *Wild Bird News,* May/June 1991.

Winterrowd, Wayne. "Hellebores: Perennial Magic in the Sleeping Garden." *The Best of Fine Gardening,* January 1992.

Index